Topographical Dictionary

OF 2885

English Emigrants

TO

NEW ENGLAND

1620 — 1650

By CHARLES EDWARD BANKS

Edited and Indexed by
ELIJAH ELLSWORTH BROWNELL

Baltimore
GENEALOGICAL PUBLISHING CO., INC.

Originally published: Philadelphia, 1937
Reprinted: Southern Book Company
Baltimore, 1957
Reissued: Genealogical Publishing Co., Inc.
Baltimore: 1963, 1969, 1976, 1981, 1992
Library of Congress Catalogue Card Number 63-4154
International Standard Book Number 0-8063-0019-1
Made in the United States of America

CONTENTS

EDITOR AND PUBLISHER'S NOTE

The following items should be carefully read and studied in order that the greatest amount of benefit may be derived from the compiling, indexing and printing of this famous Banks' Manuscript.

(1) Colonel Banks searched carefully the 41 counties and shires of England, including the City of London, and obtained from the 1,194 parishes in these respective counties, shires and the City of London, the record of 2,885 emigrants to New England from the time of the sailing of the "Mayflower" (1620) to the year 1650, inclusive.

(2) Colonel Banks began this notable research work in England, with the distinct purpose of connecting the New England emigrants with the respective parishes from whence they came. This is, by far, the most valuable portion of this compilation.

(3) There should be no doubt in the mind of any impartial reader as to the authenticity and thoroughness with which Colonel Charles Edward Banks obtained the data in this manuscript. It is evident that whenever Colonel Banks was in doubt as to the authenticity of any one of these records, he precluded that portion which was in doubt rather than to take chances that might be misleading. His record for thoroughness and precision in compiling valuable records of this character has never been questioned.

(4) Before attempting to compile, index and print the Banks' Manuscript, which no one has ever attempted to do heretofore, the editor and publisher was fully aware of the great sacrifice in time, money, and effort which he would have to forego. Nevertheless, realizing the tremendous demand for such a publication and its great value to all researchers in American genealogy, it was undertaken, not as a commercial proposition, but with one thought in mind and that was the patriotic and civic duty, as an American citizen, which he owed to the memory of his ancestors and forebears whose descendants number into the tens of thousands.

(5)   I fully realized in the compilation, indexing, and printing of this famous Banks' Manuscript, that there are thousands of our substantial American citizens who would never be able, financially, to make a research of their respective ancestors without such an edition being accessible to them in the various State and recognized genealogical libraries of the United States. Therefore, I hope that my sacrifice and efforts will be fully appreciated by the interested American public and that they may be benefited by my sincere efforts to make this edition the best record of its kind.

(6)   The editor and publisher is a descendant of John Alden and Priscilla Mullins of the Mayflower list, and is therefore, a Mayflower descendant.

The Mayflower passengers, in 1620, were not all from England, as is commonly understood, but a few were from Leyden and Amsterdam, Netherlands. Thomas Brownell and his wife, Anne (Bourne) Brownell, who came to America in 1638, are listed in this famous Banks' compilation.

Editor and Publisher.

TO MY FELLOW CITIZENS

I proudly dedicate this edition to all patriotic citizens of traditional America that they may be ever appreciative of our forefathers who made these United States of America, under the strictest interpretation of the Constitution, the greatest nation the world has ever known. Love, honor, and defend our country and perpetuate, at any cost, the basic principles of our democratic government which have made it the great nation of today.

Elijah Ellsworth Brownell

Philadelphia, Penna.
March, 1937.

vi

Charles Edward Banks

Assistant Surgeon General, U. S. P. H. S. (Retired)

Member of the Maine, New Hampshire and Massachusetts Historical Societies and of the American Antiquarian Society.

Published Works:

Col. *Alexander Rigby and the Province of Lygonia* (1885)
Life, Letters and Public Services of Edward Godfrey (1887)
History of Martha's Vineyard, Mass. (1911)
English Homes and Ancestry of the Pilgrims (1929)
The Winthrop Fleet of 1630 (1930)
Planters of the Commonwealth (1930)
Able Men of Suffolk 1638 (1931)
History of York, Maine (1931-193-).

And many articles in genealogical, historical and patriotic society, publications.

Colonel Charles Edward Banks was born in Portland, Maine, July 6, 1854, descended from Richard Bankes, the pioneer, who settled in York, Maine, 1643. On the maternal side he was a direct descendant of George Soule of the "Mayflower," and he had six other ancestors among the passengers, including Elder William Brewster. Early in life, because of the historic background of his family, he became interested in its history. Much of his spare time was spent in research, and from his methodical manner of making notes of everything he found he soon amassed a vast fund of information regarding his own and allied lines. His first trip to England was for the purpose of tracing his first American ancestors. Some months were spent in the search and as it proceeded he would encounter names of many whom he knew were amongst the first emigrants. This whetted his appetite to locate as many as possible and thus the present Dictionary was planned. Following his retirement from governmental duties, with leisure time on his hands, and with his zeal for such work unabated, he went after the search in no uncertain manner. Cultivating the acquaintance of prominent English genealogists and co-operating with one or two in the transcription of unpublished subsidies and parish registers, he soon became thoroughly familiar with the intricacies of English research. He visited all of the forty English counties and many parishes in each, in addition to spending months of work by himself and secretary in the Public Record Office, London. It was indeed a colossal task to locate almost 3000 of those who came to America between 1620 and 1650; a life work for any man.

His zeal for historical study was unflagging to the end. To his researches he brought a trained, scholarly and judicial mind, as well as a fund of sound common sense, and his keen, practical understanding of men and events made him an unusually skillful interpreter of the trends of human life and provincial government in the days of the Colonies. Of his scrupulous fidelity to accuracy of detail it seems unnecessary to speak. Distinguished in two callings it should be added that Col. Banks was an artist of no mean talents as his drawings in his various volumes bear witness. He had a hobby for extra-illustrating books, some of which were illumined by clever products of his pen and brush.

Of other genealogists who conducted researches in England, Samuel G. Drake, of Boston, was amongst the first, and produced in 1860 his "Result of Some Researches Among the English Archives for Information Relative to the Founders of New England." Hotten published a list of Emigrants to New England, but this deals mainly with those who came in the year 1635. Waters came along later with his "Genealogical Gleanings in England," but no one ever went into the matter so thoroughly as did Col. Banks. During his lifetime the Colonel spoke, on more than one occasion, of the great cost of these manuscripts.

INTRODUCTION

Colonel Charles E. Banks was universally conceded to be one of the ranking genealogists and writers on local history in America. This "Topographical Dictionary of English Emigrants to New England, 1620-1650" is unquestionably his most important genealogical work. In the local history field he is best known for his "History of Martha's Vineyard," 3 vols., and his "History of York, Maine," two volumes of which have appeared and a third is promised for subsequent publication.

The "Dictionary" comprises the records of 2885 emigrants, giving their English homes or clues to the same, the ships in which they sailed, the town in which they settled in New England and the references to the sources of such information. It is an analytical directory of English emigration for thirty years. Arranged by English counties and parishes in same, in alphabetical sequence in each county parochially, so that all emigrants from a particular parish are grouped together, it furnishes evidence of neighborhood emigration and, indirectly, clues to other possible emigrants from the same locality.

The fact that the "Index" contains names of some 500 more emigrants than are traced in the book may be accounted for thus:—The spade work was naturally done in this country. Years were spent compiling the list from authorities such as Savage's "Genealogical Dictionary," Farmer's "First Settlers of New England," "New England Historic Genealogical Register," etc. Fortified with such details as could be found in these works, in 1920 Col. Banks began his pilgrimages to England to continue his research there. The duration of his seven visits amounted in all to approximately four years and it may be said that all this time was spent in tracing the 2885 emigrants recorded. The remaining 500 names were left in the "Index" with the hope that at some future time they could be traced. His death in 1931 interfered with the completion of this plan.

A perusal of the article on succeeding pages "Genealogical Researches in England," which appeared in the "Boston Evening Transcript" in 1928, shortly after his last return from abroad, will show the intricate, laborious, not to mention costly work that the compilation of this volume entailed. Col. Banks had more knowledge of the location of early records and the procedure necessary to approach them than many English genealogists, certainly more than any American. In his specialized field, early English emigration to America, he had no equal at home or abroad. This Topographical Dictionary was the greatest effort of his life and is a monument for all time to his efforts in behalf of all seeking information regarding English emigration to America, 1620-1650.

Philadelphia, Penna.
March, 1937.

Elijah Ellsworth Brownell.

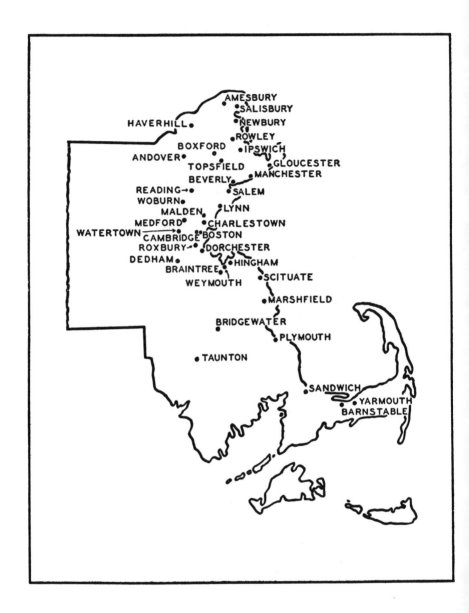

COMPARISON OF NAMES OF TOWNS IN EASTER

ASSACHUSETTS WITH THOSE IN ENGLAND

xi

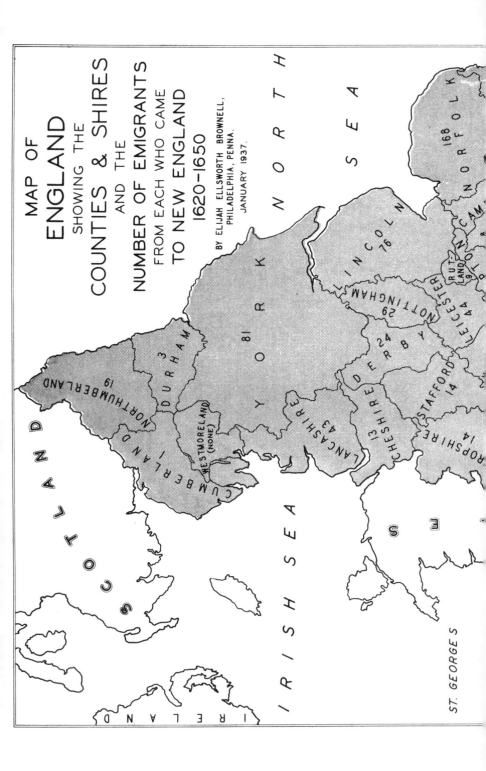

MAP OF
ENGLAND
SHOWING THE
COUNTIES & SHIRES
AND THE
NUMBER OF EMIGRANTS
FROM EACH WHO CAME
TO NEW ENGLAND
1620-1650

BY ELIJAH ELLSWORTH BROWNELL,
PHILADELPHIA, PENNA.
JANUARY 1937.

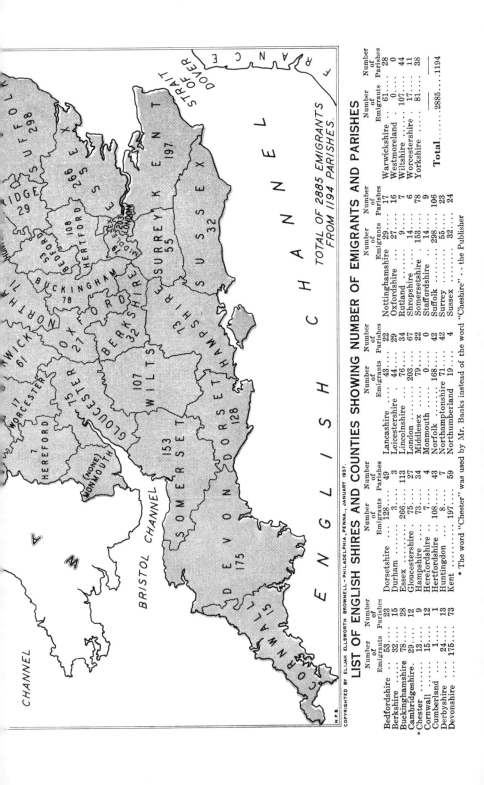

TOTAL OF 2885 EMIGRANTS FROM 1194 PARISHES.

LIST OF ENGLISH SHIRES AND COUNTIES SHOWING NUMBER OF EMIGRANTS AND PARISHES

County	Number of Emigrants	Number of Parishes
Bedfordshire	53	23
Berkshire	32	15
Buckinghamshire	78	28
Cambridgeshire	29	12
*Chester	13	9
Cornwall	15	12
Cumberland	1	1
Derbyshire	24	13
Devonshire	175	73
Dorsetshire	128	49
Durham	3	3
Essex	266	113
Gloucestershire	75	27
Hampshire	73	34
Herefordshire	7	4
Hertfordshire	108	43
Huntingdon	8	7
Kent	197	59
Lancashire	128	22
Leicestershire	44	29
Lincolnshire	76	34
London	203	67
Middlesex	79	22
Monmouth	0	0
Norfolk	168	42
Northamptonshire	71	42
Northumberland	19	4
Nottinghamshire	29	17
Oxfordshire	27	16
Rutland	9	7
Shropshire	14	6
Somersetshire	153	78
Staffordshire	14	9
Suffolk	298	106
Surrey	55	23
Sussex	32	24
Warwickshire	61	28
Westmoreland	0	0
Wiltshire	107	44
Worcestershire	17	11
Yorkshire	81	38
Total	2885	1194

* The word "Chester" was used by Mr. Banks instead of the word "Cheshire".- - the Publisher

N.P.B.

GENEALOGICAL RESEARCH IN ENGLAND

By

CHARLES EDWARD BANKS

The columns of this page have borne witness in recent years to the increasing interest of family genealogists desiring to learn something more definite than has been possible heretofore about the English origin of their immigrant ancestors. This desire is not only logical but inevitable as there is no sound reason for stopping research on this side of the Atlantic and asking no further questions as to their earlier origins. This phase of American genealogical research involves, of course, a different kind of study and a knowledge of more difficult conditions than attaches to home research in familiar surroundings. Research in England for the family connections and residence of the American ancestor at the time of his emigration must be approached and undertaken in an entirely new spirit. There is too often an easy indulgence in assuming that family names borne by prominent or historic families in England are an assurance of connection with the immigrant's family. At the outset the interested searcher should disabuse his mind of any preconceived notions as to such connections. Inquiries in this column indicate that this is a prevalent misconception, and well-meaning correspondents will answer such inquiries quoting from Burke's "Peerage" or "Landed Gentry" the occurrence of similar names as authority for linking up the humble immigrant with one of the nobility. It would save much time, labor and expense if every copy of Burke's "Peerage" and "Landed Gentry" were put on the censored list of librarians, out of the reach of amateur genealogists.

It cannot be too strongly stated that English emigrants to New England and Virginia in colonial days came from the cottages and not the manor houses. This is equally true of all the original colonies and the common chatter about "Cavaliers" peopling Virginia is entirely unjustified and can be disproved by the facts. They were of the same class of English people as those of the New England colonies, although the latter were largely dominated by the so-called Puritan influences. Everyone beginning an English search for his ancestor should start fair and not endow in advance his ancestor with a fanciful descent from nobility as the drop when the facts are established is sure to be a deserving disillusionment. The few who were in any way related to the nobility and gentry are practically well known and have been well known since their coming, and to suppose that any scion of such families concealed at the time from his children his gentle birth and allowed them and their descendants to remain ignorant of the fact is too absurd to entertain. There would be no reason for concealing it. Not only that, but Lords of the Manor had no reason to emigrate as they were practically well situated at home in the ownership of their lands, which they need not or would not abandon. Our ancestors came for the opposite reason—because they had been tenants for generations and were land hungry. Reliable investigations which have been made on the basis of such claims of noble birth have always led to proof of yeoman origin. This is not to assert that some of our emigrant ancestors were not of the younger branches of well-to-do families and it is a worthy object to establish this if possible, but the whole conception of the great transatlantic migration from the American viewpoint is not based on accident of birth but upon the quality of the great work they began in laying the foundations of a new nation in the spirit of equal opportunities and equal rights. By this it is not meant to represent them as the flotsam and jetsam of English life: they formed the backbone of English yoemanry at that period—the source of England's greatness. It would be also quite as well for the searcher to drop ideas of coats of arms in connection with the immigrant, for while it is a harmless and trivial amusement it is of no value and only confuses the object of the search. The number of families who are entitled to bear (even by good-natured courtesy) coats of arms is entirely negligible as compared to the great body of people who emigrated hither before 1700.

This present relation of personal experiences, worked out by practical dealings with conditions in England, will not cover the special form of genealogical interest which some amateurs follow in respect to "Royal Descents." This is a kind of research into prehistoric lore, quite beyond the scope of ordinary students and the documentation of it puzzles even the most expert of English historians.

Practically the initial step in carrying one's emigrant ancestor back to the parish from which he came involves a number of intensive examinations of his career in New England from the day of his landing to his death. His name may be found in certain printed lists of emigrants to New England or the Southern Colonies published by Hotten many years ago, taken from certain few Custom House lists which have been preserved out of the wreck of like documents and kept for years at local seaports of England, or in the dungeons of the Tower of London. Most of these relate to the year 1635. This book is available in all public libraries. If the name is not found therein the examination of his life and associates here must be undertaken to provide suggestions as to possible and probable connections which may have existed prior to emigration. Most of the emigrants came in neighborhood groups, often led by the Nonconforming clergymen of one of the parishes of that area. It is often possible to obtain an approximate idea of the emigrant's home if it is known with whom he emigrated or the pastor connected with that group. In the same manner these groups of emigrants went to the same town in the colonies and their former neighbors would often secure adjoining house lots and continue their old associations in the new country.

As a rule these emigrants were people in early middle life, generally married with a few young children—the kind of pioneers able to undergo the hardships of conquering a wilderness. Very few aged people undertook the dangerous ocean voyage unless accompanying their married sons or daughters. It may be assumed as a general proposition that immigrants arriving here 1630-40 (the period of the great migration) were born at the beginning of that century or shortly after. These groups contained persons closely related by marriage or of lesser degree of kinship, and often it is possible where the English location of one of the groups is known one or more of the others may also be found in the same locality. If none of these factors are present, particularly kinship by blood or marriage, the intimate associates of one's ancestor must be studied, particularly financial connections—mutual witnesses in deeds, appraisers of estates and bondsmen—as it is usual for friends and relatives to assume these obligations for each other. Through this source such connections may furnish a clue as the starting point of an investigation. This preliminary spade-work is of the utmost importance and will save much loss of time, labor and expense if thoroughly done as it is a long task to look up Zachariah Worthington (for example) "supposed to be born in England." I have in mind the compiler of a printed genealogy who even neglected to look up the grave-stone of the emigrant, which had cut on it the information that he was born in Leicestershire, England, a most vital fact which reduced to one county out of the forty in England the extent of the search.

Then there is the usual "family tradition" of the English origin of the ancestor. This may or may not be of any practical importance but the origin of it should be traced if possible and may become an important aid in the case. Frequently in case of definite statements of the parish of origin a distorted spelling will confuse one unfamiliar with the peculiar pronunciation and spelling of English localities which exist even today. Examples are found in the printed notarial records of Lechford and Aspinwall. We have no such strange transformations as Kirton for Crediton or Cissiter for Cirencester, or Sawbridgeworth which is locally pronounced Sapsearth! There is no way of unravelling these queer transformations of sound and spelling, but the searcher must be prepared to deal with such confusing local place-names. Then there are almost entire changes in the spelling of parish names, such as Agmondisham which is now written Amersham (see Pope, Pioneers of Massachusetts, page 248).

The purpose of this series of articles is to give contributors to this column, particularly inquirers who ask for the English ancestry of immigrants, some general knowledge of the peculiar phases of English research. The writer spent four years in England looking up his own ancestry as well as studying some phases of historical interest connected with emigration and settlement of New England and had to learn from practical experience, the underlying difficulties of conducting such investigations. The material sources for such research are plentiful enough but they are surrounded by all the distinctive restrictions common to English procedure and from the first one has to learn that time is an essential factor in his plans. It is impracticable to go into a record office of any kind unannounced and expect to obtain immediate access to documents desired for examination. In some probate offices only one or two searchers are allowed to work at one time, and then by previous appointment. In the principal Probate Registry, Somerset House, London, there are but fourteen seats available. The same statement as to advance appointments applies to parish registers and very few vicars will put themselves out to show their books unless considerable previous notice has been given and the time arranged.

It also should be understood as a basic difference in the character of records as compared with our own that they were at the time of emigration, and for centuries before, under ecclesiastical control, and the vast majority of what we call vital records are still in church custody. England had no civil registration of births, marriages and deaths officially established until about 1837. For only three centuries prior to that (beginning in 1538) the English church established a system of registration of baptisms, marriages and burials to be kept by the incumbents of each parish under an order of Thomas Cromwell, Lord Chancellor of the realm. Theoretically this was the first year in which actual records of the existence of an individual were officially recorded from the day of his baptism, but the local clergy did not comply generally with this injunction for one reason or another, and it took a second order twenty years later to make this registration effective. Only a small proportion of the parish registers in England in existence today begin in 1538 and that is the earliest date at which anyone can hope to find a record of the birth of an ancestor of yeoman stock. The nobility and gentry were recorded in addition to the visitations of the Heralds to those families entitled to bear coat armor.

In 1568 further provision for securing safety of these parochial registrations was taken by the church authorities, who ordered that copies of baptisms, marriages and burials should be transmitted annually to the bishop of each diocese, where they were presumed to be carefully stored for reference, but in effect they became the prey of careless custodians, who stored them in damp, inaccessible places where they became either destroyed by vermin or illegible by decay. A further provision for security was made in 1597, when it was enjoined that existing registers when written on paper should be transcribed in fair copy on permanent parchment volumes and often the two are found in custody of the vicars. These provisions for securing safety of the family records of the English people were sufficient to accomplish the worthy object of the Episcopate, but the indifference, almost criminal, of the local clergy has resulted in the loss and destruction of the earliest volumes and this, combined with like neglect of the diocesan transcripts, destroys in many cases all hopes of securing these vital records of our English ancestors.

Over two hundred volumes of marriage records of about a thousand parishes have already been printed by Phillemore & Co. of London; and several hundred additional registers are printed entirely by local or county societies and are available in any large genealogical library in the United States. These registers are the prime source of information concerning English families for three centuries following Cromwell's original injunction.

Presuming that the American seeker for his English ancestor has arrived in England, fortified with the necessary preliminary information detailed in the previous articles, he or she having a definite parish to visit, it is important to ascertain whether a register exists early enough to cover the probable birth date of the emigrant. This information can be obtained from a printed volume entitled "Key to the Ancient Parish Registers of England and Wales," compiled by the late Arthur Meredith Burke. It is unfortunately quite incomplete, often in error, but is the one most easily consulted in any public library. In my own copy, which I have annotated, there are at least a thousand additions and corrections relating to the seven thousand parishes therein listed.

If the register serves as to date, the inquirer should write to the incumbent of the living, or parish, asking for an appointment for the purpose of examining his registers. His name and address may be found in the official Clergy Directory, but it will be sufficient to use the impersonal official title "Incumbent," as if addressed personally he may be absent (as they most frequently are) "on holiday," and time will thus be wasted awaiting his reply. In his absence a curate or church warden would answer and attend to the matter. As the clergy in charge of parishes are either rectors or vicars, depending on certain legal rights, and each one is a stickler for his title, the use of "Incumbent" in addresses is a safe and proper compromise. In some cases I have found that a telegram, with a prepaid answer, would expedite the dating of an appointment, but as a rule the local clergy in rural districts are constitutionally averse to doing anything in a hurry and rather resent this "hustling" method of disturbing their village calm. Rarely will an incumbent give you immediate permission to see the registers if you arrive unannounced. As a rule the country vicars, after their typical reserve is abandoned, are glad to talk to an educated or intelligent American and often will invite his visitor to tea if the appointment is in the afternoon; and as smoking and drinking wine is a universal custom among all classes, these social amenities must be accepted without comment.

The writing of these early registers is that of the period involved in the search. If before 1600, a certain style of chirography is found and, roughly speaking, a gradual change took place after that, and in the following century a further evolution occurred whereby the succeeding entries in the course of two hundred years gradually approached our own form of writing by the Italian script. One must therefore be somewhat of an adept at reading the varied handwriting of the period about 1550 to 1650 as found in these registers or his journey will be fruitless. Few of the clergy are experts in this and are unable to aid in deciphering the early entries. Often the Christian names are entered under the Latin form, which adds to the difficulty. Registers differ in arrangement of entries, although all are chronological. Some have baptisms, marriages and burials mixed as they occur, but in the parchment copies the three classes are separated and each can be read separately.

Here one meets with the universal "fee system" so common in all English public offices, for the parish register is classed as a public record and is required to be shown on request at all reasonable hours. Examination must be conducted in the presence of the custodian and no such freedom of leisurely, unguarded use of public records exists there as with us. Naturally, as Americans are aliens, we have no legal right to require the clergy to produce their registers, but permission is rarely refused except to comply with the convenience of the vicar. It is one of the sources of his income, for he is legally entitled to a shilling for producing the register and allowing one year's entries to be examined, and a sixpence for each and every year thereafter. If he requires more than that he should be reminded that such fee is all he is entitled to by law. Each incumbent differs from another in the collection of fees. Some insist on the "last penny," others make a nominal charge, and occasionally, if the search is fruitless, no fees are asked. In case of a long search, covering, say fifty years, to get all the entries under one name, it is well to suggest a lump sum for the examination—a sort of commutation—and that is usually accepted. In my experience the English clergy are generally courteous in their dealings with American searchers, but they like to be informed whether the search is for family history or for legal purposes connected with property. In the latter case they insist on full payment of their fees.

If the searcher has been fortunate enough to find the baptism of his ancestor in a parish register whither his clue has directed him, it may happen that this is the only appearance of his family in that particular place and that they were transient residents there. The marriage of his parents is not found there and he is practically in the same position respecting the early origin of the family as when he started. It then becomes necessary to examine sources which show the general location of the family, either in that general locality or elsewhere in England.

The principal source of this information is in the probate records. The settlement of estates was from the beginning under control of the church and all records of wills and administrations of estates are to be found in the Diocesan registries located at the seats of the various bishoprics of England. The jurisdiction over wills was varied and, roughly speaking, was divided into various classes. The principal Prerogative Court of the Archbishop of Canterbury had jurisdiction over the estates of all persons owning property in more than one diocese. The recorded wills in this court begin in 1383 and are deposited in Somerset House, London. The second class of wills comprise those of testators who owned property in more than one parish in a particular diocese and these came under the control of the Bishop of the diocese in which the testator lived. The third class included testators owning property in any one parish and were subject to the jurisdiction of the archdeacon having authority in a section of the diocese where the testator lived. There are a number of variations to this classification which need not be detailed as they would confuse the searcher at the outset. Suffice it to say these exceptions must be learned by experience and ascertained in published books on the subject, such a one being Marshall's "Handbook to the Ancient Courts of Probate."

It also needs to be explained that the boundaries of a dicoese are not co-extensive with the boundaries of the counties which sometimes give the title to a bishopric. For instance, the Bishopric of Lincoln covered the counties of Lincoln, Bedford, Buckingham, Hartford, Huntington, Leicester and Northampton and early wills of testators from these counties are found in the Cathedral City of Lincoln. The Bishop of Exeter had jurisdiction over wills of residents in Devon and Cornwall, and the Bishop of Bath and Wells over Somersetshire. These are examples of the disjointed location of wills under ecclesiastical jurisdiction. An excellent guide to the location of these by counties is to be found in a handbook on the subject prepared by J. Henry Lee, an American genealogist, in 1906 and published in London that year. At Exeter, for example, are the records of twelve different probate courts—all with separate calendars and indexes which must be examined to cover any case of searching in Devon and Cornwall.

Permission to search in these courts must be obtained from the Chief Justice of the Court of Admiralty, Probate and Divorce, issued at Somerset House, Strand, London, to applicants without fee. The applicant must state the particular probate registries in which he wishes to search and on presentation of this permit to the local Registrar of Probate it gives him the privilege of search subject to the local rules which each office makes for its own convenience. This "convenience" means restricted hours and extremely limited as to seats. For example, Norwich has but two available seats and one cannot count on more than four hours for a working day in any office. As a matter of fact, the probate offices are a source of present-day revenue for current business of settling estates and the attendants have little knowledge and less interest in their ancient records and, naturally, genealogical research which provides no fees and takes up their time is regarded by them as a nuisance.

After permission has been obtained from the local probate official under the circumstances previously described, the key to recorded wills and administrations are found in the MS indexes—sometimes scarcely legible through age. In several offices these old indexes are entered by the Christian name and are practically useless. The inherent difficulties of research now confront the student. He has not the privilege of open shelves to which he can have access as, for instance, in the Boston or New York probate offices where he can help himself to the desired volume, but they must be brought to him by the clerks, generally one at a time and if it happens that the volume called for does not contain the desired will, another must be requested and will be brought whenever the leisure of the clerk permits him to give it attention from his daily duties. Thus considerable delays are sure to happen and prevent one obtaining the full benefit of even the short hours available. At Somerset House, but four volumes a day are allowed for one person and it can readily be seen that a day must be entirely lost if these four volumes happen to be without the desired information. An occasional tip judiciously placed with an attendant may expedite and break over the limitations of volumes. I have found this efficacious.

With the volumes of recorded wills in his possession the searcher is confronted with the usual problem of ancient chirography and often Latin contractions, dependent on the period searched. The earlier volumes of about 1400 present specially difficult reading, but at Somerset House the splendid collection of parchment volumes represent the highest type of engrossing and after some practice it is possible to not only decipher but read them with reasonable skill and rapidity. It should be stated that ink is not allowed to be used in these offices and only abstracts of wills are legally permitted to be made. The object of this is to confine the making of complete copies to the office force so that statutory fee for such certified copies can be collected. This provision, however, is not generally enforced and with a complaisant custodian a complete copy can be made by the searcher.

Generally speaking, the probate offices do not contain complete transcripts in volumes of all the wills in its custody, but in the files are usually found the originals which are also available for examination but only upon the payment of one shilling for the production of the original. In case a photographic reproduction of an original will is desired, one runs up against a special fee of one guinea for the privilege of such reproduction, to which must be added the cost of a local photographer to do the work.

In the event that you go to a probate office for which you have no permit in your Somerset House card authority, you can, by payment of a special fee, obtain immediate service such as looking at an original will or a volume of records, but this does not allow any copy to be made beyond the name and residence of the testator and the date of probate action. In such an emergency one has to memorize the names of beneficiaries and such other information as may be useful to him.

Wills give more general information regarding a family name and often furnish facts which parish registers cannot do. The yeomanry of England were continually moving from parish to parish as opportunities for work or improved conditions of tenancy offered. A move of a mile to an adjoining parish throws the searcher out of gear as much as if it were a removal of many miles. It should be remembered that marriages took place, in the large majority of places at the bride's home, and unless the residence of the bridegroom were specifically stated, he may have come from a distant parish. Another fact to be remembered in connection with both registers and wills is the custom at that period to baptize the eldest child at the former home of the mother. Confusing circumstances of this sort will be generally cleared up by wills and in many cases the old home of the family or the birthplace of the testator will be stated therein. Generally, testators left a certain amount of money not only to the poor of the parish where they lived at time of decease, but to another parish and this second one was generally their birthplace.

Full note should be taken of every person and place mentioned, including witnesses and overseers and accurate references to the registry, book and volume should be taken when the abstracts are made. It is well to make a carbon copy of each record to be kept in a separate receptacle in case the original is lost.

A valuable source of information for the existence and residence of adult males in England are the tax lists. These are of two kinds—general and local. The general tax lists are known as subsidies and represent the grants by Parliament to the King to collect a specified amount of money to be used for particular or general purposes and they are on deposit in the Public Record Office, London, where they can easily be consulted. They exist, for the practical purposes of this paper, from 1327 to 1675, the latter being known as the Hearth Tax and is the last general subsidy collected by the government. These subsidies are apportioned among the forty counties of England and were imposed on the well-to-do landlords and those possessed of enough property to make the collection of the tax profitable. The Hearth Tax is rather too late for use in connection with the great New England emigration prior to 1650 but is valuable for furnishing location of families who were left behind and who may have carried on the significant Christian names borne by those who emigrated. The Hearth Tax represents a tax on the number of chimneys in each house and was collected during the reign of Charles II and constitutes practically a census of the householders of that period. These subsidies which remain in the Public Record Office consist of parchment rolls on which are entered by Hundreds, tithings and parishes the residents selected for taxation, giving the valuation of their lands or their personal property and the taxes levied on the same.

In the course of several centuries of changes in deposit many of these rolls are now missing, probably through decay of the parchment, as they were stored for years in the damp dungeons of the Tower of London. Many of them are almost illegible, but others stored in more favorable locations are as clean and perfect as the day they were written.

These subsidies do not constitute an annual taxation, as they represent certain grants of money to the Sovereign at various years during his reign. For instance, the subsidies of James I are in the third, seventh, tenth, eighteenth and twenty-first years of his reign, and in Charles I the first, third, fourth and sixteenth years of his reign. In addition he attempted to collect by Royal prerogative the famous Ship Money Tax in 1634 when the King was trying to carry on the Government without the control of Parliament. It was declared illegal in 1641 and was one of the underlying causes of the Civil War. Refusals to pay were frequent and lists of delinquents were sent out for the action of the Sheriffs and some of these exist where the original tax is missing. In one of these I found Roger Goodspeed as a delinquent, our settler at Barnstable. He was living then in the parish of Windgrave, Buckinghamshire, not far from the home of the great John Hampden who led the revolt against any taxation levied without consent of Parliament.

As a rule, not many of the New England emigrants will be found in these subsidies because only a few of them were freeholders, but I came across a fair representation of them in these subsidies; for example Simon Huntingdon and Nicholas Busby of Watertown in the Norwich tax; Andrew Hallett of our Yarmouth, in Bowood, Dorset, and Rev. John Warham, who came to Dorchester and Windsor in the tax list for Crewkerne, Somerset. These subsidies vary in extent. The Devon subsidy for 1624 contains 14,000 names; Norfolk subsidy 8,000: Somerset 10,000 names and Kent 7,000. These are the largest known to me for the emigration period. The fullest subsidies, numerically speaking, which practically constitute the census for the males of any year, are those of 1327, 1524, 1568, 1593 and the Ship Money Tax above mentioned.

Local taxation, assessed annually, is to be found in the custody of the incumbents of parishes, as it was known as the Poor Rate Tax and was assessed by the wardens of each parish to support the indigent and to care for miscellaneous expenses of the parish during the ecclesiastical year. These are known as the Churchwardens' Accounts, but few of them existing as early as 1600 have survived. When they do exist they are the most valuable evidence of the existence of people in those parishes at the time they were made. When visiting a parish to consult the registers, inquiry should be made for the Churchwardens' Accounts to obtain evidence supplementary to that of baptisms, marriages and burials. The production of these books is not covered by any law or specific fees for examination but incumbents are usually courteous about showing them if they are aware of their existence. I have found such books in the church chests which were unknown to the vicar when inquiry was made for them.

Presuming that the emigrant ancestor has been practically located and possibly in some large town, the searcher will find in the Corporation Archives of the various towns and cities, records of the civil administrators and Guild Companies information of the highest value. In this connection it may clear up some confusion in the division of the local civil government in England which are different from ours to state what these differences are. Cities in England are those in which cathedrals are situated and are thus the Sees of the various Bishops. Wells, a community of 2500 people, is a "city", as is London with six million inhabitants, simply because it has a cathedral and a Bishop residing there. With us a city is established whenever it outgrows in population its old town form of government. The next division in England consists of boroughs which include the larger towns, while the word "town" is scarcely known in England in the sense that we employ it. The parish is the minimum unit of civil administration corresponding to our village or small town government.

These corporation records are of various classes but the principal and most important for genealogical purposes are the apprentice and Freeman, or Burgess Rolls which exist in the cities and boroughs, but not in the parishes. Nearly every city and borough possesses these records, extending back in some cases to the Middle Ages, but, singularly, there are none preserved in London until too late for use in connection with New England emigration. They are useful when one is able or wishes to carry his ancestral line back to the parish register period. Nearly every young boy was apprenticed and the records give his parentage and their residence and the term of his service. Many boys came into the larger towns to serve as apprentices and thus distinct clues are found for the location of his family in some distant parish. All boys were usually apprenticed from ten to twelve years of age and became free upon attaining twenty-one years, so the birth year of the apprentice can easily be determined. Frequently boys were apprenticed to their parents or near kinsmen to learn a trade long used by the family. In the same manner but less frequently girls were apprenticed to learn domestic work. This was the case of orphan girls under guardianship.

Upon terminating his service the apprentice was entitled to membership in the particular guild to which his master belonged and automatically became a freeman of the city or borough. His name was then entered on the city or borough rolls as a citizen or burgess. In London he became a citizen, in Shrewsbury a burgess. The burgess rolls are of equal value as they contain additional information respecting the freeman's family. Persons could become freemen by other methods than apprenticeship. For example, by redemption, as it was called, meaning that they bought their citizenship for a stipulated sum. This was the case with William Swift, ancestor of the famous packers of Chicago, who became a member of the London guild in this manner. The records of the Guild Companies are the private property of the company to which they relate and access to them is difficult to obtain. This is true in large cities like London. Personal inspection cannot be made and a fee of a guinea is demanded by most clerks for a report on a particular name. But this is not the universal rule. The Merchant Tailors Company of London are very liberal and courteous in furnishing whatever information they have without a fee.

Other Corporation Records will include valuable and often particularly important information on the object of the search. These comprise Ward lists of residents, local tax lists, leases of property and transactions of the Mayors' or Burgesses' Courts covering the infractions of local laws. Bristol has a splendid set of these records extending back to the Middle Ages and intelligently arranged for examination under very liberal conditions. The same may be said of Plymouth, Shrewsbury, Southampton, Ipswich and other like boroughs too numerous to specify. It would be, however, ungracious to omit mention of the records of the City of London, now in the Guildhall, which have recently been made available for examination by the City Archivist. They are divided into appropriate classes, mostly indexed for easy reference, and are generally placed at the disposal of the searcher without any of the needless restriction which some smaller places throw around their records London has a special jurisdiction over the estates of its citizens. It was an unwritten law which became an invariable custom that freemen of the city should dispose of their estates in three equal parts—one to his wife, if surviving him, one to his children and the remaining third for his own disposition in personal bequests. This was usually referred to in wills as the "laudable custom" of the city. The City Chamberlain was charged with supervision of the third bequeathed to children to see that they received their portions. The records of this official supervision are contained in volumes labeled "Orphans Recognizances" and should be consulted always whenever the emigrant ancestor has been located in London. It should be here remarked that hundreds of emigrants from the great city came to New England in the seventeenth century, more than is generally known. Locating an ancestor in a parish in London after it has been determined that he came from that city, is a difficult problem. Over four score churches with their parish registers were destroyed in the Great London Fire of 1666 out of a total of 106 edifices, but many of the remaining registers have been printed. Do not overlook London in any search for an ancestor whose residence is unknown.

As previously set forth, a large part of the domestic life of the people of England was under the control of ecclesiastical authorities. It has been explained what relation the church had to the settlement of estates, attending to the probate business, which in our first settlement was immediately changed and this function of government assigned to civil authorities where it properly belonged. Another more vital function was also exercised by the church authorities in every community. The Bishops and Archdeacons in each diocese were the constituted authorities over the daily lives and actions of the people, fulfilling what we should understand as local courts of limited civil and criminal jurisdiction. These church functionaries took cognizance of infractions of the church canons and local parish laws as a matter of course, but in addition to this they had authority to deal with infractions of the moral laws such as violation of the marriage vow, illicit cohabitations, breaches of promise of marriage, slander and petty larceny. Ecclesiastically they took cognizance of infractions of church discipline such as absence from communion or other non-attendance, failure to observe the requirements of the prayer book in relation to the ritual, neglect in payment of tithes and encroachment on church property. In addition to this the clergy had authority to issue licenses of marriage, licenses to teach school and permits to practice midwifery, and to grant dispensations respecting fast days. The records of all these intimate associations with the daily lives of the people are to be found in the Act Books of the Consistory and Archdeaconal Courts of the several dioceses.

Some of the records extend to several hundred volumes and, as may be inferred from this general survey, they are of the utmost importance and value, ranging in my opinion of nearly equivalent value to probate and parish records. Nearly every adult in nearly every parish got into the toils of the clergy sooner or later—generally sooner—and it is not infrequently the case that more can be learned of a particular individual from these diocesan records than from wills or registers. The licenses of marriage, for example, are of the highest value as they give not only the age and residence of the principals but the names of the sureties, usually parents or kinfolks of the contracting parties. Not all marriages were consummated by license as the ordinary folk were married by banns proclaimed three times in the parish house without the fee required by a license. The other forms of ecclesiastical jurisdiction cited above followed the individual from the cradle to the grave. Regular trials were had in all classes involving moral turpitude and testimony taken in the form of depositions by witnesses, all of which were recorded at length in a special set of volumes. The depositions taken in these ecclesiastical courts are of unusual value as they give more personal particulars of the deponents than were required by the civil courts. These deponents stated not only their age and present residence and how long they had lived there, but all former residences and length of time in each and their place of birth. In addition to this it was customary to state why and how they remembered certain events in order to add strength to their testimony.

Violations of the church ritual were common charges and became uniformly so about the time of the New England emigration—such as refusal to kneel at communion, to bow at the name of Jesus and publicly scoffing at the church services. Punishment for these infractions was public acknowledgement of the offence the following Sabbath or excommunication if a refusal to obey was persistently maintained. This was all the "persecution" that the Puritans suffered and of which so much has been written. It was the non-conforming clergy who felt the heavy hand of the church at that period as they were the leaders in the revolt.

These valuable records, scarcely ever consulted by the average searcher, are now in custody of the Registrars of each diocese and may be found in every cathedral city. Some are more complete than others. Bristol, for instance, lost most of its ecclesiastical records a century ago in the riots during the Corn Law agitations. These diocesan Act Books are not easy of approach. The custodians, usually solicitors, more concerned with current business than sixteenth century tomes, have no facilities in their offices for convenient examination of these ancient folios. They are not public records like parish registers and there is no obligation to produce them from the lofts or towers of cathedrals—the usual location of them. Nevertheless they can be seen with a little diplomacy or a proper introduction. The usual fee must be paid for this privilege which is generally a guinea a day. I have obtained the most valuable material from them and it is worth it on any important search. It is generally understood that nobody is allowed to examine them, under the present Bishop's attitude, as he has no interest in the object of such searches.

One class of documents which are valuable with us in America for the solution of family descents are deeds of property found in the county registries of the several States. Nothing has been said about similar documents in England because such do not exist, and deeds of property such as we have had from the earliest settlement of this country were unknown in England, the nobility and landed gentry having absorbed most of the area of the Kingdom for themselves and maintained an oligarchy of landlords and tenants for centuries. Only now and then was one of the "villains" (Serfs) able to break out of bondage and have a certain amount of liberty to call a small piece of land his own with some restrictions in favor of the greater overlord. This more or less fortunate class are described as freeholders and as such could dispose of their rights. The manner of disposal approached somewhat our form of land transfers by warranty deeds but it was so complicated by legal red tape that it required several different processes to complete the transaction. These documents are known as the Pedes Finium or Feet of Fines, indicating that the grantor had to pay a fine for the privilege of selling his property. The sale included an appearance in the King's Court, the "Querrant" being the purchaser and the "Deforcient" the seller. No description of the property was given beyond the total acreage and whether houses and buildings were on the property in a specified parish. No boundaries were given or abuttors named. This deed was then engrossed three times on one piece of parchment—two of them side by side and one across the end of these two. They were then cut apart in a waving line, one being given to the purchaser, another to the seller, and the end copy or foot of the parchment was filed in the Rolls Office. Hence the name Feet of Fines. These Feet are now in the Public Record Office, London, and the calendars of them by regnal years, extending to nearly a hundred volumes from the Middle Ages almost to modern times, engrossed in almost microscopic legal script, are available for examination. It requires long practice to decipher them and they scarcely repay the time and trouble of their examination.

The reason for this is that so few of the emigrants were freeholders. The vast majority of these fines relate to transactions of the landed gentry and nobility, but if a good clue exists these should not be overlooked. I have found in the Yorkshire Fines a sale in 1611 by Gov. William Bradford of his property in that county descended to him from his grandfather. The original "Feet" are generally in fine condition but the difficulty of reading them is great owing to the engrossment being in contracted and sometimes marvellous Latin.

The other form of land tenure by copyhold takes us into a private class of document very difficult to consult. They are in custody of solicitors of manors and the owners generally resent any inquiry into their private property holdings. These are the Manor Rolls and are the property of the present owners of the ancient manors of England, either descended to them by inheritance or purchase. These manor rolls record the annual doings of the Courts Baron held by the Lord of the Manor for the yearly round-up of his tenants to pay him homage, but particularly for the collection of rents. It was a sort of sweating affair in which the Lord of the Manor extorted from these helpless tenants various "customary" fines. For example, if a tenant died during the year his poor widow or successor had to pay a "fat beeste" to the Lord for the privilege of renewing the lease. If the tenant's daughter married another fine was exacted, and so on without end.

At the conclusion of the annual court the tenant was given a copy of the record which renewed his yearly lease and thus originated the word "Copyholder" because he held his property by a copy of the Manor Roll. Naturally he could not sell the land, but in the gradual humanization of England he was able to dispose of the rights in his lease-hold. The Public Record Office has many of these Manor Rolls recently deposited, particularly of the Royal Manors and those owned by the Ecclesiastical Commissioners. Americans descended from Colonial emigrants can have real pride in claiming descent from these copyholders who had the courage to break away from this hopeless bondage and establish a nation of freemen and freeholders. Any one of these men and women who braved the "vast and furious ocean", as Bradford phrased it, is worth a dozen of those lords who fattened for ages on the labor of their tenants.

But one more class of records remains to be considered by the searcher if he has not already located and elaborated his pedigree, namely the judicial records of England. It will not be worth time or space to go into an explanation of the intricacies of the various courts and their jurisdictions as they are numerous and bewildering. The King's Bench, the Chancery Courts, the County Courts (Quarter Sessions), and the Manor Courts are enough to specify here as covering all that the average American searcher could profitably include in his program. The court records are not mentioned now as in many cases of inferior importance to other sources of genealogical material. On the contrary, the Chancery Courts contain some of the most valuable evidences relating to families that can be found in England. The writer has found in them more important facts than in any other source. In one Chancery suit was obtained a complete story of the residence, parentage, marriage, names of children and emigration to New England of a prominent Colonial governor whose ancestry had been sought in vain for some years. In another the exact time when an emigrant sailed from England, and in another a complete family pedigree was given. These examples could be multiplied in which residence in New England or emigration hither formed a part of the pleadings. For this reason the writer considers the records of the Chancery Courts of the highest value because of their character and the splendid facilities for consulting them in the Public Record Office, Chancery Lane, London. The great parchments on which are recorded the pleas and answers of the litigants offer little difficulty in reading and they are so arranged that most all the documents in a suit are found together or can be easily obtained.

The Chancery Courts are the courts of equity as distinguished from the courts which deal with statute law. The Chancery judges heard cases in which the plaintiff had no remedy by law but had an equitable claim to something which he tried to establish by evidence. A typical example would be the loss of title deeds by which the ownership of property could not be shown if a sale were impending and evidence would be introduced to show that the plaintiff and his father or grandfather had always lived on it unmolested and the verdict in his favor on the evidence would confirm his title by a court record. At that time the actual possession of title deeds or feet of fines were as important as actual residence on the property. In these pleadings a full statement of the family pedigree and succession of owners would be given as far back as possible—sometimes several generations—and the testimony of old neighbors offered to support the claim. In no other class of documents can such information be found. Many of these suits, however, are staged simply to get a verdict of record. The plaintiff would sue a friend for slander in "giving out speeches" that his title was not good. The issue would be joined, testimony introduced and a verdict secured that the alleged slander was never uttered and that the title held good in law. These records date from about 1400 but are of little value as early as that to an American searcher looking for his emigrant ancestor.

In the course of a lifetime nearly every adult in England got into these Chancery Court records either as defendant or witness or was mentioned in the testimony. These suits have been arranged chronologically in the Record Office and manuscript records of them are all in existence. In addition some of these calendars have been printed with a brief description of the details of each suit and the location of the property or residence of the parties. For the period most important to Americans, 1600-1700, these printed calendars are of little help. The suits for the reign of Charles 1 (1625-1649) are printed in four volumes with only the surnames of the plaintiffs given alphabetically and the defendants helter skelter in the many thousands of cases. "Wilson vs. Tozer" is a little help for the plaintiff's name, but for Tozer one has to go through the entire list of four volumes outside of letter T. The calendar for the reign of James I (1603-25), has been printed with particulars of each suit A to K alphabetically arranged. The Chancery Court was so big that it had six divisions and "The Six Clerks," as they were called, kept separate records during the seventeenth century. Only one division (Reynardson's) has had its calendar printed. The Court of Requests, sometimes called the poor man's court, has not been catalogued after 1600 and its many thousands of cases with depositions and other records are tied up in over three hundred great bundles, but they contain much material relating to New England. I speak of this from a long and complete examination of the suits in this court. Many searchers for our early emigrants stop too early in the Chancery Courts, as I learned by experience. In one instance a suit as late as 1690 gave information of the ancestor, his emigration and the family connections. One of our countrymen who came over while I was there found his ancestor in the first suit he called for in the Record Office, but this was only a piece of luck that cannot be expected as a regular occurrence. Of course, odd surnames help greatly in any kind of a search. Associated documents in these suits are the Chancery and Exchequer Depositions and the Court Books recording the reports of the Masters in Chancery and the decisions of the judges, which always add important facts. In one of these I found that the defendant had fled "as is suspected to New England." The suspicion was correct. He had.

The quarter sessions are the criminal courts of the counties and the records are at the various county seats. These contain like valuable records. In those days there were so many things that were "criminal" which are now adjusted by less drastic means that the word criminal need have no deterrent effect. Several of these County Records have been printed (Somerset, Worcester). The Courts Leet of the Manors were like our Police Courts and took cognizance of violations of manor laws or customs. If able to get permission to see these rolls the searcher will find that they often give valuable information about the tenants.

By this time the searcher has probably found his ancestor and secured most of his life story up to the time of his emigration and I leave him, with my congratulations, to enjoy the fruits of his labor. For with all these records available few will miss the quarry if persistent and intelligent detective work is followed through.

NOTE

The important Manuscript material found in the library of Col. Charles E. Banks at the time of his death in 1931, was distributed as follows:

The following 44 titles, in 56 volumes, are in the Congressional Library, Washington, D. C.

ALLEN. Manuscript and printed Genealogical Notes on the Allen Family in America and England, collected and arranged by Charles E. Banks. Laid in are numerous letters showing the result of researches made in tracing the family. About 80pp., 8vo, cloth.

This family History is fairly complete, and apparently was being prepared for printing.

BANKS, CHARLES E. (Compiler). Topographical Dictionary of English Emigrants to New England, 1620-1650. Maps, 405pp., and Index of Names and Places. 4to, buckram.

FORTUNE (The). Passengers of the Fortune, Thomas Barton, Master, 1621. Printed and in MSS. The manuscript material consists mainly of genealogical data, collected by Col. Banks, in England. About 150pp., 4to.

GENEALOGICAL NOTES. Five oblong folio scrap-books, with 1 vol. Index, (Names and Places). Total of 1455pp., in loose-leaf folders.

An invaluable collection of MSS. genealogical data, collected by Col. Banks during his many years research work, in this country and England. For the most part, the material was gathered in England, from Parish and Diocese Records, Tax Lists, Wills and Court Records, etc. Nearly all are from records prior to 1620.

GENEALOGICAL NOTES. Four oblong folio scrap-books, 769pp., in all. Bound in loose-leaf folders. MSS.

Similar to preceding, but smaller. Typewritten Index gives 350 families.

LECHFORD (England) LIST. Miscellaneous Lists, Subsidies, Protestations, etc. Manuscript Notes made by Col. Banks. In 2 vols. of about 200pp. each. Oblong folio, in loose-leaf binder.

The Lists are followed by extended notes on the families of Gardiner, Pepperell, Cleeves, Morton, Hilton, Jordan, Purchase, Royal and Standish.

MAYFLOWER (The). The Mayflower Passengers. Printed and in MSS. The manuscript material consists mainly of genealogical material, collected by Col. Banks, in England. Nearly 200pp., 4to, cloth.

PRINCE. Manuscript and typewritten Genealogical Notes on the Prince Family. In 4 vols. of about 200pp., each. 8vo, cloth.

With genealogical tables, and Index of males. Apparently about ready for publication.

(WINTHROP, John). Genealogical Notes, from the Medical Journal of Gov. John Winthrop, Jr., 1657-1669. Manuscript scrap-book of about 140pp. Oblong folio, in loose-leaf binder.

Compiled by and in handwriting of Col. Banks. Extracted from original Journal in Mass. Historical Society. Typewritten index contains over 160 names. Separate index of cases extends to 13pp.

BEDFORDSHIRE Subsidy Rolls, (Charles I and James I), Public Record Office Reference 72/279, 72/266, 72/269. 80pp., including indices of 139 places and around 1,000 Names. 4to, cloth. MSS.

BOCKING & BRAINTREE Subsidies, 1523-1636. P. R. O. Reference 108/163 15 H VIII. (1523). 53pp., and 23pp. Index. 4to, cloth. MSS.

BOXTED, Essex. Marriages, 1600-1617. 4pp., small 4to, boards. MSS.

BUCKINGHAMSHIRE Subsidy Rolls, 1620-1628. P. R. O. Reference 79/275 to 80/286. 112pp., and Index of over 1,000 Names. 4to, cloth. MSS.

BUCKS Marriages, from Parish Register and Bishop's Transcript of Great Missenden County, Bucks, 1575-1640. 40pp., 12mo, cloth. MSS.

CAMBRIDGESHIRE Subsidy Rolls, 1625-1629. P. R. O. Reference 83/384 to 83/395. 96pp., and Index of over 1,000 Names. 4to, cloth. MSS.

DEVONSHIRE RECORDS. 1, Exeter Subsidy. 2, Royal Loan. 3, Notes, Registers. 4, Dartmouth Protestation Roll. 5, Saint Petrox Transcript. 6, Notes, Plymouth Corporation and Church Records, 1627-61. (168pp.). 4to, buckram. Typewritten and MSS.

DEVON Marriages. Bishop's Transcripts, St. Petrox, Dartmouth County, Devon, 1590-1653. (53pp.), small 4to, boards, MSS.

DEVON Subsidy, 1624. P. R. O. Reference 102/463. 328pp., fully indexed. 4to, half morocco, Typewritten and in MSS.

DORSET. County of Dorset Lay Subsidy Rolls, 1623-1628. P. R. O. Reference 105/307 to 105/322. 186pp., and Index. 4to, cloth, MSS.

ESSEX. Calendar of Wills. Archdeaconries of Bocking, Goodeaster, and Writtle. Small 4to, boards. MSS.

ESSEX County Subsidy Rolls, 1605-1628. P. R. O. Reference 111/573 to 112/638. 192pp. and Index. 4to, cloth. MSS.

ESSEX. Ship Subsidy Money, 1636. 319pp., and Index. 4to, cloth. MSS.

EXCHEQUER DEPONENTS. Vol. 1, 1559-1620. Thick folio, buckram. The names of 43,625 Deponents in the "Exchange Depositions by Commission", from 1 Elizabeth to 18 James I, are arranged in 8 geographical groups, according to the Counties to which the documents relate. England and Wales are completely covered in the list. Two copies of this volume were made. One for Col. Banks, the other for Mr. R. Holworthy, of London, at combined cost of $1,000.00.

EXETER. Marriage Licenses of the Diocese of Exeter, from the Bishop's Register. Edited by Col. J. L. Vivian. Part 1, 121pp., and typewritten Index (Grooms only). Exeter, 1887. Printed and typewritten.

GLOUCESTER Subsidy Rolls, 1620-1625. P. R. O. Reference 116/485 to 116/518. 177pp., and Index. 4to, cloth. MSS.

HAMPSHIRE LAY Subsidies, 1623-1628. P. R. O. Reference 175/490 to 175/529. 218 pp., carefully indexed. 4to, cloth. MSS.

HERTFORDSHIRE Subsidy Rolls, 1610-1629. P. R. O. Reference 121/313 to 121/335. 85pp. and Index. Royal 8vo, cloth. MSS.

HINGHAM, Norfolk, Parish Register, 1600-1645. Marriages, 248pp., and Index. Royal 8vo, half roan. MSS.

HUNTINGDONSHIRE Lay Subsidies. P. R. O. Reference 122/180 to 122/204. 54pp., and Index. 4to, cloth. MSS.

KENT Subsidy Rolls, 1623-1628. P. R. O. Reference 128/610 to 128/636. 287pp., and Index (7,000 names). 4to, buckram. MSS.

LEICESTERSHIRE Subsidy Rolls 1620-1628. P. R. O. Reference 134/286. 93pp., and Index (Persons 94, places 127). 4to., cloth. MSS.

LONDON. A Directory of the House-Holders of London, 1638. 363pp. and Index. 4to, buckram. Hectographed.

A copy of MSS. Codex No. 272 in Lambeth Palace Library. Comprises list of house-holders, or occupiers of shops, etc. in 94 parishes.

LONDON MARRIAGES. (Savoy, Southwark, Whitechapel) 142pp., double column, and Index. 4to, cloth. Typewritten.

Contains 3,800 marriages recorded in three above parishes.

LONDON SUBSIDIES 1595 to 1641, and Rent Rolls, 1638. 81pp., and Index. 4to, cloth. Typewritten and in MSS.

NORFOLK County Subsidies 1598-1640. P. R. O. Reference 152/494 to 153/619. 332pp., and Index. 4to, cloth. MSS.

NORFOLK. Register of Caston. Marriages 1539-1700. 22pp., and Index. 8vo, cloth, 1926. MSS.

NORTHAMPTONSHIRE Lay Subsidies, 1609-1628. P. R. O. Reference 157/392 to 238/129. 114pp., and Index. 4to, cloth. MSS.

OXFORDSHIRE Lay Subsidies. 1620-1629. P. R. O. Reference 163/445— 18 James I, to 164/474, 4 Charles I. 120pp., and Index. 4to, cloth.

RUTLAND Subsidies. P. R. O. Reference 165/188, etc. 23pp., and Index. Royal 8vo, cloth. MSS.

SOMERSETSHIRE Lay Subsidies, 1620-1628. P. R. O. Reference 171/350 to 172/390. 412pp., and Index, 4to, cloth.

These subsidies comprise about 10,000 names.

STEPNEY. A List of the Inhabitants of Stepney, 1640. Including the hamlets of Limehouse, Poplar, Blackwall, Bethnall Green, etc. Alphabetically arranged, from the Protestation Rolls, by C. E. Banks. 4to, buckram. Typewritten.

SURREY County Subsidy Rolls, 1620-1628. P. R. O. References 186/407 to 186/441. 135pp., and Index. 4to, cloth. MSS.

WARWICKSHIRE Subsidy Rolls, 1620-1628. P. R. O. Reference 193/285 to 194/315. 95pp., and Index. 4to, cloth. MSS.

WILTSHIRE Subsidy Rolls, 1609-1628. P. R. O. Reference 199/367 to 199/400. 203pp., and Index. 4to, cloth. MSS.

The Following Manuscripts, compiled by Col. Charles E. Banks, are in the Bangor Public Library, Bangor, Maine.

PIONEERS OF MAINE. Two folio volumes, alphabetically arranged, mostly typewritten, with Pedigrees of every Maine Settler known to the author. Numerous Pedigree Charts and Coats of Arms. About 1,000pp., boards and heavy buckram. (only copy in existance).

YORK (Maine) Records. 134 typed pages; covers all known records from Charter of Agamenticus, 1641, down to 1699. Tipped in at end are 20pp. Records to about 1720. (2) Records, 21pp. typed, mostly Records of Town Meetings from 1732 to about 1780; indexed. (3) Estates, about 300pp. typed, in alphabetical order, of early land Grants, Deeds, etc., in York. (4) Notes, 14pp., typed, mostly bibliographical, giving titles of books relating to York. In all, 4 vols., folio, uniformly bound in boards and heavy buckram.

MANUSCRIPT. Typed and printed genealogical memoranda, collected by Col. Banks at home and in England. In 23 cardboard containers. Six consist of extracts from English Records, Wills, etc. remainder pertain to early settlers in America. Much of this material has never been published.

INDEX, Names and Places, in MSS., to Bancroft's "History of the United States", and Palfrey's "History of New England." About 50pp. 16mo, boards, n.p., n.d.

MANUSCRIPT SCRAP BOOK, 39pp., listing early Maine State Officials, from about 1635 to 1667. At beginning is 4pp. list of names, probably early settlers of York. Also list of subscribers to Submission List of 1658 from Falmouth and Scarboro, and signers of Petition to King Charles II, May, 1668. 8vo, cloth.

MAINE PLACE NAMES, scrap book of 42 leaves, typed and MSS. of unusual Maine Place Names, with their derivations, or mention of where first found. First 2pp. deal with Indian derivation of Agamenticus; laid in, 5pp. correspondence from Mrs. Fannie H. Eckstorm regarding this. Bound at end, 2pp. Index of Places found in Maine deeds. Folio, loose-leaf binder.

The Following Manuscripts are in the New England Historic Genealogical Society, Boston, Massachusetts.

CROWE, Norcross, French, Keayne and Horton Families. Genealogical data from English Records, comp. by Charles E. Banks. 10pp.

CUTTS FAMILY. Genealogical data from English Records, compiled and in hand of Charles E. Banks. 25pp.

DORSET Protestation Returns, preserved in the House of Lords, 1641-2. Edited by E. A. Fry. 180pp. With Typed Index, 158pp., compiled by C. E. Banks. 1912.

EXETER Diocesan Kalendar, 1924. 62pp. Exeter, (1923). Pages 5-31 have marginal notes in Col. Banks' hand, giving dates of parish registers before 1630.

LEA, J. Henry. Genealogical research in England, Scotland and Ireland. Interleaved. 1906. Annotated by Col. Banks, giving corrections and locations of records not noted by Lea.

LIST OF MEMBERS, First Church, Boston, 1630. From Banks' papers.

MAINE FAMILIES of Yeamans, Yeo, Yelas, Young and York. MSS. Genealogical notes, compiled by Chas. E. Banks. 13pp.

MILITIA LISTS in Public Records Office, London, 1531-1544. Typed from working copy in hand of Chas. E. Banks.

OAKES Family, compiled by Chas. E. Banks. About 20pp., MSS. and printed matter, latter from "Old Times", Portland c. 1891. Bound in is "The Wyman Family", by Col. Banks. MSS. Genealogical table and 1 p. printed matter from "Old Times". 8vo, cloth, n. p., n. d.

PARISH REGISTERS in Manuscript, in College of Arms, London, Eng. From typed copy in Chas. E. Banks' papers.

PEDDOK. Manuscript Notes (8pp.) on the Peddok, Pidoke, Peddocke Family. Compiled by Banks.

PRINCE FAMILY. Miscellaneous collection of MSS. Notes, compiled by Banks.

RECORDS OF THE COUNCIL FOR N. E., 10pp. Typed Index, compiled by Charles E. Banks. Cambridge, 1877.

SOMERSET, England. Index to Licence Books, containing Marriage Licences, Administration and Probate Acts, with Names of Bondsmen, Citations, Licences to Preach, Teach, practice Surgery, etc. In Archdeaconries of Bath and Wells and Taunton. 24 folio pages, mimeographed. In loose-leaf binder.

SOULE. Miscellaneous Notes on the Soules, from English Records. Collected by C. E. Banks, 1880-1920. 23pp. printed and typed and in MSS. 8vo. cloth, 1921.

SUFFOLK, England. Ship-Money Returns for Suffolk, 1639-40. Transcribed by V. B. Redstone, 255pp. (printed), Ipswich, 1904. Subsidies and Militia for Suffolk, 1609-1635, transcribed from Original Documents, and Indexed by Chas. E. Banks. 237 leaves MSS. Calendar of Wills in Archdeaconry of Suffolk, 1600-1660, 223pp. of photostat facsimiles of original MSS. Vol., with typed index. 3 vols., uniformly bound in half polished calf. V. p., v. d.

YORK, Maine. Censuses of, 1790 to 1850, lacking 1830-40. Compiled and in hand of Chas. E. Banks.

KEY

to

VARIOUS ABBREVIATIONS

found in the

REFERENCE COLUMN

A. H. A. — Historic Ancient & Honorable Artillery Co., 4 v., 1895.

Als.—Alias.

Asp. — Aspinwall Notarial Records. (Boston Record Commissioners' Reports, Vol. 32).

Austin — Genealogical Dictionary of Rhode Island, 1887.

B. T. or Boston T. — Boston Evening Transcript.

Banks Mss. — Charles E. Banks Mss. in Library of Congress.

Bond — Genealogies of Early Settlers of Watertown, 1860.

Bradford — History of Plimouth Plantation, 1896.

C. E. B. — Banks Mss. in Congressional Library, Washington, D. C.

C. of A. — Mss. in College of Arms, London.

D. L. J. — Donald Lines Jacobus (Genealogist).

Drake — History and Antiquities of Boston, 1856.

Ess. Inst. — Essex Institute Publications.

Farmer — First Settlers of New England, 1829.

History of Jericho, Vermont — by Hayden, Stevens, Wilbur & Barnum, 1916.

Hotten — Original Lists of Persons . . . who went to American Plantations, 1874.

Hoyt — Old Families of Salisbury and Amesbury, Mass., 1897-1916.

Key to Various Abbreviations Found in the Reference Column

(*Continued*)

Hubbard — General History of New England, 1848.

Hutchinson — History of Massachusetts Bay, 3 v., 1760-1828.

Jacobus — New Hampshire Genealogical Magazine.

Lechford — Thomas Lechford's Notebook, 1885.

M. H. S. — Massachusetts Historical Society.

Mass. Bay Rec. — Massachusetts Bay Records.

Mayf. Desc. — The Mayflower Descendant.

N. E. G. R. — New England Historic Genealogical Register.

N. Y. G. & B. R. — New York Genealogical & Biographical Record.

P. C. C. — Prerogative Court of Canterbury Archives.

P. R. O. — Mss. in State Paper Dept., Public Record Office, London.

Perley — History of Salem, 3v., 1924-1928.

Plain Dealing — Thomas Lechford's "Plain Dealing", 1642.

Pope — Pioneers of Massachusetts, 1900.

Riker — Annals of Newton, Long Island.

Savage — Genealogical Dictionary of First Settlers of New England, 4 v., 1860-1862.

Stiles — History of Ancient Windsor, Conn., 1859.

Stone Gen. — Gregory Stone Genealogy.

Trel. Papers — Trelawney Papers.

Vincent — Vincent's History of Pequot War, 1637.

Waters, or Waters and Emmerton — Genealogical Gleanings in England, 1885.

Wyman — Genealogies and Estates of Charlestown, 2 v., 1879.

TOPOGRAPHICAL DICTIONARY

OF 2885

ENGLISH EMIGRANTS

TO

NEW ENGLAND

1620 — 1650

BEDFORDSHIRE

NAME OF THE EMIGRANT	ENGLISH PARISH NAME	SHIPS NAME	NEW ENGLAND TOWN	VARIOUS REFERENCE
NEALE, Francis	Bolnehurst		Salem, Mass. Casco Bay	Banks Mss.
BUNKER, George	Chalgrove		Charlestown, Massachusetts	Banks Mss.
GIDDINGS, George	Clapham	Planter	Ipswich, Mass.	Banks Mss.
ODELL, William	Cranfield		Concord	N.E.G.R. 60/91
WHEELER, George	Cranfield		Concord	Banks Mss.
Isaac	Cranfield		Charlestown, Massachusetts	Banks Mss.
Joseph	Cranfield		Concord	Banks Mss.
Obadiah	Cranfield		Concord	Banks Mss.
Thomas	Cranfield		Concord Fairfield	Banks Mss.
Timothy	Cranfield		Watertown Concord	Banks Mss.
LAWTON, George	Cranfield		Newport, R. I.	Banks Mss.
HAINES, Richard	Dunstable		Salem, Mass.	Aspinwall
BUCKMASTER, Thomas	Dunstable		Boston, Mass.	Banks Mss.
HAYNES, William	Dunstable		Salem, Mass.	Aspinwall
LYNDE, Thomas	Dunstable		Charlestown, Massachusetts	Aspinwall
LONG, Robert	Dunstable	Defence	Charlestown, Massachusetts	Savage Gen. Dict.
SYMMES, Rev. Zachariah	Dunstable		Charlestown, Massachusetts	Savage Gen. Dict.
HOUGHTON, John	Eaton Bray	Abigail	Dedham, Mass.	Pope

BEDFORDSHIRE

NAME OF THE EMIGRANT	ENGLISH PARISH NAME	SHIPS NAME	NEW ENGLAND TOWN	VARIOUS REFERENCE
BALDWIN, Sylvester	Flitwick		Norwich, Conn.	Banks Mss.
ALLING, Roger	Kempston		New Haven, Connecticut	Jacobus N. H. Gen. Magazine
FELT, George	Leighton Buzzard		Charlestown, Massachusetts	Banks Mss.
KEZAR, George	Leighton Buzzard		Lynn, Massachusetts	Aspinwall
SAYER, William	Leighton Buzzard		Salem, 1640 Wenham, 1643 Newbury, 1645	Parish Register
BREED, Allen	Leighton Buzzard		Lynn, Massachusetts	
ROBINSON, John	Mapershall		Haverhill, Massachusetts	N.E.G.R. 63/35
STILES, Francis	Millbrook		Windsor	Farmer
Henry	Millbrook		Windsor	Farmer
John	Millbrook		Windsor	Farmer
WILLIAMSON, Michael	Oakeley	Planter	Ipswich, Mass. Newport, R. I.	Banks Mss. Lechford
GALE, Edmund	Oakeley		Cambridge, Mass.	Banks Mss.
BULKELEY, Rev. Peter	Odell	Susan & Ellen	Cambridge, Mass. Concord	N.E.G.R. 23/303
MELLOWES, Abraham	Odell		Charlestown, Massachusetts	Banks Mss.
PICKETT, Christopher	Pulloxhill		Scarboro, Maine	Banks Mss.
SHALLER, Michael	Rosseter		Boston, Mass.	Banks Mss.
INGERSOLL, Richard	Sandy		Salem, Mass.	Genealogy

BEDFORDSHIRE

NAME OF THE EMIGRANT	ENGLISH PARISH NAME	SHIPS NAME	NEW ENGLAND TOWN	VARIOUS REFERENCE
SPENCER, Gerrard	Stotfold		Cambridge, Mass. Lynn, Mass.	Boston T. 29/12/24
Michael	Stotfold		Cambridge, Mass. Lynn, Mass.	Boston T. 29/12/24
Thomas	Stotfold		Cambridge, Mass. Hartford, Conn.	Boston T. 29/12/24
William	Stotfold		Cambridge, Mass. Hartford, Conn.	Boston T. 29/12/24
NORTON, Henry	Streatley		York, Maine	Banks Mss.
Walter	Streatley		Charlestown, Massachusetts York, Maine	Banks Mss.
CLAYDON, Richard	Sutton		Salem, Mass.	Pope
HANSCOMBE, Thomas	Sutton		Salem, Massachusetts	Mass. Bay Rec. 1/35
SPOFFORD, John	Toddington		Rowley, Mass.	Banks Mss.
LUDDINGTON, William	Turvey		Malden, Mass. New Haven, Connecticut	Banks Mss.
GODFREY, William	Woburn		Watertown	N.E.G.R. 63/32 Aspinwall
SAYER, Francis	Woburn		Southampton, Long Island	Banks Mss.
BRACEY, Rev. John	Wootton		New Haven, Connecticut	Banks Mss.
Thomas	Wootton		Ipswich, Mass.	Banks Mss.
CLARKE, Carew (3) [Thomas (2) John (1)]	?		Newport, Rhode Island	Austin Gen. Dict. 43-47

BEDFORDSHIRE

NAME OF THE EMIGRANT	ENGLISH PARISH NAME	SHIPS NAME	NEW ENGLAND TOWN	VARIOUS REFERENCE
SAYER,				
Job	?		Lynn, Mass. Southampton	Banks Mss.
Thomas	?		Chelsea Southampton	
FOOTE, Pasco	?		Salem, Massachusetts	Perley 1/368

Total number of Emigrants from Bedfordshire is 53 from 23 Parishes.

BERKSHIRE

NAME OF THE EMIGRANT	ENGLISH PARISH NAME	SHIPS NAME	NEW ENGLAND TOWN	VARIOUS REFERENCE
AVERY, William	Arborfield		Dedham, Massachusetts	N.E.G.R. 63/362
BULLOCK, Edward	Barkham	Elizabeth	Dorchester	Aspinwall
AVERY, William	Barkham		Dedham, Massachusetts	N.E.G.R. 63/362
DAVENPORT, Richard	Binfield		Salem, and Boston, Mass.	Waters
HATHORNE, William	Binfield		Dorchester Salem, Mass.	N.E.G.R. 67/258
KNIGHT, William	Binfield		Salem, Mass.	Banks Mss.
DAVENPORT, Richard	Bray		Salem, Mass.	Pope
HATHORNE, John	Binfield		Salem, Mass.	Pope
SMITH, Richard	Burghfield		Sudbury, Mass.	Pope
COBBETT, Thomas	Newbury		Ipswich, Mass.	Waters 98
PARKER, Joseph	Newbury	Confidence	Newbury	N.E.G.R. 60/60
KELLY, John	Newbury		Newbury	
COLLIER, Thomas	Reading		Hull, Massachusetts	N.E.G.R. 60/60
CLEMENT, Augustine	Reading	James	Dorchester	N.E.G.R. 61/61
COGGSWELL, John	Reading	Angel Gabriel	Ipswich, Massachusetts	N.E.G.R. 15/177 Mass. Arc. 39/506
DAMON, John	Reading		Reading, Massachusetts	N.E.G.R. 60/61
LARKIN, William	Reading		Reading, Massachusetts	N.E.G.R. 63/318
SANDS, James	Reading		Portsmouth, Rhode Island	Austin Gen. Dict.

BERKSHIRE

NAME OF THE EMIGRANT	ENGLISH PARISH NAME	SHIPS NAME	NEW ENGLAND TOWN	VARIOUS REFERENCE
WHEELER, Thomas	Reading	James	Boston, Mass.	Banks Mss.
COWDREY, William	Reading		Lynn, Mass. Reading, Mass.	Banks Mss.
PRINCE, John	Shefford (East)		Watertown	Banks Mss.
WILDER, Martha	Shiplake	Confidence	Hingham, Massachusetts	N.E.G.R. 60/60
BUSHNELL, Francis	Thatcham	Planter	Boston, Mass. Salem, Mass. Norwalk, Conn.	Banks Mss.
John	Tilehurst	Hopewell	Salem, Mass.	Banks Mss.
MYLAN, Humphrey	Warfield		Boston, Mass.	Banks Mss.
John	Warfield		Boston, Mass.	Banks Mss.
ABDY, Matthew	Wantage	Abigail	Boston, Massachusetts	P. C. C. Pell p. 275
KEAYNE, Robert	Windsor (New)	Defence	Boston, Massachusetts	Banks Mss.
MANSFIELD, John	Windsor (New)	Susan & Ellen	Boston, Massachusetts	Pope
CLEMENT, Augustine	Wokingham	James	Dorchester	Pope
MATTHEWS, Thomas	Wokingham		Boston, Mass.	Pope
PARKER, Nathan	Newbury		Newbury	Parker Genealogy

Total number of Emigrants from Berkshire is 32 from 15 Parishes.

BUCKINGHAMSHIRE

NAME OF THE EMIGRANT	ENGLISH PARISH NAME	SHIPS NAME	NEW ENGLAND TOWN	VARIOUS REFERENCE
HUNT, Ephraim	Agmondsham		Weymouth, Mass.	Aspinwall
PUTNAM, John	Aston Abbotts		Salem, Massachusetts	Genealogy
LAKE, Henry	Aston Abbotts		Salem, Massachusetts	
BRANDON, William	Aston Clinton		Milford, Connecticut	Aspinwall
BALDWIN, Henry	Aston Clinton		New Haven, Connecticut	N.E.G.R. 26/295
John	Aston Clinton		Norwich, Connecticut	N.E.G.R. 38/160
Sylvester	Aston Clinton		Norwich, Connecticut	Banks Mss.
NORWOOD, Francis	Aston Clinton		Gloucester, Massachusetts	Banks Mss.
BRYAN, Alexander	Aylesbury		Milford, Connecticut	Miner Gen. Page 81
SAXTON, Thomas	Aylesbury		Boston, Massachusetts	Banks Mss. Subsidy
KING, Daniel	Beaconsfield		Lynn, Mass.	Pope
BARNEY, Jacob	Bradenham		Salem, Mass.	Pope
MONTAGUE, Richard	Burnham		Boston, Mass. Salem, Mass. Wethersfield	Savage
SALE, Edward	Chesham		Weymouth, Mass. Charlestown, Massachusetts Edgartown Rehoboth	Banks Mss.
RUSSELL, Henry	Chalfont St. Giles		Weymouth, Massachusetts	Pope
John	Chalfont St. Giles		Dorchester	Lechford

BUCKINGHAMSHIRE

NAME OF THE EMIGRANT	ENGLISH PARISH NAME	SHIPS NAME	NEW ENGLAND TOWN	VARIOUS REFERENCE
WEEDON, James	Chesham	Martin	Newport, Rhode Island	N.E.G.R. 76/115
TATE, Edward	Chesham		Marblehead, Massachusetts Weymouth, Mass.	N.E.G.R. 65/1
WHITMAN, John	Chesham		Weymouth, Massachusetts	N.E.G.R. 65/67
Zachariah	Chesham	Elizabeth	Weymouth, Mass. Milford, Conn.	N.E.G.R. 65/67
PRESTON, William	Chesham	Truelove	Dorchester New Haven, Connecticut	N.E.G.R. 65/64
SEABROOK, Robert	Chesham			Donald L. Jacobus
HALSEY, George	Chesham		Dorchester	P. C. C. Brent 250
TWICHELL, Benjamin	Chesham		Dorchester	Twichell Genealogy
Joseph	Chesham		Dorchester	Banks Mss.
LOVETT, Daniel	Chesham		Salem, Mass.	Banks Mss.
WEEDON, William	Chesham		Newport, R. I.	Banks Mss.
BRINLEY, Francis	Datchet		Newport, Rhode Island	Austin 256 P. C. C. May 193
GROVER, Samuel	Chesham		Charlestown, Massachusetts	Banks Mss.
Thomas	Chesham		Charlestown, Massachusetts	Banks Mss.
BALDWIN, Nathaniel	Cholesbury		Fairfield, Connecticut	Jacobus Old Fairfield, 22
GOODWIN, Christopher	Emberton		Charlestown, Massachusetts	Banks Mss.

BUCKINGHAMSHIRE

NAME OF THE EMIGRANT	ENGLISH PARISH NAME	SHIPS NAME	NEW ENGLAND TOWN	VARIOUS REFERENCE
HIGBY, Edward	Ivinghoe		New London, Connecticut	Banks Mss.
GRIGGS, George	Lavendon	Hopewell	Boston, Mass.	Pope
HUNT, Enoch	Lee		Weymouth, Massachusetts	N.E.G.R. 8/357
WHITMAN, Zachary	Lee	Elizabeth	Weymouth, Mass. Milford, Conn.	Banks Mss.
HOWELL, Edward	Marsh Gibbon		Lynn, Massachusetts	Lechford
RAWSON, Edward	Marris		Boston, Mass.	Waters
LANE, Job	Missenden Great		Dorchester	Aspinwall
GOULD, Zaccheus	Missenden Great		Lynn, Massachusetts	Banks Mss.
BISCO, Nathaniel	Missenden Great		Watertown	N.E.G.R. 39/83
GOULD, Jeremiah	Missenden Great		Weymouth, Massachusetts	Banks Mss.
BALDWIN, George	Missenden Great		Boston, Massachusetts	Banks Mss.
NEALE, John	Missenden Great		Salem, Massachusetts	Banks Mss.
STALLION, Edward	Missenden Great		New London, Connecticut	Banks Mss.
HUNT, Peter	Missenden Great		Weymouth, Mass. Rehoboth	Banks Mss.
HAWES, Richard	Missenden Great	Truelove	Dorchester	Banks Mss.
KIRKLAND, Nathaniel	Newport Pagnell	Hopewell	Lynn, Massachusetts	N.E.G.R. 48/67
Philip	Newport Pagnell	Hopewell	Lynn, Massachusetts	N.E.G.R. 48/67
ODELL, William	Newport Pagnell		Concord	Banks Mss.

BUCKINGHAMSHIRE

NAME OF THE EMIGRANT	ENGLISH PARISH NAME	SHIPS NAME	NEW ENGLAND TOWN	VARIOUS REFERENCE
WORCESTER, Rev. William	Olney		Salisbury, Connecticut	N.E.G.R. 53/328
FULLER, John	Olney		Boston, Mass.	Lechford
GAYNES, Henry	Olney		Lynn, Massachusetts	N.E.G.R. 63/283
PARTRIDGE, William	Olney		Lynn, Mass. Salisbury, Conn.	N.E.G.R. 63/283 Aspinwall
PURRIER, William	Olney		Ipswich, 1638 Salisbury, 1639 Southold, L. I.	Hotten N.E.G.R. 55/378
FARRINGDON, Edmund	Olney	Hopewell	Long Island, New York	N.E.G.R. 55/301
COOPER, John	Olney	Hopewell	Lynn, Massachusetts	N.E.G.R. 55/301
DEXTER, Gregory	Olney		Providence, Rhode Island	R. I. Hist. Society
NEWHALL, Anthony	Olney		Lynn, Mass.	Banks Mss.
STREAM, John	Oving		Weymouth, Mass Hingham, Mass. Milford, Conn.	Banks Mss.
NEALE, Francis	Risborough Princes		Casco Bay Salem, Mass.	Banks Mss.
John	Risborough Princes		Salem, Massachusetts	Banks Mss.
BARSTOW, George	Risborough Princes	Truelove	Dedham, Massachusetts	Banks Mss.
William	Risborough Princes	Truelove	Dedham, Massachusetts	Banks Mss.
PARSLOW, William	Saunderton		Sandwich	Banks Mss.
KIRKLAND, Philip, Jr.	Sherrington	Hopewell	Lynn, Massachusetts	N.E.G.R. 48/68 Waters, 203

BUCKINGHAMSHIRE

NAME OF THE EMIGRANT	ENGLISH PARISH NAME	SHIPS NAME	NEW ENGLAND TOWN	VARIOUS REFERENCE
TOPPING, Richard	Soulbury		Boston, Massachusetts	Waters' 606
PHILLIPS, Nicholas	Wendover		Weymouth, Mass.	Banks Mss.
HUMPHREY, Jonas	Wendover		Dorchester, Massachusetts	N.E.G.R. 63/278
RANDALL, Robert	Wendover		Dorchester	N.E.G.R. 8/357
GIBSON, Christopher	Wendover		Dorchester Boston, Mass.	N.E.G.R. 65/65
TOPPING, Thomas	Whitchurch		Wethersfield Milford, Conn.	Banks Mss.
GOODSPEED, Roger	Wingrave		Barnstable, Mass.	Banks Mss.
BROWNE, Chad	Wycombe (High)	Martin	Providence, Rhode Island	N.E.G.R. 65/84
KING, Daniel	Wycombe (High)		Lynn, Massachusetts	N.E.G.R. 65/84
YOUNG, Rowland	Wycombe (High)		York, Maine	Banks Mss.
FENN, Benjamin	?		Milford, Conn.	Banks Mss.
WESTON, John	?		Salem, Massachusetts	Perley Salem 3/44

Total number of Emigrants from Buckinghamshire is 78 from 28 Parishes.

CAMBRIDGESHIRE

NAME OF THE EMIGRANT	ENGLISH PARISH NAME	SHIPS NAME	NEW ENGLAND TOWN	VARIOUS REFERENCE
NASH, Samuel	Burrough Green		Weymouth, Massachusetts	Lechford
* MOTT, Adam	Cambridge	Defence	Portsmouth, Rhode Island	Austin Gen. Dict. p. 344
SKINNER, Edward	Cambridge		Cambridge, Mass.	Pope
FEARING, John	Cambridge		Hingham, Mass.	Pope
HAWLE, Matthew	Cambridge		Hingham, Massachusetts	Cushing Mss.
BOARDMAN, Andrew	Cambridge		Cambridge, Mass.	
William	Cambridge		Cambridge, Massachusetts	Essex Inst. Vol. 27
ANNABLE, Anthony	Cambridge	Anne	Plymouth, Massachusetts	All Mss. Par. Reg.
DAY, Stephen	Cambridge		Cambridge, Massachusetts	Essex Inst. Vol. 27
CUDWORTH, James	Cambridge		Scituate	N.E.G.R. 14 & 22
GILSON, William	Cambridge		Scituate	Banks Mss.
GOTT, Charles	Cambridge	Abigail	Salem, Mass.	Banks Mss.
BLOSSOM, Thomas	Cambridge		Plymouth, Mass.	Bradford
NASH, Samuel	Comberton		Weymouth, Mass.	Lechford
COOLIDGE, John	Cottenham		Watertown	N.E.G.R. 80/401
ORMESBY, Richard	Ellsworth		York, Maine	Banks Mss.

* The great-great-great-great-great-great-grandfather of Elijah Ellsworth Brownell - - the Publisher.

CAMBRIDGESHIRE

NAME OF THE EMIGRANT	ENGLISH PARISH NAME	SHIPS NAME	NEW ENGLAND TOWN	VARIOUS REFERENCE
DESBOROUGH, Isaac	Eltisley	Hopewell	New Haven, Connecticut	N.E.G.R. 41/53
John	Eltisley		New Haven, Connecticut	N.E.G.R 41/53
Samuel	Eltisley		New Haven, Connecticut	N.E.G.R. 41/53
PECK, Paul	Eltisley		New Haven, Connecticut	Banks Mss.
MITCHELL, Experience	Eltisley	Anne	Plymouth, Mass.	Banks Mss.
ALCOCK, George	Impington		Roxbury	Banks Mss.
WARNER, George	Leverington		New Haven, Connecticut	Banks Mss.
NASH, Samuel	Papworth		Weymouth, Mass.	Lechford
MEAD, Gabriel	Wisbeach		Dorchester	Banks Mss.
KILBOURNE, Thomas	Wood Ditton	Increase	Wethersfield, Connecticut	Genealogy
PRATT, John	Wood Ditton		Cambridge, Mass. Hartford, Conn.	Banks Mss.
PRIME, Mark	?		Rowley, Mass.	Banks Mss.
SACKETT, Simon	"Isle of Ely"		Cambridge, Massachusetts	Riker History Newtown 344

Total number of Emigrants from Cambridgeshire is 29 from 12 Parishes.

*CHESTER

NAME OF THE EMIGRANT	ENGLISH PARISH NAME	SHIPS NAME	NEW ENGLAND TOWN	VARIOUS REFERENCE
HEALD, John	Alderley		Concord	J. G. B.
BOOTH, Richard	Gt. Budworth		Fairfield, Connecticut	Jacobus Old Fairfield, 87.
JONES, Edward	Chester		Charlestown, Massachusetts	Harl. Mss. 1972 fo. 44d.
BANCROFT, Thomas	Cheadle		Dedham, Mass. Reading, Mass. Lynn, Mass.	Essex Antiq. 2 /94
HARRISON, Richard	Kirby, (West)		New Haven, Connecticut Branford, Conn.	N.E.G.R. 70/
MASSEY, Jeffrey	Knutsford		Salem, Mass.	
HILTON, Edward	Northwich		Dover, N. H.	Banks Mss.
William	Northwich	Fortune	Plymouth 1623 Dover, N. H. 1624	Banks Mss.
BOSTWICK, Arthur	Taperly		Stratford, Conn.	Genealogy
WITTER, William	Knutsford? Frodsham		Lynn, Massachusetts	Banks Mss.
RATLIFFE, Robert	Knutsford?	Anne	Plymouth, Mass.	
INCE, Gabriel	?		New Haven, Connecticut	Banks Mss.
Jonathan	?		New Haven, Connecticut	Banks Mss.

Total number of Emigrants from Chester is 13 from 9 Parishes.

* The word "Chester" was used by Mr. Banks instead of the word "Cheshire" - - the Publisher

CORNWALL

NAME OF THE EMIGRANT	ENGLISH PARISH NAME	SHIPS NAME	NEW ENGLAND TOWN	VARIOUS REFERENCE
BONYTHON, Richard	Breage, St.		Saco, Maine	Banks Mss.
ARCHER, Henry	Blazey, St.		Roxbury Ipswich, Mass.	N.E.G.R. 64/348
GILL, Arthur	Enoder, St.		Richmond's Id. Dorchester	Banks Mss.
NOWELL, Peter	Falmouth		Salem, Mass. York, Maine	Banks Mss.
PETER alias DICK-WOOD, Hugh	Fowey	Defence	Salem, Mass.	Pope
FREETHEY, William	Landrake		Richmond Island, Maine York, Maine	Banks Mss.
ANGIER, Sampson	Launceton		York, Maine	Banks Mss.
WISE, Humphrey	Launceton		Ipswich, Mass.	Banks Mss.
CARVEATH, Ezekiel	Menhenniot		Boston, Mass.	Banks Mss.
HUNKING, Hercules	Saltash St. Stephen's		Portsmouth, Rhode Island	Banks Mss.
MITCHELL, Paul	Sheviock		Saco, Maine	Trelawney Papers
HILL, Peter	St. Teath		Richmond Id. Saco, Maine	Banks Mss.
WILLIAMS, Richard	?		Saco, Maine	Banks Mss.
Thomas	?		Saco, Maine	Banks Mss.
LIBBY, John	?		Scarboro, Maine	Trelawney Papers

Total number of Emigrants from Cornwall is 15 from 12 Parishes.

CUMBERLAND

NAME OF THE EMIGRANT	ENGLISH PARISH NAME	SHIPS NAME	NEW ENGLAND TOWN	VARIOUS REFERENCE
NICHOLSON, Edmund	Bootle		Portsmouth, Rhode Island	Austin Gen. Dict. Page 139

Total number of Emigrants from Cumberland is 1 from 1 Parish.

DERBYSHIRE

NAME OF THE EMIGRANT	ENGLISH PARISH NAME	SHIPS NAME	NEW ENGLAND TOWN	VARIOUS REFERENCE
ALSOP, Joseph	Alsop	Elizabeth and Anne	New Haven, Connecticut	Visit. Derby
SHELDON, Godfrey	Bakewell		Scarboro, Maine	Banks Mss.
LEFFINGWELL, Thomas	Croxhall		Norwich, Connecticut	History Norwich Page 189
OLDHAM, John	Derby	Anne	Plymouth, Mass.	Banks Mss.
COTTON, Rev. John	Derby	Griffin	Boston, Mass.	Savage
SHELDON, Isaac	Bakewell		Windsor Northampton	N.E.G.R. 80/378
TOMLINSON, Henry	Derby		Milford, Conn. Stratford, Conn.	Jacobus Fairfield Page 609
STARBUCK, Edward	Draycot		Dover, New Hampshire	Coffin Farmer
PEAT, John	Duffield		Hopewell	Pope
SMITH, Henry	Haddon Hall		Hingham, Massachusetts	Cushing Mss.
LUDLOW, Anthony	Matlock		Hempstead, Long Island	Boston T. 25 Oct. 1926
Obadiah	Matlock		Hempstead, Long Island	Boston T. 25 Oct. 1926
FLYNT, Rev. Henry	Matlock		Braintree, Massachusetts	N.E.G.R. 56/313 Mass. Bay Rec. 25/19
BOURNE, Thomas (Bowne?)	Matlock		Charlestown and Boston, Mass.	N.E.G.R. 55/300
FLINT, Thomas	Matlock		Concord	N.E.G.R. 56/315

18

DERBYSHIRE

NAME OF THE EMIGRANT	ENGLISH PARISH NAME	SHIPS NAME	NEW ENGLAND TOWN	VARIOUS REFERENCE
LUDLAM, Clarence	Matlock		Southampton, Long Island	N.E.G.R. 56/316
William	Matlock		Southampton, Long Island	N.E.G.R. 56/316
WOODIS, William	Matlock		Concord	N.E.G.R. 56/317
JOYCE, John	Mickleover		Sandwich Yarmouth	N. Y. Gen. Biog. Reg.
BANCROFT, John	Swarketon		Lynn, Massachusetts	N.E.G.R. 56/197
GREGSON, Thomas	Thurvaston		New Haven, Connecticut	Familiae Minorum Gentium 1/216 ms. 99 Waters 1/563
HUNLOCK, John	Wingerworth		Boston, Massachusetts	Visit. Derby
STORER, William	Wirksworth		Dover, New Hampshire	Banks Mss.
ALLESTREE, Ralph			Boston, Massachusetts	P. C. C. Derby

Total number of Emigrants from Derbyshire is 24 from 13 Parishes.

DEVONSHIRE

NAME OF THE EMIGRANT	ENGLISH PARISH NAME	SHIPS NAME	NEW ENGLAND TOWN	VARIOUS REFERENCE
FROST, Nicholas	Alwington		Kittery, Maine	Banks Mss.
WINTER, John	Ashprington		Richmond I'd., Maine	Banks Mss.
PARSONS, Jeffrey	Ashprington		Gloucester, Massachusetts	History Gloucester Page 120
OTIS, John	Barnstable		Hingham, Massachusetts	N.E.G.R. 11/282 57/65
ALLEN, Thomas	Barnstable		Barnstable, Mass.	Pope
COLLACOT, Richard	Barnstable		Dorchester	N.E.G.R. 66/87
MAVERICK, Rev. John	Beaworthy	Mary and John	Dorchester	
BRAWNE, Michael	Berry Pomeroy		Dover, N. H.	Banks Mss.
UPHAM, John	Bicton		Weymouth, Massachusetts	Boston T. 22 Apr. 8 28 Sept. 25
SMALL, Edward	Bideford		Isles of Shoals	Genealogy
Francis	Bideford		Kittery, Maine	Genealogy
PROUT, Timothy	Bideford		Boston, Massachusetts	N.E.G.R. 55/106
GARDE, Roger	Bideford		York, Maine	Banks Mss.
SUMMERS, Henry	Bideford	Abigail	Woburn, Mass.	Wyman
SHURT, Abraham 1st conveyancer of land from an Indian to a white man.	Bideford		Pemaquid, Maine	Banks Mss.
Adam	Bideford		Maine	Banks Mss.

DEVONSHIRE

NAME OF THE EMIGRANT	ENGLISH PARISH NAME	SHIPS NAME	NEW ENGLAND TOWN	VARIOUS REFERENCE
LARREBEE, William	Bigbury		Dorchester	Banks Mss.
CARTER, John	Branscombe		Charlestown, Massachusetts	Suffolk Deeds 14/264
ALLYN, Matthew	Braunton		Cambridge, Massachusetts Hartford, Connecticut	Lechford N.E.G.R. 48/496 57/212
Thomas	Braunton		Cambridge, Massachusetts Barnstable, Massachusetts	Lechford N.E.G.R. 48/496 57/212
MADDOCKS, Henry	Brent, South		Saco, Maine Watertown	Banks Mss.
FROST, John	Brixham		York, Maine	Banks Mss.
START, Edward	Brixham		York, Maine	Banks Mss.
CONANT, Christopher	Budleigh, East	Anne	Plymouth, Mass. Charlestown, Massachusetts	Pope
Roger	Budleigh, East		Cape Ann Salem, Mass.	Genealogy
COFFIN, Tristram	Brixton		Salisbury	Genealogy
COLCORD, Edward	Bovey Tracy		Salem, Mass. Dover Hampton, Conn.	Banks Mss.
LANE, Ambrose	Coffinswell		Portsmouth, R. I.	Banks Mss.
Sampson	Coffinswell		Portsmouth, R. I.	Banks Mss.
GILBERT, Humphrey	Compton		Ipswich, Mass.	Banks Mss.
FROST, Nicholas	Clyst S. Mary		Kittery, Maine	Banks Mss.

DEVONSHIRE

NAME OF THE EMIGRANT	ENGLISH PARISH NAME	SHIPS NAME	NEW ENGLAND TOWN	VARIOUS REFERENCE
POOLE, William	Colyton		Taunton, Massachusetts	Som. N&Q. 19/75
NEWTON, Anthony	Colyton		Dorchester	N.E.G.R. 49/385
DRAKE, Thomas	Colyton		Weymouth, Mass.	
FROST, Nicholas	Combe-in-Teignhead		Kittery, Maine	Banks Mss.
JEFFRIES, Gregory	Cookbury		Cape Porpus, Maine	Banks Mss.
HELE, William	Cornwood		Cambridge, Mass.	
HILL, Roger	Cullompton		Saco, Maine	Banks Mss.
CHRISTOPHER, Christopher	Churston Ferrers		New London, Connecticut	History N. L. p. 317
Jeffrey	Churston Ferrers		New London, Connecticut	Hist. N. L. p. 317
CHAMPERNOWNE, Francis	Dartington		Kittery, Maine	History Kittery
BASTER, Richard	Dartmouth		Newport, Rhode Island	Austin Gen. Dict. Page 15
PIPER, Nathaniel	Dartmouth		Ipswich, Mass.	
LADD, Daniel	Dartmouth	Mary and John	Ipswich, Mass. Salisbury, Mass.	N.E.G.R. 38/345
DEERING, George	Dartmouth		Richmond I'd., Maine	Trelawney Papers
Roger	Dartmouth		Kittery, Maine	Banks Mss.
MANNING, Nicholas	Dartmouth		Pemaquid, Maine	Banks Mss.
WEYMOUTH, Robert	Dartmouth		Kittery, Maine	Banks Mss.

DEVONSHIRE

NAME OF THE EMIGRANT	ENGLISH PARISH NAME	SHIPS NAME	NEW ENGLAND TOWN	VARIOUS REFERENCE
DIAMOND, John	Dartmouth		Kittery, Maine	Banks Mss.
HARDING, Stephen	Denbury		Providence, Rhode Island	Banks Mss.
CROOKER, Francis	Exeter		Marshfield, Massachusetts	Genealogy
William	Exeter		Wethersfield, Connecticut	Genealogy
WARHAM, Rev. John	Exeter	Mary and John	Dorchester Windsor	Pope
JACKMAN, James	Exeter		Newbury	Farmer
MANSFIELD, John	Exeter		New Haven, Connecticut	Banks Mss. Winthrop Journal
Robert	Exeter		Lynn, Mass.	Genealogy
TROWBRIDGE, Thomas	Exeter		Dorchester	N.E.G.R. 59/291
DUNCAN, Nathaniel	Exeter		Dorchester	Pope
COGAN, John	Exeter		Boston, Massachusetts	Aspinwall Lechford
FOSTER, Reginald	Exeter		Ipswich, Massachusetts	N.E.G.R. 30/83
SAFFIN, John	Exeter St. Paul's		Scituate Boston, Mass.	Banks Mss.
MILLS, Thomas	Exeter		Saco, Maine	N.E.G.R. 69/189
WADE, Nicholas	Fremington		Scituate	Banks Mss.
BOWDEN, Ambrose	Holbeton		Scarboro, Maine	Banks Mss.
HINKSON, Philip	Holbeton		Scarboro, Maine	Banks Mss. Aspinwall

DEVONSHIRE

NAME OF THE EMIGRANT	ENGLISH PARISH NAME	SHIPS NAME	NEW ENGLAND TOWN	VARIOUS REFERENCE
AVERY, Christopher	Ipplepen		Gloucester, Massachusetts	Babcock & Families
WINTER, John	Harberton		Richmond I'd., Maine	Banks Mss.
BURT, Henry	Harberton		Springfield	Banks Mss.
WINSOR, Walter	Hemiock		Isles of Shoals	Banks Mss.
TURRELL, Daniel	Instow		Boston, Mass.	Savage
COAKER, Richard	Kingsbridge			Waters 178
FORD, Stephen	Kingsbridge		Isles of Shoals	Banks Mss.
ROGERS, William	Kingsbridge		Nantucket, Massachusetts	History Martha's Vineyard
PITCHER, Andrew	Kenton		Dorchester	Pope
SEELEY				
George	King's Teignton		Isles of Shoals	Aspinwall
John	King's Teignton		Isles of Shoals	Aspinwall
Richard	King's Teignton		Isles of Shoals	Aspinwall
LITTLEJOHN, George	Kingsweare		Portsmouth, New Hampshire	Banks Mss.
SHAPLEIGH, Nicholas	Kingsweare		Kittery, Maine	History Kittery
TREWORGIE, James	Kingsweare		Kittery, Maine	History Kittery
DEERING, Roger	Loddiswell		Kittery, Maine	Banks Mss.
MUNJOY, George	Littleham		Boston, Mass. Casco Bay	Banks Mss.

DEVONSHIRE

NAME OF THE EMIGRANT	ENGLISH PARISH NAME	SHIPS NAME	NEW ENGLAND TOWN	VARIOUS REFERENCE
STRANGE, George	Littleham		Dorchester	Banks Mss.
VENNER, Thomas	Littleham		Salem, Mass.	Banks Mss.
ROE, Anthony	Meavy		Portsmouth, New Hampshire	Banks Mss.
PHIPPEN, Joseph	Membury		Hingham, Mass.	Banks Mss.
THORNE, John	Moulton, South		Cambridge, Mass.	Pope
LEWIS, Philip	Northam		Portsmouth, New Hampshire	Banks Mss.
GEE, Peter	Newton Ferrers			Pope 297
HATCH, Philip	Newton Ferrers		Richmond I'd., Maine York, Maine	Trelawney Papers Banks Mss.
CREBER, Moses	Newton Ferrers		Portsmouth, New Hampshire	Banks Mss.
PENWELL, Clement	Newton Ferrers			Banks Mss.
Walter	Newton Ferrers		Saco, Maine	Banks Mss.
TETHERLY, Gabriel	Northam		Kittery, Maine	Banks Mss.
William	Northam		Kittery, Maine	Banks Mss.
LARKHAM, Rev. Thomas	Northam		Dover, N. H.	Banks Mss.
CADE, James	Northam		Hingham, Massachusetts	N.E.G.R. 68/61 Lechford
MATTHEWS, Francis	Ottery, S. Mary			Banks Mss.
ADAMS, Robert	Ottery, S. Mary		Salem, Massachusetts	N.E.G.R. 59/322

DEVONSHIRE

NAME OF THE EMIGRANT	ENGLISH PARISH NAME	SHIPS NAME	NEW ENGLAND TOWN	VARIOUS REFERENCE
CLAPP, Nicholas	Ottery Ven		Dorchester	Pope
Thomas	Ottery Ven		Weymouth, Mass.	Pope
WELLS, Joseph	Ottery Ven		Roxbury	Pope
MARTIN, Richard	Ottery, S. Mary		Rehoboth	Boston T. Oct.6,1924
PHENICK (Phoenix), John	Paignton		Kittery, Maine	Banks Mss.
YEO, Allen	Paignton		Salem, Mass.	Banks Mss.
CHAPIN, Samuel	Paignton		Springfield	Genealogy
NEWCOMB, Andrew	Paignton		Boston, Mass.	Banks Mss.
STETSON, Robert	Paignton		Duxbury	Banks Mss.
NICK, William	Paignton		Marblehead, Massachusetts	Banks Mss.
SNELLING, William	Plympton (St. Mary)		Newbury	Pope
BEALE, Arthur	Plympton (S. Maurice)		York, Maine	Banks Mss.
GAYER, William	Plymouth		Nantucket, Massachusetts	Banks Mss.
PHINNEY, Robert	Plymouth		Plymouth, Mass.	Banks Mss.
MATTHEWS, Walter	Plymouth		Isles of Shoals	Banks Mss.
COLLINS, Christopher	Plymouth		Braintree, Mass.	Aspinwall
THOMSON, David	Plymouth	Jonathan	Dover, New Hampshire 1623	Trelawney Papers & Banks Mss.

DEVONSHIRE

NAME OF THE EMIGRANT	ENGLISH PARISH NAME	SHIPS NAME	NEW ENGLAND TOWN	VARIOUS REFERENCE
HUNNEWELL, Ambrose	Plymouth		Sagadahoc, Maine	N.E.G.R. 54/144
WINTER, John	Plymouth		Richmond Island, Maine	Trelawney Papers & Banks Mss.
HAM, William	Plymouth		Portsmouth, R. I.	Banks Mss.
GIBBONS, Edward	Plymouth		Mass. Bay Boston, Mass	Pope
MARTIN, Francis	Plymouth		Falmouth, Maine	Trelawney Papers
BRAY, John	Plymouth		Kittery, Maine	Banks Mss.
GARY, William	Plymouth		Nantucket, Massachusetts	Banks Mss.
KING, Thomas	Plymouth		Richmond I'd., Maine Hampton, N. H. Exeter, N. H.	Pope
NAZITER, Michael	Sidbury (See P. 27)		Saco, Maine	Banks Mss.
CLAPP, Edward	Salcombe (Regis)		Dorchester	Pope
WEEKS, George	Salcombe (Regis)		Dorchester	Pope
CLAPP, Roger	Salcombe (Regis)	Mary and John	Dorchester	Pope
WALTON, Rev. William	Seaton		Marblehead, Massachusetts	Ext.Ct. Files 45/12
BULLY, Nicholas	Stoke Fleming		Saco, Maine	Banks Mss.
MILBURY, Henry	Stoke-in-Teignhead		York, Maine	Banks Mss.
Richard	Stoke-in-Teignhead		York, Maine	Banks Mss.
JEFFRIES, Gregory	Stoke-in-Teignhead		Arundel, Maine	Banks Mss.

DEVONSHIRE

NAME OF THE EMIGRANT	ENGLISH PARISH NAME	SHIPS NAME	NEW ENGLAND TOWN	VARIOUS REFERENCE
POTUM, Charles	Stoke-in-Teignhead		Scarboro, Maine	Banks Mss.
MINCK, George	Stoke-in-Teignhead		Boston, Massachusetts	Aspinwall
BEDFORD, Nathan	Stoke, Gabriel		Scarboro, Maine	Banks Mss.
JAMES, William	Shebbeare		Boston, Mass.	Banks Mss.
PARKMAN, Elias	Sidmouth		Dorchester	N.E.G.R. 55/322
SMITH, Abraham	Sidbury (see p. 26)		Charlestown, Massachusetts	Pope
BUNKER, James	Slapton		Dover	Banks Mss.
CROCKETT, Thomas	Stoke Gabriel		Kittery, Maine York, Maine	Banks Mss.
BURRINGTON, Bartholomew	Teignmouth (West)		Isles of Shoals	Banks Mss.
HAM, William	Teignmouth (East)		Richmond I'd., Maine Portsmouth, New Hampshire	Banks Mss.
PUDDINGTON, George	Tiverton		York, Maine	Putnam Magazine
Robert	Tiverton		Portsmouth, New Hampshire	Putnam Magazine
COGAN, John	Tiverton		Boston, Mass.	Lechford
MARSHALL, Christopher	Tiverton		Boston, Mass. Piscataqua	P. C. C. Aylett 112
NEWCOMB, Andrew	Tor Mohun		Isles of Shoals	Banks Mss.
PARSONS, Joseph	Torrington		Springfield	N.E.G.R. 1/266

DEVONSHIRE

NAME OF THE EMIGRANT	ENGLISH PARISH NAME	SHIPS NAME	NEW ENGLAND TOWN	VARIOUS REFERENCE
PARSONS, Benjamin	Torrington		Springfield	Savage 3/361
BABBAGE, Christopher	Totnes		Salem, Massachusetts	N.E.G.R. 68/58
BARTLETT, Nicholas	Totnes		Salem, Mass. Casco Bay	Banks Mss.
TRIPE, Gabriel	Totnes		Kittery, Maine	Banks Mss.
NEWCOMB, Andrew	Thrushelton		Isles of Shoals	Banks Mss.
KING, James	Ugborough		Suffolk, Connecticut	N.E.G.R. 58/347 46/370 Genealogy
William	Ugborough		Suffolk, Connecticut	N.E.G.R. 58/347 46/370 Genealogy
GARNESEY, William	Uploman		York, Maine	Banks Mss.
BURGESS, John	Westleigh		Richmond Island, Maine	Banks Mss.
DRAKE, John	Winscombe		Boston, Mass.	Banks Mss.
ALGER, Andrew	Yealmpton		Scarboro, Maine	Banks Mss.
Arthur	Yealmpton		Scarboro, Maine	Banks Mss.
Tristram	Yealmpton		Scarboro, Maine	Banks Mss.
GILLETT, Jonathan	?		Dorchester	N.E.G.R. 47/168
MULFORD, John	?		Southampton, Long Island	N.E.G.R. 34/172
William	?		Southampton, Long Island	N.E.G.R. 34/173

DEVONSHIRE

NAME OF THE EMIGRANT	ENGLISH PARISH NAME	SHIPS NAME	NEW ENGLAND TOWN	VARIOUS REFERENCE
WESTCOTT, Stukeley	?		Salem, Mass.	Banks Mss.
EVELETH, Sylvester	?		Boston, Mass. Gloucester, Mass.	Banks Mss.
SOUTHMEAD, William	?		Gloucester, Massachusetts	Subsidy, Visit'n
HOPPIN, Stephen	?			C. A. H.
CHICHESTER, James	?		Taunton, Mass.	Banks Mss.
BENHAM, John	Town of Plymouth	Mary and John	Dorchester, Massachusetts	History of Jericho, Vt. page 382
John (Son of John)	Town of Plymouth	Mary and John	Dorchester, Massachusetts	History of Jericho, Vt. page 382
Joseph (Son of John)	Town of Plymouth	Mary and John	Dorchester, Massachusetts	History of Jericho, Vt. page 382
EELLS, Maj. Samuel			Dorchester, Mass. about 1633	History of Cuyahoga Co.O.P.351
HODGES, Nicholas	Abbotsham		Isles of Shoals and Rye, N. H.	Banks Mss.

Total number of Emigrants from Devonshire is 175 from 73 Parishes.

DORSETSHIRE

NAME OF THE EMIGRANT	ENGLISH PARISH NAME	SHIPS NAME	NEW ENGLAND TOWN	VARIOUS REFERENCE
DENSLOW, Nicholas	Allington	Mary and John	Dorchester Windsor	Banks Mss.
RANDALL, Philip	Allington		Dorchester Windsor	Banks Mss.
THISTLE, Jeffrey	Abbotsbury		Marblehead, Massachusetts	Essex Prob.
RABY, John	Abbotsbury			P. C. C. Berkeley 246
WAY, Henry	Allington	Mary and John	Dorchester	Banks Mss.
KERLEY, Edmond (Edward)	Ashmore	Confidence	Sudbury, Massachusetts	N.E.G.R. 61/60
William			Sudbury, Massachusetts	N.E.G.R. 61/60
WHITE, William	Beaminster	Mayflower	Plymouth, Massachusetts	Banks Mss.
POMEROY, Eltweed	Beaminster		Dorchester Windsor	N.E.G.R. 59/215
HOSKINS, John	Beaminster		Dorchester Windsor	Banks Mss.
SIBLEY, John	Bradpole		Salem, Mass.	Aspinwall
DUTCH, Osmond	Bridport		Gloucester, Mass.	Lechford
BETSCOMBE, Richard	Bridport		Hingham, Mass.	Lechford
HALLETT, William	Bridport		Newton, Long Island, New York	Mss. College of Arms
MILLARD, Thomas	Bridport		Gloucester, Mass.	Pope
COGGAN, Henry	Bridport		Taunton, Mass.	Banks Mss.
COOKE, Aaron	Bridport		Dorchester Windsor Northampton	Banks Mss.

DORSETSHIRE

NAME OF THE EMIGRANT	ENGLISH PARISH NAME	SHIPS NAME	NEW ENGLAND TOWN	VARIOUS REFERENCE
CHIPMAN, John	Brinspittle		Barnstable, Massachusetts	N.E.G.R. 4/23
MEECH, John	Bredy (Long)		Charlestown, Massachusetts	Banks Mss.
LONG, Joseph	Broadmayne			
LASKIN, Hugh	Broadwindsor		Salem, Mass.	Banks Mss.
BEERE, John	Burton Bradstock		Newport, Rhode Island	Banks Mss.
HUMPHREY, John	Chaldon		Dorchester	N.E.G.R. 65/86
WILLIS, Nathaniel	Chettle		Boston, Mass. Bridgewater	Aspinwall
WYETH, Nicholas	Chardstock		Cambridge, Mass.	Banks Mss.
STONE, John	Chideock		Hull, Mass.	Aspinwall
GALLOP, John	Chideock		Boston, Mass. Gloucester, Mass.	Aspinwall
ORCHARD, Giles	Chideock		Boston, Mass.	Banks Mss.
ARNOLD, Thomas	Cheselborne	Plain Joan	Providence, Rhode Island	Austin 246
DODGE, Richard	Coker, East		Beverly	Genealogy
GARDINER, ——	Compton (Over)	Bachelor	Long Island, New York	Dorset Prot. Roll p. 34
DAVENPORT, Richard	Dorchester		Salem, Mass.	Genealogy
WOODBURY, John	Dorchester		Salem, Mass.	Banks Mss.
WAY, George	Dorchester		Dorchester	Banks Mss.

DORSETSHIRE

NAME OF THE EMIGRANT	ENGLISH PARISH NAME	SHIPS NAME	NEW ENGLAND TOWN	VARIOUS REFERENCE
PURCHASE, Aquila	Dorchester		Dorchester	Whiteway Diary
Thomas	Dorchester		Pejepscot, Maine	Banks Mss.
CAPEN, Bernard	Dorchester		Dorchester	Whiteway Diary
UPSALL, Nicholas	Dorchester	Mary and John	Dorchester	Banks Mss.
TERRY, Stephen	Dorchester	Mary and John	Dorchester Windsor	N.E.G.R. 55/223 53/460
SWIFT, Thomas	Dorchester		Dorchester	Banks Mss.
FORD, Thomas	Dorchester		Dorchester	Pope
HANNAM, William	Dorchester	Mary and John	Dorchester Windsor, Conn.	Pope
DYER, George	Dorchester	Mary and John	Dorchester	Banks Mss.
HORSFORD, William	Dorchester		Dorchester Windsor	Banks Mss.
SMITH, Henry	Dorchester	Mary and John	Dorchester Springfield	Banks Mss.
SANFORD, Mrs. Frances, widow	Dorchester	Mary and John	Dorchester Springfield	Banks Mss.
BUSHRODE, Thomas	Dorchester		Boston, Mass. Virginia	Banks Mss.
ROSSITER, Bryan	Dorchester		Dorchester	M. H. S. 111/10
SNOOKE, James	Fifehead Magdalen		Weymouth, Massachusetts	Savage
BRACKENBURY, Richard	Folke or Holnest	Abigail	Salem, Massachusetts	Banks Mss.
William	Folke or Holnest	Abigail	Salem, Massachusetts	Banks Mss.

DORSETSHIRE

NAME OF THE EMIGRANT	ENGLISH PARISH NAME	SHIPS NAME	NEW ENGLAND TOWN	VARIOUS REFERENCE
EAMES, Anthony	Fordington		Charlestown, Massachusetts	P. C. C. 71 Soame
SPRAGUE, Ralph	Fordington		Charlestown & Salem, Mass.	Genealogy
Richard	Fordington		Charlestown & Salem, Mass.	Genealogy
William	Fordington		Charlestown & Salem, Mass.	Genealogy
CANTERBURY, William	Frampton		Salem, Massachusetts	Perley Salem 3/117
BERRY, Edmond	Frampton		Salem, Mass.	Banks Mss.
CROAD, Richard	Frampton		Salem, Mass.	Banks Mss.
BARTLETT, Robert	Frampton		Marblehead, Massachusetts	Essex Antiq. 7/59
BASCOMBE, Thomas	Fordington		Dorchester Windsor, Conn.	Banks Mss.
GREENE, John	Gillingham		Salem, Mass. Warwick, R. I.	College of Arms
MORRIS, Edmund	Kington Magna		Roxbury	Pope
MEECH, John	Kingston Russell		Charlestown, Massachusetts	Banks Mss.
HILL, Ignatius	Lyme Regis		Dorchester Windsor	N.E.G.R. 39/79 Waters
James	Lyme Regis		Dorchester Windsor	N.E.G.R 39/79 Waters
William	Lyme Regis		Dorchester Windsor, Conn.	N.E.G.R. 39/79 Waters

DORSETSHIRE

NAME OF THE EMIGRANT	ENGLISH PARISH NAME	SHIPS NAME	NEW ENGLAND TOWN	VARIOUS REFERENCE
HUMPHREY, Michael	Lyme Regis		Windsor, Connecticut	Stiles History Windsor
GALLOP, Humphrey	Mosterton	Mary and John	Dorchester Windsor	Ut infra
John	Mosterton	Mary and John (1630)	Dorchester	Wheeler Stonington Page 381
CHIPMAN, Thomas	Marshwood Vale	Increase	Yarmouth	N.E.G.R. 15/79
NEWBERRY, Thomas	Marshwood Vale		Dorchester Windsor	Genealogy
HOLLARD, Angell (See page 36)	Netherbury		Weymouth, Mass. Boston, Mass.	Banks Mss.
STICKLAND, John	Overmoigne		Charlestown, Massachusetts	Banks Mss.
GIBBS, Giles	Perrott, South		Dorchester Windsor	Banks Mss.
MOORE, Miles	Powerstock		Guildford	Banks Mss.
GOODNOW, Thomas	Shaftsbury	Confi-dence	Sudbury, Massachusetts	Pope
KING, Thomas	Shaftsbury		Sudbury, Mass.	Pope
SCOVILL, John	Shapwick			Hoppin Genealogy
GILBERT, William	Sherborne		Boston, Massachusetts	Essex Inst. V. 27
BALCH, John	Sherborne		Salem, Mass.	
ELWELL, Robert	Stoke Abbot		Dorchester	Pope

DORSETSHIRE

NAME OF THE EMIGRANT	ENGLISH PARISH NAME	SHIPS NAME	NEW ENGLAND TOWN	VARIOUS REFERENCE
DOLBEAR,				
Samuel	Stoke Abbot		Marblehead, Massachusetts	Pope
Tristram	Stoke Abbot		Salem, Massachusetts	Pope
HALLET, Andrew	Stoke Abbot		Dorchester Yarmouth	Banks Mss.
JOLLIFFE, John	Stour, East		Boston, Mass.	Banks Mss.
DERBY,				
John	Sturtle		Yarmouth	Boston T. 15 Apr., 1908
Richard	Sturtle		Plymouth, Massachusetts	Boston T. 15 Apr., 1908
SNOW, William	Sturtle		Plymouth, Mass.	Banks Mss.
HOLMAN, John	Swyre		Dorchester	N.E.G.R.
WADE, Richard	Symondsbury		Dorchester Sandwich	Banks Mss.
PEACH, John	Symondsbury		Salem, Mass.	Pope
ARNOLD, William	Tolpuddle		Hingham, Massachusetts	N.E.G.R. 33/435
LOMBARD, Bernard	Thorncombe		Dorchester	Banks Mss.
COOKE, Aaron	Thorncombe	Mary and John	Dorchester	Banks Mss.
SPRAGUE,				
Ralph	Upway	Lions Whelp	Salem, 1629 Massachusetts	Pope
Richard	Upway	Lions Whelp	Salem, 1629 Massachusetts	Pope
William	Upway	Lions Whelp	Salem, 1629 Massachusetts	Pope

DORSETSHIRE

NAME OF THE EMIGRANT	ENGLISH PARISH NAME	SHIPS NAME	NEW ENGLAND TOWN	VARIOUS REFERENCE
HOYT, Simon (Haight, Hait, or Hoit)	Upway	Lions Whelp or Abigail 1629	Charlestown & Salem, Mass. Dorchester Windsor, Conn.	Historical Record of Putnam Co. New York
STOWER, ——	Upway	Lions Whelp	Charlestown, Mass. 1629	
DEDENNETT, Alexander	Wareham		Kittery, Maine	Banks Mss.
DENNETT, John	Wareham		Kittery, Maine	Banks Mss.
KITCHEN, John	Weymouth		Salem, Mass.	Pope
WOOD, John	Weymouth		Weymouth, Mass.	Pope
WOODCOCK, John	Weymouth		Roxbury	Pope
WHITMARSH, John	Weymouth			
UPHAM, John	Weymouth		Charlestown, Massachusetts	Wyman
PHIPPEN, David	Weymouth		Hingham, Mass.	Pope
DIBBLE, Thomas	Weymouth		Dorchester	Pope
BABER, Francis	Weymouth		Scituate	Pope
CHICKEN, Joseph	Weymouth		Weymouth, Mass.	Pope
HUSTED, Robert	Weymouth		Braintree, Mass.	Pope
FORD, John	Weymouth		Weymouth, Mass.	Pope
HOBLE, John	Weymouth		Springfield	Pope
HOLLARD, Angel (See page 34)			Weymouth, Mass.	Pope

DORSETSHIRE

NAME OF THE EMIGRANT	ENGLISH PARISH NAME	SHIPS NAME	NEW ENGLAND TOWN	VARIOUS REFERENCE
JESSUP, Walter	Weymouth			Pope
KING, William	Weymouth		Salem, Mass.	Pope
KINGMAN, Henry	Weymouth		Weymouth, Mass.	Pope
CORNISH, James	Weymouth		Saybrook, Conn.	Banks Mss.
CHIPMAN, John	Whitchurch		Plymouth, Mass. Barnstable, Massachusetts	Boston T. 15 Apr., 1908
PALMER, Walter	Yetminster		Charlestown, Massachusetts	Banks Mss.
BEERE, Edward	?		Newport, R. I.	Austin 17
HALLETT, William	?		Newtown, Long Island	Riker Page 403
FAWNE, John	?		Ipswich, Mass.	Banks Mss.
PORTER, John	?		Hingham, Massachusetts	Perley Salem 2/161
DENSLOW, Nicholas	Allington	Mary and John	Dorchester Windsor	Banks Mss.
BAULSTON, William	?		Boston, Mass. Newport, R. I.	Banks Mss.
EEDES, William	?	Lion's Whelp	Salem, Massachusetts	Suff. Deeds 1/16
HAIGHT, John		Abigail	Salem, Massachusetts 1629	Hist. Rec. of Putnam Co., N. Y. P. 452

Total number of Emigrants from Dorsetshire is 128 from 49 Parishes.

DURHAM

NAME OF THE EMIGRANT	ENGLISH PARISH NAME	SHIPS NAME	NEW ENGLAND TOWN	VARIOUS REFERENCE
WATTS, Henry	Cockfield		Scarboro, Maine	W.G.Davis
WILKINSON, Lawrence	Lanchester		Providence, Rhode Island	Austin
WATSON, John	Whickham		Cambridge, Massachusetts	Aspinwall

Total number of Emigrants from Durham is 3 from 3 Parishes.

ESSEX

NAME OF THE EMIGRANT	ENGLISH PARISH NAME	SHIPS NAME	NEW ENGLAND TOWN	VARIOUS REFERENCE
LOVERING, John	Ardleigh		Watertown	Aspinwall Lechford N.E.G.R. 56/184
PEPYS, Richard	Ashen	Francis	Boston, Mass.	Banks Mss.
PAGE, Abraham	Baddow Magna		Boston, Massachusetts	Suff. Deeds 1/66
PEASE, John	Baddow Magna	Francis	Salem, Mass. Edgartown, Massachusetts	History M. V.
Robert	Baddow Magna	Francis	Salem, Mass. Enfield, Conn.	Pope
POLLARD, John	Belchamp		Boston, Mass.	Pope
LAKE, John	Benfleet, N.		Boston, Mass.	
BENTON, Andrew	Bentley			N.E.G.R. 60/300
MARVIN, Matthew	Bentley Magna	Increase	Hartford, Connecticut	Genealogy
Reginald	Bentley Magna	Increase	Hartford, Connecticut	Genealogy
ADAMS, Ferdinando	Barking		Dedham, Mass.	Banks Mss.
HILLS, Joseph	Billericay	Susan & Ellen	Charlestown, Massachusetts	Essex Inst. Mss.
MARTIN, Christopher	Billericay	Mayflower	Plymouth, Massachusetts	Bradford
PROWER, Solomon	Billericay	Mayflower	Plymouth, Massachusetts	Bradford
ROSCOE, William	Billericay	Increase	Cambridge, Mass. Hartford, Conn.	N.E.G.R. 55/379
BROWNE, Peter	Billericay	Mayflower	Plymouth, Massachusetts	Banks Mss.

ESSEX

NAME OF THE EMIGRANT	ENGLISH PARISH NAME	SHIPS NAME	NEW ENGLAND TOWN	VARIOUS REFERENCE
WALFORD, Thomas	Birdbrook		Portsmouth, R. I. Charlestown, Massachusetts	Banks Mss.
WHIPPLE John	Bocking		Ipswich, Massachusetts	N.E.G.R. 78/449
Matthew	Bocking		Ipswich, Massachusetts	N.E.G.R. 56/274
GOODWIN, Ozias	Bocking		Hartford, Connecticut	Mem. Hist. Hartford
William	Bocking		Hartford, Connecticut	Mem. Hist. Hartford
STACEY, Thomas	Bocking		Ipswich, Mass.	Banks Mss.
FITCH, Thomas	Bocking		Norwalk, Connecticut	College of Arms
STEBBINS, Rowland	Bocking	Francis	Roxbury Springfield	N.E.G.R. 5/71 Banks Mss.
STACEY, Simon	Bocking		Ipswich, Mass.	Banks Mss.
HARDING, Abraham	Boreham		Boston, Mass.	Lechford
Robert	Boreham		Boston, Mass. Newport, R. I.	Pope Aspinwall
WARNER, William	Boxted		Ipswich, Mass.	Banks Mss.
LUMPKIN, Richard	Boxted		Ipswich, Mass.	Banks Mss.
WELLS, Thomas	Boxted	Susan & Ellen	Ipswich, Massachusetts	Banks Mss.
HOWE, Edward	Boxted		Watertown	Stone Gen. P. 69
WARNER, John	Boxted	Increase	Ipswich, Mass.	Banks Mss.
MORE, Isaac	Boxted	Increase	Windsor	Banks Mss.

ESSEX

NAME OF THE EMIGRANT	ENGLISH PARISH NAME	SHIPS NAME	NEW ENGLAND TOWN	VARIOUS REFERENCE
CLEARE, George	Boxted		Plymouth, Mass. Dedham, Mass. Newport, R. I.	Banks Mss.
HART, Stephen	Braintree		Cambridge, Mass. Hartford, Conn. Farmington	Genealogy
TALCOTT, John	Braintree		Hartford, Connecticut	N.E.G.R. 56/275
HAWKINS, Robert	Braintree		Charlestown, Massachusetts	N.E.G.R. 56/274
LOOMIS, Joseph	Braintree	Susan and Ellen	Windsor	Lechford
WADSWORTH, William	Braintree		Cambridge, Mass. Hartford, Conn.	Day Hist. Disc. 1843
JOSSELYN, Henry	Braintree		Gloucester, Mass.	Banks Mss.
SANFORD, Zachary	Braintree		Saybrook, Conn.	Hinman
BRAINERD, David	Braintree		Hartford, Connecticut	History Haddam, Conn.
BUTLER, Richard	Braintree		Cambridge, Mass. Hartford, Conn.	History Weth.
BARNARD, Robert	Branstone		Salisbury	Banks Mss.
BAKER, Launcelot	Braxted (Magna)		Boston, Massachusetts	Banks Mss.
COLBRON, William	Brentwood (See next page)		Boston, Massachusetts	Mass.Arch. Vol. 100
GOODALE, Robert	Braxted (Magna)	Elizabeth	Salem, Massachusetts	Banks Mss.
STONE, Gregory	Bromley, Magna		Watertown Cambridge, Mass.	Genealogy
Simon	Bromley, Magna	Increase		

ESSEX

NAME OF THE EMIGRANT	ENGLISH PARISH NAME	SHIPS NAME	NEW ENGLAND TOWN	VARIOUS REFERENCE
HOWE, Edward	Bromley, Magna		Watertown	N.E.G.R. 63/285
CLARKE, Jeremy	Bromfield			Banks Mss.
VINCENT, William	Bromfield		Edgartown, Mass. M.V.	History Martha's Vineyard
BODFISH, Robert	Bromfield		Lynn, Mass.	Banks Mss.
BROWNE, Edmund	Brentwood		Boston, Mass.	Banks Mss.
ALLEN, Samuel	Bumpstead Steeple		Braintree, Massachusetts	Banks Mss.
CORNELL, Richard	Bumpstead Steeple		Rhode Island	N.E.G.R. 54/433
HEMPSTEAD, Robert	Bumpstead Steeple		New London, Connecticut	Banks Mss.
PELHAM, Herbert	Bures		Cambridge, Mass.	Aspinwall
BARNARD, John	Burnham	Francis	Cambridge, Mass. Hartford, Conn. Hadley, Mass.	Banks Mss.
WHALE, Philemon	Canfield (Magna)		Sudbury, Massachusetts	Banks Mss.
WALFORD, Thomas	Castle Hedingham		Charlestown, Massachusetts Portsmouth, R. I.	Banks Mss.
PRENTICE, Valentine	Chelmsford		Roxbury	Banks Mss.
TURNER, Robert	Chelmsford		Boston, Mass.	Pope
ROGERS, John	Chelmsford		Watertown	Aspinwall 9
KNIGHT, Alexander	Chelmsford		Ipswich, Massachusetts	Vincent War, 1637
BUMSTEAD, Thomas	Chelmsford		Roxbury	S. P. Dom. 358 Essex Ship Money

ESSEX

NAME OF THE EMIGRANT	ENGLISH PARISH NAME	SHIPS NAME	NEW ENGLAND TOWN	VARIOUS REFERENCE
WILKINSON, Lawrence	Chelmsford		Providence, R. I.	Banks Mss.
BROOKS, Gilbert	Chelmsford	Blessing	Scituate	Banks Mss.
OGDEN, John	Chelmsford		Hartford, Conn.	Banks Mss.
STOUGHTON, Israel	Coggeshall		Dorchester	Stiles Windsor 11/722
FINCH, Samuel	Coggeshall		Roxbury	Banks Mss.
CRANE, Robert	Coggeshall			N.E.G.R. 4/179
NICHOLS, Thomas	Coggeshall		Hingham, Mass.	Lechford
FRENCH, Richard	Coggeshall		Concord Cambridge, Mass.	Middlesex Court Rec.
KEMPTON, Manasseh	Colchester	Anne	Plymouth, Mass.	Burrage
HOSIER, Samuel	Colchester		Watertown	Lechford
REED, Thomas	Colchester		Sudbury, Massachusetts	N.E.G.R. 63/200
WHALE, Philemon	Colchester		Sudbury, Massachusetts	N.E.G.R. 53/302 63/36
SPOONER, William	Colchester		Plymouth, Massachusetts	N.E.G.R. 23/407
BACON, Daniel	Colchester		Charlestown, Massachusetts Newton, L. I.	N.E.G.R. 21/369
DRAKE, Robert	Colchester		Hampton, Connecticut	History Martha's Vineyard
BLAND, John	Colchester		Watertown Edgartown, Massachusetts	History Martha's Vineyard
AUSTIN, Francis	Colchester		Dedham, Mass.	Banks Mss.

ESSEX

NAME OF THE EMIGRANT	ENGLISH PARISH NAME	SHIPS NAME	NEW ENGLAND TOWN	VARIOUS REFERENCE
CLOYES, John	Colchester		Watertown	Banks Mss.
PINGREE, Aaron	Colchester		Ipswich, Mass.	Pope
Moses	Colchester		Ipswich, Mass.	Pope
JENNINGS, William	Colchester		Charlestown, Massachusetts	Pope
BOOSEY, James	Colchester		Wethersfield, Connecticut	Banks Mss.
BROCK, Henry	Colchester		Dedham, Massachusetts	P. C. C. 165 Fines
BRACKETT, Anthony	Colne, Engaine		Portsmouth, R. I.	Banks Mss.
POWELL, Michael	Colne, Wake		Dedham, Mass.	Banks Mss.
HARVEY, Joseph	Colne, Engaine			Pope
BRACKETT, Thomas	Colne, Engaine		Portsmouth, Rhode Island	Banks Mss.
SHEPARD, Rev. Thomas	Colne, Earl's		Charlestown, Massachusetts	Savage
HARLAKENDEN, Roger	Colne, Earl's	Defence	Cambridge, Massachusetts	N.E.G.R. 15/328
LAPPINGWELL, Michael (See page 45)	Colne, White		Cambridge, Mass.	Banks Mss.
HAYNES, John	Copford	Griffin	Cambridge, Mass. Hartford, Conn.	Farmer
ALLIS, William	Dagenham		Boston, Massachusetts	P. C. C. 130 Ruthen
BARNARD, Bartholomew	Debden		Hartford, Conn.	Banks Mss.
CHUTE, Lionell	Dedham		Ipswich, Mass.	Pope
PAGE, John	Dedham		Dedham, Massachusetts	N.E.G.R 26/75

ESSEX

NAME OF THE EMIGRANT	ENGLISH PARISH NAME	SHIPS NAME	NEW ENGLAND TOWN	VARIOUS REFERENCE
PLUMB, George	Inworth		New London, Connecticut	D. L. J.
HOWE, Abraham	Hatfield (Broadoak)		Roxbury	Banks Mss.
LEATHERLAND, William	Kelvedon		Boston, Mass.	Banks Mss.
BREADCAKE, Thomas	Leigh		Salem, Mass.	Banks Mss.
BIRDSEY, John	Kelvedon		Milford, Conn. Stratford, Conn. Fairfield, Conn.	Banks Mss.
GROOME, Samuel	Langham		Salisbury	Pope
JUDD, Thomas	Langley		Cambridge, Mass. Hartford, Conn. Farmington	Banks Mss.
WING, Robert	Lawford	Francis	Boston, Mass.	Lechford
PEMBERTON, John	Lawford		Boston, Massachusetts	N.E.G.R. 39/61
CAMMOCK, Thomas	Maldon		Scarboro, Maine	Trelawney Papers
MILLS, Joseph	Maldon	Susan and Ellen	Charlestown, Massachusetts	Pope
RUCK, Thomas	Maldon		Salem and Charlestown, Massachusetts	N.E.G.R. 34/194 66/358
PRATT, Richard	Maldon		Charlestown, Massachusetts	Wyman
BROWNING, Malachi	Maldon		Watertown Edgartown, Massachusetts	History Martha's Vineyard
MASON, Hugh	Maldon	Francis	Watertown	Banks Mss.
TYNDAL, Arthur	Maplestead Magna	Arbella	Boston, Massachusetts	Winthrop Mss.

ESSEX

NAME OF THE EMIGRANT	ENGLISH PARISH NAME	SHIPS NAME	NEW ENGLAND TOWN	VARIOUS REFERENCE
NAYLOR, Edward	Easter, High		Boston, Mass.	Banks Mss.
STEELE, George	Fairstead		Hartford, Conn.	Banks Mss.
OLMSTEAD, Nicholas	Fairstead		Cambridge, Massachusetts	N.E.G.R. 59/355
Richard	Fairstead		Fairfield, Connecticut	N.E.G.R. 59/355
STEELE, John	Fairstead		Hartford, Conn.	Banks Mss.
PORTER, John	Felstead		Dorchester Hartford, Conn. Windsor	
CULLICK, John	Felstead		Hartford, Connecticut	Mem. Hist.Hart.
LORD, Richard	Felstead		Cambridge, Mass. Hartford, Conn.	Banks Mss.
OLMSTEAD, James	Fairstead	Lion	Boston, Mass. Hartford, Conn.	Banks Mss.
Nehemiah	Fairstead		Fairfield, Conn.	Banks Mss.
SAYWARD, Henry	Farnham		Salisbury Hampton, N. H. York, Maine	Banks Mss.
SHEDD, Daniel	Finchingfield		Braintree, Mass.	Genealogy
STEBBINS, Martin	Fordham		Roxbury	Banks Mss.
MORSE, Samuel	Foxearth	Increase	Dedham, Massachusetts	N.E.G.R. 19/265
WARNER, William	Gt. Horkesley		Ipswich, Massachusetts	Parker Ruggles Gen. 430
GRANT, Matthew	Hadleigh Castra		Dorchester	Banks Mss.

ESSEX

NAME OF THE EMIGRANT	ENGLISH PARISH NAME	SHIPS NAME	NEW ENGLAND TOWN	VARIOUS REFERENCE
CORLET, Elijah	Halstead	Increase	Cambridge, Mass.	Banks Mss.
COGGESHALL, John	Halstead	Lyon	Roxbury Newport, R. I.	
HOOD, John	Halstead		Lynn, Massachusetts	N.E.G.R. 56/184
John (Weaver)	Halstead		Cambridge, Mass.	Lechford
FRENCH, William	Halstead	Francis	Cambridge, Massachusetts	N.E.G.R. 44/367
WAINWRIGHT, Francis	Halstead		Ipswich, Mass.	Aspinwall
DOANE, John	Ham, East		Plymouth, Mass. Eastham, Mass.	Banks Mss.
GRAVES, John	Harlow		Roxbury	Lechford
BAKER, James	Harwich		Newport, R. I.	Austin p.14
*ALDEN, John	Harwich	May-flower	Plymouth, Massachusetts	Banks Mss.
MORRILL, Abraham	Hatfield (Broadoak)		Cambridge, Massachusetts	
Isaac	Hatfield (Broadoak)		Roxbury	
HOWE, James	Hatfield (Broadoak)		Ipswich, Massachusetts	N.E.G.R. 8/133
WARNER, Andrew	Hatfield (Broadoak)		Cambridge, Mass. Hartford, Conn. Hadley, Mass.	Genealogy
FAIRCHILD, Thomas	High Laver		Stratford, Conn.	Banks Mss.
PRESTON, Edward	Heybridge		Boston, Mass.	Banks Mss.
RAWLINS, Jasper	Ingatestone		Roxbury	Banks Mss.

*Ancestor of Elijah Ellsworth Brownell - - the publisher.

† The great-great-great-great-great-great-great-grandfather of Francis Herbert Brownell (7).

ESSEX

NAME OF THE EMIGRANT	ENGLISH PARISH NAME	SHIPS NAME	NEW ENGLAND TOWN	VARIOUS REFERENCE
SPARHAWK, Nathaniel	Dedham		Cambridge, Massachusetts	N.E.G.R. 19/125
COLE, Stephen	Dedham		Boston, Mass.	Banks Mss.
SHERMAN, John	Dedham	Elizabeth	Watertown	
SALTER, Theophilus	Dedham		Ipswich, Mass.	Banks Mss.
WATSON, George	Dedham		Plymouth, Mass.	Banks Mss.
SHERMAN, Philip (born Feb. 5, 1610)	Dedham		Roxbury, 1633 Newport, R. I.	N.E.G.R. 66/157
COOPER, John	Dedham		Cambridge, Massachusetts	N.E.G.R. 67/92
HINSDALE, Robert	Dedham		Dedham, Mass.	Boston T.
ANGIER, Edmund	Dedham		Cambridge, Mass.	Savage
SHERMAN, Rev. John	Dedham		Watertown	Pope
Richard	Dedham		Boston, Mass.	Pope
COLLINS, Edward	Dedham		Cambridge, Mass.	Pope
BARNARD, John	Dedham	Elizabeth	Watertown	Banks Mss.
SHERMAN, Edmund	Dedham		Watertown	
SMITH, Francis	Dunmow		Roxbury	Banks Mss.
LEPPINGWELL, Michael (See page 44)	Donyland, East		Cambridge, Mass.	Banks Mss
MUNNINGS, Edmund	Denge	Abigail	Dorchester	Waters
BELKNAP, Abraham	Epping		Lynn, Mass.	Banks Mss

ESSEX

NAME OF THE EMIGRANT	ENGLISH PARISH NAME	SHIPS NAME	NEW ENGLAND TOWN	VARIOUS REFERENCE
WHITE, John	Messing		Cambridge, Mass. Hartford, Conn.	N.E.G.R. 55/25
BUSH, Reynold	Messing		Cambridge, Massachusetts	N.E.G.R. 63/98
COLE, Samuel	Mersea		Boston, Mass.	Aspinwall
WARD, John	Mersea, East		Ipswich, Mass.	Pope
ROGERS, John	Moulsham (part of Chelmsford)		Watertown	Aspinwall
COLE, Thomas	Navestock		Salem, Mass.	Pope
PARTRIDGE, John	Navestock		Dedham, Massachusetts	N.E.G.R. 57/50
CONVERSE, Allen	Navestock		Charlestown, Massachusetts	Genealogy
Edward	Navestock		Charlestown, Massachusetts	Genealogy
ELIOT, Rev. John	Nazing		Roxbury	Savage
HOLMES, George	Nazing		Roxbury	N.E.G.R. 58/21
GRAVES, John	Nazing		Roxbury	Lechford
PAYSON, Edward	Nazing	Hopewell	Roxbury	Winter Mem. of Pilgrim Fathers (1884)
CURTIS, William	Nazing		Roxbury	Pope
PAYSON, Giles	Nazing	Hopewell	Roxbury	Pope
RUGGLES, John	Nazing		Roxbury	Pope
Thomas	Nazing		Roxbury	Eliot Ch. Re.

ESSEX

NAME OF THE EMIGRANT	ENGLISH PARISH NAME	SHIPS NAME	NEW ENGLAND TOWN	VARIOUS REFERENCE
ELLIOTT, Francis	Nazing		Braintree, Mass.	Pope
CAMP, Nicholas	Nazing		New Haven, Connecticut	Banks Mss.
SHELLEY, Robert	Nazing	Lion	Boston, Mass.	Banks Mss.
KING, Thomas	Norton, Cold	Blessing	Scituate	Genealogy
CLARKE, Nicholas	Nazing	Lion	Cambridge, Mass.	Banks Mss.
ELLIOTT, Jacob	Nazing		Roxbury	Pope
SPARHAWK, Nathaniel	Notley		Cambridge, Massachusetts	N.E.G.R. 56/275 E. & W. Gleanings page 115
ELLIOTT, Phillip	Nazing		Roxbury	Pope
LYMAN, Richard	Ongar, High		Roxbury Hartford, Conn.	Hills Gen. Banks Mss.
BANGS, Edward	Panfield	Anne	Plymouth, Mass. Eastham, Mass.	Banks Mss.
BRITTERIDGE, Richard	Prittlewell	Mayflower	Plymouth, Massachusetts	Pilgrim Story
CULLICK, John	Prittlewell		Hartford, Conn. Boston, Mass.	Suff.Deeds 4/435
PLAISTOW, Josias	Ramsden Crays (prob. Stanford-le-hope)		Boston, Massachusetts	Subsidy
POULTER, John	Rayleigh		Billerica, Mass.	Savage
BRIGHT, Rev. Francis	Rayleigh		Charlestown, Massachusetts	Pope
PARKER, John	Rayleigh		Billerica, Massachusetts	N.E.G.R. 66/180

ESSEX

NAME OF THE EMIGRANT	ENGLISH PARISH NAME	SHIPS NAME	NEW ENGLAND TOWN	VARIOUS REFERENCE
TAINTOR, Charles	Rochford		Fairfield, Connecticut	Banks Mss.
POWELL, Michael	Romford		Dedham, Massachusetts	P.R.O.S.P. Dept.V.388 Ship Money
JOSSELYN, Thomas	Roxwell	Increase	Hingham, Mass.	N.E.G.R.
BROWNE, John	Roxwell	Winthrop Fleet	Salem, Mass. 1630	Mass.Bay Record
Samuel	Roxwell	Winthrop Fleet	Salem, Mass. 1630	Mass.Bay Record
SHARPE, Thomas	Sandon		Boston, Massachusetts	Banks Mss. N.E.G.R. 21/178
FOOTE, Nathaniel	Shalford		Hartford, Connecticut	Noyes Gilman Anc.
CONVERSE, Edward	Shenfield		Charlestown, Massachusetts	N.E.G.R. 59/176
HARWOOD, George	Shenfield		Boston, Mass.	Banks Mss.
Henry	Shenfield		Charlestown, Massachusetts	Mss. Banks
MARION, John	Stebbing		Watertown	N.E.G.R. 56/275
WARD, Rev. Nathaniel	Stondon Massey		Ipswich, Massachusetts	N.E.G.R. 37/58
PIGGE, Thomas	Saffron Walden		Roxbury	Banks Mss.
MINOT, George	Saffron Walden		Dorchester	N.E.G.R. 1/171 Banks Mss.
RICE, Nicholas	Saffron Walden		Boston, Massachusetts	Aspinwall
BOADE, Henry	Strambridge Magna		Saco, Maine Wells, Maine	Banks Mss.

ESSEX

NAME OF THE EMIGRANT	ENGLISH PARISH NAME	SHIPS NAME	NEW ENGLAND TOWN	VARIOUS REFERENCE
PYNCHON, William	Springfield	Arbella	Dorchester Springfield, Mass.	Savage
SANFORD, Thomas m. Sarah ———	Stansted Montfichet		Dorchester Hartford, Conn.	Genealogy
BULLOCK, Henry	St. Lawrence	Abigail	Charlestown, Massachusetts	Pope
WITHAM, Peter	Steeple		Boston, Mass. Kittery, Maine	London Marr. Lic.
SANFORD, Robert	Stansted Montfichet		Hartford, Connecticut	Genealogy
FAUNCE, John	Stow, Maris		Plymouth, Mass.	Banks Mss.
Manasseh	Stow, Maris		Plymouth, Mass.	Banks Mss.
BURR, Simon	Stisted		Hingham, Mass.	Banks Mss.
HUBBARD, William	Tendring	Defence	Ipswich, Mass.	Pope
NEALE, Jeremiah	Terling		Easthampton, Massachusetts	Banks Mss.
WELD, Rev. Thomas	Terling		Roxbury	N.E.G.R. 36/36 54/442
WESTLEY, William	Thaxted		Hartford, Conn.	Banks Mss.
COLEMAN, Edward	Thorrington		Boston, Mass.	
EAMES, Anthony	Thurrock, Grays		Charlestown, Massachusetts	Banks Mss.
HILLS, Thomas	Upminster		Roxbury Hartford, Conn.	Hills Genealogy
William	Upminster		Roxbury Hartford, Conn.	Hills Genealogy
DADE (Y), William	Wanstead		Charlestown, Massachusetts	Banks Mss.

ESSEX

NAME OF THE EMIGRANT	ENGLISH PARISH NAME	SHIPS NAME	NEW ENGLAND TOWN	VARIOUS REFERENCE
LOTT, Robert	Waltham		Charlestown, Massachusetts	Banks Mss.
AMES, William	Walthamstow	Lyon	Boston, Mass.	Banks Mss.
HENEY, John	Waltham Abbey		Roxbury	Banks Mss.
IERCE, Richard	Waltham Abbey		Newport, Rhode Island	Aspinwall
HENEY, William	Waltham Abbey		Roxbury	Banks Mss.
IORRIS, Edward	Waltham Abbey	Confi- dence	Roxbury	Banks Mss.
HASE, William	Wivenhoe		Roxbury Yarmouth	Banks Mss.
VAITE, John	Wethersfield		Malden, Massachusetts	N.E.G.R. 28/62
ASEY, John	Wethersfield		Hartford, Conn.	Banks Mss.
OSSELYN, Henry	Willingdale Doe		Scarboro, Maine	N.E.G.R.
ARSONS, Hugh	Witham		Portsmouth, Rhode Island Springfield	Banks Mss.
VAITE, Thomas	Wethersfield		Ipswich, Massachusetts	N.E.G.R. 32/188
OSSELYN, John	Willingdale Doe		Scarboro, Maine	N.E.G.R.
TEBBING, Edward	Woodham Mortimer		Cambridge, Massachusetts Hartford, Conn.	Banks Mss.
HADWICK, Charles	Woodham Ferrer		Watertown	Banks Mss.
POONER, Thomas	Writtle		Salem, Mass.	Banks Mss.
LUMB, John	Yeldham (Great)		Dorchester Wethersfield, Connecticut	P. F. 148

ESSEX

NAME OF THE EMIGRANT	ENGLISH PARISH NAME	SHIPS NAME	NEW ENGLAND TOWN	VARIOUS REFERENCE
COOK,				
Col. George	Yeldham (Great)	Defence	Cambridge, Massachusetts	Pope
Joseph	Yeldham (Great)	Defence	Cambridge, Massachusetts	N.E.G.R. 56/184 Pope
SYMONDS,				
Samuel	Yeldham (Great)		Ipswich, Massachusetts	Pope
William	Yeldham (Great)		Ipswich, Massachusetts	Pope
READE, Thomas	Wickford		Salem, Mass.	Banks Mss.
GILBERT, Matthew	?		New Haven, Connecticut	Jacobus
WESTWOOD, William	?	Francis	Cambridge, Massachusetts Hartford, Conn.	Mem.Hist. Hartford Page 268
MYGATT, Joseph	?	Griffin	Cambridge,Mass. Hartford, Conn.	Banks Mss.
MORSE, Joseph	?	Elizabeth	Watertown	Banks Mss.
STONE, William	?		Guildford	Banks Mss.
SYMONDS, Mark	?		Ipswich, Mass.	Banks Mss.
WOODFORD, Thomas	?	William & Francis	Boston, Mass. Roxbury	Banks Mss.
AGAR, William	?		Watertown	Banks Mss.
THROCKMORTON,				
George	?	Lyon	Boston, Mass.	Banks Mss.
John	?	Lyon	Boston, Mass. Salem, Mass. Providence, R. I.	Banks Mss.

Total number of Emigrants from Essex is 266 from 113 Parishes.

GLOUCESTERSHIRE

NAME OF THE EMIGRANT	ENGLISH PARISH NAME	SHIPS NAME	NEW ENGLAND TOWN	VARIOUS REFERENCE
OLDER, Christopher	Alveston		Newport, R. I.	Austin 102
ALL, Edmond	Almondsbury		Lynn, Mass.	Aspinwall
LETCHER, Edward	Bagendon		Boston, Mass.	Pope
ROWN, John	Bristol		Pemaquid, Maine	Banks Mss.
ARR, Barnabas	Bristol	James	Dorchester	Pope
NIGHT, Robert	Bristol		Boston, Mass.	Pope
OUGHTY, Francis	Bristol		Dorchester	Pope
ILL, Zebulon	Bristol		Gloucester, Mass.	Pope
TETSON, William	Bristol		Boston, Mass.	Pope
RMITAGE, Thomas	Bristol	James	Ipswich, Mass.	Pope
ILLEY, William	Bristol		Boston, Mass.	N. H. Arch.
YNN, Henry	Bristol		Boston, Mass. York, Maine	N. H. Arch.
ERRISH, William	Bristol		Newbury, Mass.	Farmer
HIPPS, James	Bristol		Sheepscot, Maine	Banks Mss.
LIVER, John	Bristol		Newbury, Mass.	Suff. Deeds 1/51
AREY, James	Bristol		Charlestown, Massachusetts	Wyman
HIPWAY, John	Bristol		Portsmouth, New Hampshire	Banks Mss.
ATON, Francis	Bristol	Mayflower	Plymouth, Mass. (1620)	Banks Mss.

GLOUCESTERSHIRE

NAME OF THE EMIGRANT	ENGLISH PARISH NAME	SHIPS NAME	NEW ENGLAND TOWN	VARIOUS REFERENCE
BURDETT, (Burden), George	Bristol		Boston, Mass.	Wyman
HOOKE, William	Bristol		York, Maine	YorkDeeds
NEWMAN, George	Bristol		York, Maine	Trelawney Mss.
CUTT, John	Bristol		Portsmouth, New Hampshire	Banks Mss.
Richard	Bristol		Portsmouth, New Hampshire	Banks Mss.
Robert	Bristol		Portsmouth, New Hampshire	Banks Mss.
RUSSELL, Richard	Bristol		Charlestown, Massachusetts	Wyman
OLIVER, John (linen draper)	Bristol		Newbury, Mass.	Aspinwall
BREWSTER, Francis	Bristol		New Haven, Connecticut	Banks Mss.
PICKMAN, Nathaniel	Bristol		Salem, Mass.	Savage
PRICE, Walter	Bristol		Salem, Massachusetts	Perley 2/120
HILL, John	Bristol		Salem, Massachusetts	Perley 2/203
SYMONS, Henry	Bristol		Boston, Mass.	Banks Mss
OLIVER, Thomas	Bristol	William & Francis	Boston, Massachusetts	Savage
VAUGHAN, William	Bristol	Fellow-ship	Hartford, Connecticut	Wyllys Mss.
MARCHANT, Walter	Bristol		Pemaquid, Maine	Lechford 377
WEARE, Peter	Charfield		York, Maine	Banks Mss

G L O U C E S T E R S H I R E

NAME OF THE EMIGRANT	ENGLISH PARISH NAME	SHIPS NAME	NEW ENGLAND TOWN	VARIOUS REFERENCE
KIDMORE, Thomas	Codrington		Cambridge, Massachusetts	Military List 1608
ᵛILLIAMS, Richard	Eastington		Taunton	Aspinwall
AWSON, Christopher	Filton		Boston, Mass.	Aspinwall
DDIS, William	Frampton on Severn		Gloucester, Massachusetts	Banks Mss.
ᵗOARE, Leonard	Gloucester		Boston, Mass.	Pope
ᵗANSON, Thomas	Gloucester		New Haven, Connecticut	Banks Mss.
OARE, John	Gloucester		Scituate	History Scituate
UGGE, John	Gloucesteᵗ		Boston, Mass.	Waters 554
ARNES, William	Gloucester		Gloucester, Mass.	Waters 607
ALL, Edmond	Hill		Lynn, Mass.	Aspinwall
Edward	Henbury		Duxbury	Lechford
UCE, Harke	Horton		Scituate Tisbury, Massachusetts	History Martha's Vineyard
Henry	Horton		Scituate Tisbury, Massachusetts	History Martha's Vineyard
LISS, Thomas	Painswick			Chan. Pro. James 1 B 38/34
EARCE, John	Panington			Aspinwall
OLE, Richard	Rangeworthy		Newbury	N.E.G.R. 38/74 42/250

GLOUCESTERSHIRE

NAME OF THE EMIGRANT	ENGLISH PARISH NAME	SHIPS NAME	NEW ENGLAND TOWN	VARIOUS REFERENCE
HAGBOURNE, Samuel	Rockhampton		Roxbury	P. C. C. 276 Brent Pope
GOOCH, John	Slimbridge		York, Maine	Banks Mss.
HAMMOND, William	Slimbridge		Kittery, Maine	Banks Mss.
DAVIS, Barnabas	Tewkesbury	Blessing	Charlestown, Massachusetts	Pope
TRACEY, Thomas	Tewkesbury		Salem, Mass. Wethersfield Norwich, Connecticut	Caulkins History Norwich 201
THAYER, Richard m. Dorothy Mortimore	Thornbury		Braintree, Massachusetts	N.E.G.R. 60/281 64/185
Thomas m. Margery	Thornbury		Braintree, Massachusetts	N.E.G.R. 60/281 64/185
DOLE, Richard	Thornbury		Newbury	N.E.G.R. 42/250
POOR, John	Thornbury		Newbury	N.E.G.R. 42/250
THURSTON, Daniel	Thornbury		Newbury	N.E.G.R. 42/250
BADGER, Giles	Westbury on Severn		Newbury	P. C. C. Nabbes 20
SKIDMORE, Thomas	Westerleigh		Cambridge, Massachusetts	N.E.G.R. 55/379 Genealogy Lechford
SPENCER, Thomas	Winchcomb		Kittery, Maine	Parish Register
CHADBOURNE, Humphrey	Winchcomb		Kittery, Maine	Parish Register
WILLIAMS, Richard	Wheatonhurst		Taunton, Massachusetts	P.C.C. 292 Ayloffe

GLOUCESTERSHIRE

NAME OF THE EMIGRANT	ENGLISH PARISH NAME	SHIPS NAME	NEW ENGLAND TOWN	VARIOUS REFERENCE
ILLIAMS, Richard	Wotton sub Edge		Taunton, Massachusetts	Aspinwall
IMBERLEY, Thomas	Wotton sub Edge		Dorchester New Haven, Connecticut	Banks Mss.
OPKINS, Stephen	Wotton sub Edge	May-flower	Plymouth, Massachusetts	Banks Mss.
EVAN, Arthur	Yate		Glastonbury, Connecticut Tisbury, Mass	History Martha's Vineyard
OLLISTER, John	?		Wethersfield, Connecticut	Banks Mss.
ORRIS, Edward	?		Salem, Massachusetts	Perley Salem 2/82
MITH, Richard	?		Taunton Kingston, R. I.	Austin Gen. Dict.
IMMOCK, Thomas	?		Scituate	Banks Mss.
ERNALD, Reginald	?		Portsmouth, New Hampshire	Banks Mss.

Total number of Emigrants from Gloucestershire is 75 from 27 Parishes

HAMPSHIRE

NAME OF THE EMIGRANT	ENGLISH PARISH NAME	SHIPS NAME	NEW ENGLAND TOWN	VARIOUS REFERENC
SEDGWICK, Robert	Andover		Charlestown, Massachusetts	Pope
BACHILER, Stephen	Barton Stacey	William & Francis	Lynn, Massachusetts	Pope
FRY, John	Basingstoke	Bevis	Newbury	N.E.G.R. 8/226
CARMAN, John	Bishops Stoke	Plough	Boston, Mass. Hempstead, Long Island	Banks Mss.
DUMMER, Richard	Bishops Stoke	Whale	Newbury	Pope
Stephen	Bishops Stoke	Bevis	Newbury	Pope
AUSTIN, Richard	Bishops Stoke	Bevis	Charlestown, Massachusetts	Pope
NELSON, Thomas	Bishops Stoke		Rowley, Mass.	Waters 83
FROST, William	Binstead		Oyster Bay, New York	New York Wills
BECKLEY, Richard	Bourne S. Mary (Tradition)		Wethersfield, Connecticut	Stiles History of Wethersfield
HOOKE, Rev. William	Bramshot		Taunton, Mass. New Haven, Connecticut	Banks Mss.
FIELD, Robert	Eling	James	Boston, Mass.	Pope
WHITEHEAD, Daniel	Exbury		Hempstead, Long Island	Banks Mss
PLYMPTON, Thomas	Goodworth Clatford	Jonathan	Sudbury, Massachusetts	Banks Mss.
HART, Stephen	Hartley Wintley		Cambridge, Mass. Hartford, Conn.	Banks Mss.
MOODY, William	King's Samborne		Newbury	Banks Mss

HAMPSHIRE

NAME OF THE EMIGRANT	ENGLISH PARISH NAME	SHIPS NAME	NEW ENGLAND TOWN	VARIOUS REFERENCE
ALCONER, Edmond	Kingsclere		Andover	Visit. Hants. Aspinwall
EARCE, Augustine	Longstock	Confidence	Barnstable, Massachusetts	Banks Mss.
ASTON, Nicholas	Lymington	Mary & John	Newport, Rhode Island	AustinGen. Dict. p. 292
IFIELD, William	Littleton	Hercules	Hampton, New Hampshire	Banks Mss.
OODMAN, Edward	Milford	James	Newbury	Pope
ALKER, Richard	Newton Stacey		Lynn, Mass.	Pope
ALMADGE, Robert	Newton Stacey		Boston, Mass. New Haven, Connecticut	Lechford N.E.G.R. 81/132
Thomas	Newton Stacey		Lynn, Mass.	Pope
William	Newton Stacey		Boston, Mass.	Lechford
HERBURNE, Henry	Odiham		Portsmouth, New Hampshire	N.E.G.R. 58/227
URT, John	Penton Mewsey	Defence	Sudbury, Massachusetts	N.E.G.R. 36/407 48/288
ARNES, Richard	Penton Mewsey	Jonathan	Braintree, Massachusetts	Pope
LANCHARD, Thomas	Penton Mewsey	Jonathan	Braintree, Massachusetts	Pope
OYES, Peter	Penton Mewsey	Confidence	Sudbury, Massachusetts	N.E.G.R. 60/59
OKER, Henry	Penton Mewsey		Sudbury, Massachusetts	N.E.G.R. 60/357
UTTER, John	Penton Mewsey	Confidence	Sudbury, Massachusetts	Hotten
WILLOUGHBY, Francis	Portsmouth		Charlestown, Massachusetts	Wyman

HAMPSHIRE

NAME OF THE EMIGRANT	ENGLISH PARISH NAME	SHIPS NAME	NEW ENGLAND TOWN	VARIOUS REFERENCE
WILLOUGHBY, William	Portsmouth		Charlestown, Massachusetts	Wyman
HOLT, Nicholas	Romsey	James	Newbury	Pope
SMITH, Thomas	Romsey	James	Ipswich, Mass.	Pope
EASTMAN, Roger	Romsey	Confidence	Salisbury	Genealogy
FOSTER, William	Romsey		Charlestown, Massachusetts	N.E.G.R. 25/
BIDGOOD, Richard	Romsey		Boston, Massachusetts	N.E.G.R. 60/60
PARKER, Joseph	Romsey	Confidence	Newbury	N.E.G.R. 60/60
KNIGHT, John	Romsey	James	Newbury	Pope
Richard	Romsey		Newbury	Pope
EMERY, Anthony	Romsey	James	Newbury Kittery, Maine	Pope
John	Romsey	James	Newbury	Pope
GORE, John	Southampton		Roxbury	Aspinwall
MAYHEW, Thomas	Southampton		Watertown Edgartown, Massachusetts	History Martha's Vineyard
*ALDEN, John	Southampton	Mayflower	Plymouth, Massachusetts	Bradford
GORE, Richard	Southampton	Elizabeth and Anne	Roxbury	
DUMMER, Thomas	Stoneham, North	Bevis	Newbury	Pope
MUSSEY, Robert	Stoneham, South		Ipswich, Massachusetts	Banks Mss.

*Ancestor of Elijah Ellsworth Brownell - - the publisher.

HAMPSHIRE

NAME OF THE EMIGRANT	ENGLISH PARISH NAME	SHIPS NAME	NEW ENGLAND TOWN	VARIOUS REFERENCE
UMMER, Richard	Stoneham, South	Whale	Newbury	Banks Mss.
ORTER, Roger	Sutton, Long	Confidence	Watertown	N.E.G.R. 60/59
ABIN, William	Tichfield		Rehoboth, Mass.	
ITTLEFIELD, Edmund	Tichfield		Exeter Wells, Maine	N.E.G.R. 67/347
IMBERLAKE, Henry	Tichfield		Newport, Rhode Island	Banks Mss.
ENT, Stephen	Tytherley (W)	Confidence	Newbury	Banks Mss.
ARCH, Hugh	Tytherley (W)	Confidence	Newbury	
ADLER, Anthony	Tytherley (W)	Confidence	Newbury Salisbury	Banks Mss.
UY, Nicholas	Upton Gray	Confidence	Watertown	N.E.G.R. 60/59 61/258
AINTOR, Joseph	Upton Gray	Confidence	Watertown	Pope
ENT, Edward	Wallop, Middle		Newbury	Banks Mss.
Richard	Wallop, Upper	Mary and John	Newbury	Banks Mss.
ONDAY, Hugh	Wallop, Nether		Newbury	Waters 187
ALLINGFORD, Nicholas	Wallop, Nether	Confidence	Newbury	Waters 187
LSLEY, John	Wallop, Nether	Confidence	Newbury	Waters 187
ENT, Stephen	Wallop, Nether	Confidence	Newbury	Waters 187
LSLEY, William	Wallop, Nether	Confidence	Newbury	Waters 187

HAMPSHIRE

NAME OF THE EMIGRANT	ENGLISH PARISH NAME	SHIPS NAME	NEW ENGLAND TOWN	VARIOUS REFERENCE
BENT, John	Weyhill	Confidence	Sudbury, Massachusetts	N.E.G.R. 49/65 Lechford
LOKER, Henry	Weyhill		Sudbury, Massachusetts	N.E.G.R. 60/357
OSGOOD, John	Wherwell		Andover	N.E.G.R. 20/24
William	Wherwell		Andover	N.E.G.R. 20/24
BACHILER, Rev. Stephen	Wherwell	William and Francis	Lynn, Massachusetts	Savage
CARPENTER, William	Wherwell	Bevis	Weymouth, Mass. Rehoboth, Mass.	Pope

Total number of Emigrants from Hampshire is 73 from 34 Parishes.

HEREFORDSHIRE

NAME OF THE EMIGRANT	ENGLISH PARISH NAME	SHIPS NAME	NEW ENGLAND TOWN	VARIOUS REFERENCE
EAVER, Edmond	Aymestray	Planter		
James	Aymestray	Planter		
ATTOCKS, David	Cloddock		Roxbury	P.C.C. Aylett 104
USSELL, Richard (appr. Bristol, 1628)	Hereford		Charlestown, Massachusetts	Wyman
INGRY, Aaron	Upton Bishop		Ipswich, Mass.	Aspinwall
Moses	Upton Bishop		Ipswich, Mass.	Aspinwall
EDFERN, Isabel	Upton Bishop		Ipswich, Mass.	Aspinwall

Total number of Emigrants from Herefordshire is 7 from 4 Parishes.

HERTFORDSHIRE

NAME OF THE EMIGRANT	ENGLISH PARISH NAME	SHIPS NAME	NEW ENGLAND TOWN	VARIOUS REFERENCE
LATHAM, Carey s. Nicholas bp. 10 Nov. 1613	Aldenham		New London, Connecticut Cambridge, Massachusetts	Par. Reg. N.E.G.R. 61/385
PLATT, Richard	Aldenham		New Haven, Connecticut	Tradition Par. Reg. Aldenham
GROVER, Thomas	Aldenham		Charlestown, Massachusetts Malden, Mass.	Banks Mss.
BURNAP, Thomas (Belknap)	Aston		Lynn, Massachusetts	Ess. Inst. 56
EELS, John	Aldenham		Dorchester	Banks Mss
BURNAP, Isaac	Amwell, Great		Salem, Massachusetts	Perley Salem 2/234
HEATH, Isaac	Amwell, Little	Hopewell	Roxbury	Banks Mss
William	Amwell, Little	Lyon	Roxbury	Banks Mss
BUNKER, George	Bengeo		Topsfield	Banks Mss
TAPPE, Edmond	Bennington		Milford, Connecticut	N.E.G.R 54/352 57/298
HOWE, Edward	Berkhamstead		Lynn, Mass. 1635	Banks Mss.
PITKIN, William	Berkhamstead		Hartford, Connecticut	N.E.G.R. 66/160
RICE, Edmund	Berkhamstead		Sudbury, Mass.	Savage
SCOTT, Richard	Berkhamstead		Providence, Rhode Island	N.E.G.R. 66/87
DANE, John	Berkhamstead		Roxbury	Pope
DARVILL, Robert	Berkhamstead (West)		Sudbury, Massachusetts	Aspinwall

HERTFORDSHIRE

NAME OF THE EMIGRANT	ENGLISH PARISH NAME	SHIPS NAME	NEW ENGLAND TOWN	VARIOUS REFERENCE
HOWE, Ephraim	Berkhamstead (North Church)		Lynn, Mass. 1638	Banks Mss.
GOULD, Jeremy (Rich. 5, 4, Thos. 3) (Rich, 2, Thos. 1)	Bovingdon		Newport, Rhode Island	Austin Gen. Dict. Page 304
Thomas	Bovingdon		Charlestown, Massachusetts	Banks Mss.
BURWELL, John	Bovingdon		Milford, Connecticut	Hinman
HUMBERSTONE, Henry	Bramfield		New Haven, Connecticut	Banks Mss.
HANCHETT, Thomas	Braughing		Boston, Mass. Braintree, Mass. Roxbury	Banks Mss.
MORLEY, John	Cheshunt		Braintree, Massachusetts	Banks Mss.
Ralph	Cheshunt		Charlestown, Massachusetts	Banks Mss.
HAYNES, John	Codicote	Griffin	Hartford, Conn.	
CURTIS, Zaccheus	Dunton	James	Salem, Mass.	Hotten
AXTELL, Thomas	Gatesden (Gaddesden?)		Marlboro	N.E.G.R. 53/227
WELCH, Thomas	Graveley		Milford, Conn.	Banks Mss.
CLARK, "Deacon" George	Hatfield (Bishops)		Milford, Connecticut	Subsidy
HOWE, Daniel	Hemel Hempstead		Lynn, Mass. 1636	Banks Mss.
BETTS, Richard	Hemel Hempstead		Ipswich, Massachusetts	N.E.G.R. 55/300
AXTELL, Thomas	Hemel Hempstead		Sudbury, Massachusetts	Banks Mss.

HERTFORDSHIRE

NAME OF THE EMIGRANT	ENGLISH PARISH NAME	SHIPS NAME	NEW ENGLAND TOWN	VARIOUS REFERENCE
FURNELL, John	Hertford		Cambridge, Mass.	Pope
STONE, Rev. Samuel	Hertford		Cambridge, Mass.	Pope
LUCAS, Simon	Hitchin			Waters
DRAPER, Nathaniel	Hitchin		Sheepscot, Maine	Banks Mss.
WHITTEMORE, Thomas	Hitchin		Charlestown, Massachusetts	N.E.G.R. 21/169 Wyman
TARBOX, John	Ippolitts		Lynn, Mass.	Banks Mss.
WEEDON, William	Kings Langley		Newport, R. I.	Banks Mss.
PRUDDEN, James	Kings Walden		Milford, Conn.	Banks Mss.
HALL, Thomas	Kings Walden		Newbury	N.E.G.R. 31/83
GOLD, Nathan	Kings Langley		Fairfield, Conn.	Banks Mss.
WHITTRIDGE, William	Lilley	Elizabeth	Ispwich, Mass.	Banks Mss.
CLARKE, George	Munden, Magna		Milford, Connecticut	History Winsor 2/155
BRANDON, William	Puttenham		Milford, Conn.	Aspinwall
MORRIS, William	Royston		Plymouth, Massachusetts	Plymouth Colonial Records Vol. 1/64
PARKER, Richard	Royston		Boston, Massachusetts	N.E.G.R. 51/298
HEWES, Joshua	Royston		Roxbury	Banks Mss.
FORDHAM, Rev. Robert	Sacombe		Sudbury, Mass. Southampton, Long Island	Miner Genealogy Page 143

HERTFORDSHIRE

NAME OF THE EMIGRANT	ENGLISH PARISH NAME	SHIPS NAME	NEW ENGLAND TOWN	VARIOUS REFERENCE
SEAMER, Richard	Sawbridg-worth		Hartford, Connecticut	J. G. B.
PERRY, John	Sawbridg-worth		Roxbury	Banks Mss.
FITCH, Zachary	St. Albans		Reading, Massachusetts	N.E.G.R. 57/415 63/162
PEABODY, Francis	St. Albans	Planter	Hampton, New Hampshire	N.E.G.R. 2/154
PROCTOR, Robert	St. Albans		Concord, New Hampshire	N.E.G.R. 57/416
HARVEY, Richard	St. Albans	Planter	Salem, Mass.	Pope
BACON, Francis	St. Albans		Boston, Mass.	Pope
LAWRENCE, Henry	St. Albans		Charlestown, Massachusetts	Banks Mss.
OLNEY, Thomas	St. Albans	Planter	Salem, Massachusetts	College of Arms
LANG, Robert	St. Albans		Charlestown, Massachusetts	Boston T. 17 Aug. 1925
TUTTLE, John	St. Albans	Planter	Ipswich, Massachusetts	College of Arms
LAWRENCE, John	St. Albans	Planter	Newtown, Long Island	N.E.G.R. 45/85
William	St. Albans	Planter	Newtown, Long Island	N.E.G.R. 45/85
STETSON, Robert	St. Albans		Duxbury	Banks Mss.
AXTELL, Nathaniel	St. Albans		New Haven, Connecticut	N.E.G.R. 44/50
WILCOXON, William m. Margaret	St. Albans	Planter	Concord, Mass. 1635	Pope
SAVAGE, Thomas	St. Albans	Planter	Boston, Mass.	Savage

HERTFORDSHIRE

NAME OF THE EMIGRANT	ENGLISH PARISH NAME	SHIPS NAME	NEW ENGLAND TOWN	VARIOUS REFERENCE
GIDDINGS, George	St. Albans	Planter	Ipswich, Mass.	Pope
PERLEY, Allen	St. Albans	Planter	Ipswich, Mass.	Pope
FELLOWES, William	St. Albans	Planter	Ipswich, Mass.	Pope
COWLEY (Cooley), Benjamin	St. Albans		Springfield	Banks Mss.
WHITTEMORE, Lawrence	Stanstead Abbot	Hopewell	Roxbury	Hotten
DAY, Robert	Stanstead Abbot	Hopewell	Cambridge, Mass. Hartford, Conn.	Hotten
PEACOCK, William	Stanstead Abbot	Hopewell	Roxbury	Hotten
THRALL, William	Sandridge		Windsor, Conn.	
PRATT, John	Stevenage		Dorchester	Banks Mss.
FOWLER, William	Stevenage		Milford, Connecticut	N.E.G.R. 54/354 57/298
ABBOTT, George	Stortford Bishop's		Roxbury	N.E.G.R. Jan. 1931
DENNISON, Edward	Stortford Bishop's		Roxbury	N.E.G.R. 46/127
GARY, Arthur	Stortford Bishop's		Roxbury	N.E.G.R. 70/
DANE, John	Stortford Bishop's		Roxbury, Mass. Ipswich, Mass.	N.E.G.R. 8/148
WELCH, Thomas	Stortford Bishop's		Charlestown, Massachusetts Milford, Connecticut	N.E.G.R. 54/354 57/298 S. P. Dom. 376/106
DENNISON, Daniel	Stortford Bishop's		Roxbury	N.E.G.R. 46/127

HERTFORDSHIRE

NAME OF THE EMIGRANT	ENGLISH PARISH NAME	SHIPS NAME	NEW ENGLAND TOWN	VARIOUS REFERENCE
DENNISON,				
George	Stortford Bishop's		Roxbury	N.E.G.R. 46/127
William	Stortford Bishop's		Roxbury	Genealogy
NORTON,				
Rev. John	Stortford Bishop's		Ipswich, Massachusetts	Pope
William	Stortford Bishop's	Hopewell	Ipswich, Massachusetts	Pope
CHANDLER, William	Stortford Bishop's		Roxbury	N.E.G.R. Jan. 1931
HOLLOMAN, Ezekiel	Tring		Warwick, Rhode Island	Austin Gen. Dict.P.102
SWEETZER, Seth	Tring		Charlestown, Massachusetts	Aspinwall Wyman
EARLE, Ralph	Stortford Bishop's		Newport, Rhode Island	Banks Mss. Par. Reg.
CHAUNCEY, Rev. Charles	Ware		Plymouth, Massachusetts	N.E.G.R. 10/105
HALE, Thomas	Watton at Stone	Hector	Newbury	N.E.G.R. 35/370 64/186 Banks Mss.
KING,				
Daniel	Watford		Lynn, Massachusetts	N.E.G.R. 66/125
David	Watford		Lynn, Massachusetts	N.E.G.R. 46/415
SKIDMORE, George	Watford			Parish Reg.
PRIOR,				
John	Watford	Hopewell	Scituate	Lechford
Thomas	Watford	Hopewell	Scituate	Lechford
GOULD, Nathan	Watford		Salisbury	Pope

HERTFORDSHIRE

NAME OF THE EMIGRANT	ENGLISH PARISH NAME	SHIPS NAME	NEW ENGLAND TOWN	VARIOUS REFERENCE
RICHARDSON, Ezekiel	Westmill		Charlestown, Massachusetts	N.E.G.R. 51/299
Samuel	Westmill		Charlestown, Massachusetts	N.E.G.R. 51/299
Thomas	Westmill		Charlestown, Massachusetts	N.E.G.R. 51/299
WYMAN, Francis	Westmill		Charlestown, Massachusetts Woburn, Mass.	N.E.G.R. 43/56
John	Westmill		Charlestown, Massachusetts Woburn, Mass.	N.E.G.R. 43/56
PENNIMAN, James	Widford		Boston, Mass.	Pope
MILES, Richard	Wormeley		Milford, Connecticut	N.E.G.R. 54/354 S. P. Dom. 376/106
CORNELL, Thomas	?		Boston, Mass.	Austin 54
ESTEN, Thomas	?		Providence, R. I.	Austin 294
CANFIELD, Matthew	?		Norwalk, C nn.	Banks Mss.

Total number of Emigrants from Hertfordshire is 108 from 43 Parishes.

HUNTINGDON

NAME OF THE EMIGRANT	ENGLISH PARISH NAME	SHIPS NAME	NEW ENGLAND TOWN	VARIOUS REFERENCE
ASTWOOD, James	Abbotsley		Boston, Mass.	Banks Mss.
John	Abbotsley		New Haven, Connecticut	Banks Mss.
SYLVESTER, Nathaniel	Brampton		Shelter Island, Long Island	Waters
PARRISH, Judith	Bythorne		Boston, Mass.	Banks Mss.
BAYES, Thomas	Catworth		Dedham, Mass. Edgartown, Mass.	Banks Mss.
LEETE, William	Diddington		Guildford, Connecticut	Visit. Hunts.
PHILBRICK, Thomas	Elton		Watertown	Banks Mss.
HAWKINS, Richard	St. Ives		Boston, Massachusetts	Rugg Anne Hutch. page 241

Total number of Emigrants from Huntingdon is 8 from 7 Parishes.

KENT

NAME OF THE EMIGRANT	ENGLISH PARISH NAME	SHIPS NAME	NEW ENGLAND TOWN	VARIOUS REFERENCE
BANKES, Richard	Alkham		Scituate York, Maine	C. E. B.
CURTIS, William	Ash, near Sandwich		Scituate	Banks Mss.
CHAMBERS, Thomas	Ash, near Sandwich		Scituate	Banks Mss.
CURTIS, John	Ash, near Sandwich		Scituate	Banks Mss.
Richard	Ash, near Sandwich		Scituate	Banks Mss.
Thomas	Ash, near Sandwich		Scituate York, Maine	Banks Mss.
EDGARTON, Richard	Ashford		Norwich, Conn.	Banks Mss.
BUTLER, Nicholas	Ashford		Dorchester Edgartown, Massachusetts	History Martha's Vineyard
STARR, Comfort	Ashford		Duxbury	Pope
HATCH, William	Ashford	Castle	Scituate	Lech. 92 Genealogy
CAMPION, Thomas	Ashford			Pope
PATCHEN, Joseph	Ashford	Hercules	Cambridge, Massachusetts Roxbury	N.E.G.R. 75/219 79/108
NEALEY, Thomas	Ashford	Hercules		N.E.G.R. 75/219 79/108
DUNCAN, Samuel	Ashford	Hercules	Cambridge, Massachusetts	N.E.G.R. 75/219 79/108
POPE, John	Ashford		Dorchester Boston, Massachusetts	N.E.G.R. 75/219 79/108

KENT

NAME OF THE EMIGRANT	ENGLISH PARISH NAME	SHIPS NAME	NEW ENGLAND TOWN	VARIOUS REFERENCE
GILL, John	Ashford		Dorchester	N.E.G.R. 75/219 79/108
JENKINS, Richard	Ashford		Dorchester	N.E.G.R. 75/219 79/108
TURVEY, John	Ashford	Hercules	Cambridge, Massachusetts	N.E.G.R. 75/219 79/108
WINES, Faint-not	Ashford	Hercules	Charlestown, Massachusetts	N.E.G.R. 75/219 79/108
ROUSE, Faithful	Ashford		Charlestown, Massachusetts	Pope
PANTRY, William	Ashford		Hartford, Conn.	Banks Mss.
DAYTON, Ralph	Ashford		New Haven, Connecticut Easthampton, Long Island	New Hamp. Genealogical Magazine 3/528
MASTERSON, Richard	Ashford		Plymouth, Mass.	Banks Mss.
HAYWOOD, Thomas	Aylesford		Cambridge, Mass.	Pope
VINAL, John	Biddenden		Scituate	Banks Mss.
Stephen	Benenden		Scituate	Banks Mss.
POST, Richard	Biddenden		Woburn, Massachusetts	N.E.G.R. 66/350
BEALE, Thomas	Biddenden		Cambridge, Massachusetts	N.E.G.R. 66/350
STEDMAN, Isaac	Biddenden		Scituate	N.E.G.R. 66/76
BISBEECH, Thomas	Biddenden		Scituate	N.E.G.R. 67/34

KENT

NAME OF THE EMIGRANT	ENGLISH PARISH NAME	SHIPS NAME	NEW ENGLAND TOWN	VARIOUS REFERENCE
SEALIS, Richard	Biddenden		Scituate	N.E.G.R. 65/320
POST, Thomas	Biddenden		Scituate	N.E.G.R. 66/350
FOSTER, Hcpestill	Biddenden	Elizabeth	Dorchester	Banks Mss.
HILL, Hercules	Boughton-under Blean		Scituate	N.E.G.R. 66/87
FOSTER, Thomas	Biddenden	Hercules	Weymouth, Mass. Braintree, Mass.	Banks Mss.
SCOTCHFORD, John	Brenchley		Concord	Waters
CHAPFILL, John	Bromley		Lynn, Mass.	Aspinwall
PAGE, Edward	Canterbury	Hercules	Boston, Massachusetts	N.E.G.R. 75/217 79/108
FARLEY, John	Canterbury	Hercules	Charlestown, Massachusetts	N.E.G.R. 75/217 79/108
ENGLAND, John	Canterbury	Hercules	Plymouth and Charlestown, Massachusetts	N.E.G.R. 75/217 79/108
KNOWLTON, Thomas	Canterbury		Hingham, Massachusetts	Amer. Hist. Soc. Pub.
PALMER, Abraham	Canterbury		Charlestown, Massachusetts	Banks Mss.
JOHNSON, Edward	Canterbury	Hercules	Woburn, Massachusetts	Genealogy N.E.G.R. 67/177
STARR, Thomas	Canterbury	Hercules	Boston, Mass.	Pope
BUCK, John	Canterbury	Hercules		
CUSHMAN, Robert	Canterbury	Fortune	Plymouth, Mass.	Pope
Thomas	Canterbury	Fortune	Plymouth, Mass.	Pope

KENT

NAME OF THE EMIGRANT	ENGLISH PARISH NAME	SHIPS NAME	NEW ENGLAND TOWN	VARIOUS REFERENCE
BACHELOR, Henry	Canterbury	Hercules	Ipswich, Mass.	Pope
John	Canterbury	Hercules	Salem, Mass.	Pope
Joseph	Canterbury	Hercules	Salem, Mass.	Pope
FESSENDEN, John	Canterbury		Cambridge, Mass.	Pope
RICHARDSON, Henry	Canterbury	Hercules		Pope
SYMMES, Rev. Zachariah	Canterbury	Griffin	Charlestown, Massachusetts	Pope
WARD, William	Canterbury		Sudbury, Mass.	Pope
CHEEVER, Bartholomew	Canterbury		Boston, Mass.	Pope
CHILTON, James	Canterbury	Mayflower	Plymouth, Massachusetts	Banks Mss.
GRANGER, Thomas	Canterbury	Hercules	Scituate	N.E.G.R. 75/218 79/108
HARNETT, Edward	Canterbury	Hercules	Salem, Massachusetts	N.E.G.R. 75/218 79/108
CHEEVER, Daniel	Canterbury		Cambridge, Mass.	Pope
ROOT, Josiah	Chart, Great	Hercules	Salem, Mass.	Genealogy
HUDSON, Francis	Chatham		Boston, Mass.	Farmer
CHAPFILL, John	Chiddingstone		Lynn, Mass.	Aspinwall
STOWE John	Cranbrook		Dorchester	Waters
Nathaniel	Cranbrook		Dorchester	Waters

KENT

NAME OF THE EMIGRANT	ENGLISH PARISH NAME	SHIPS NAME	NEW ENGLAND TOWN	VARIOUS REFERENCE
STOWE,				
Samuel	Cranbrook		Dorchester	Waters
Thomas	Cranbrook		Dorchester	Waters
ENSIGN, Thomas	Cranbrook		Scituate	N.E.G.R. 66/87
SHEAFE, Jacob	Cranbrook		Guildford, Connecticut	N.E.G.R. 55/213
EDDY, John	Cranbrook		Plymouth, Mass. Watertown	Genealogy
TWISDEN, John	Denton		Scituate York, Maine	Banks Mss.
CLARK, Dennis	Dartford			Pope
BECK, Henry	Dover	Blessing	Portsmouth, Rhode Island	N. Y. Gen. & Biog. Rec.
BACHELOR, Henry	Dover	Hercules	Ipswich, Mass.	Pope
PONTUS, William	Dover		Plymouth, Mass.	Davis
HOWES, Thomas	Eastwell		Yarmouth	N.E.G.R. 66/356
ROOT,				
Joshua	Eastwell		Salem, Mass.	Banks Mss.
Josiah	Eastwell		Beverly, Mass.	Banks Mss.
Richard	Eastwell		Lynn, Mass. Salem, Mass. Fairfield	Banks Mss.
Thomas	Eastwell		Salem, Mass.	Banks Mss.
MASON, Elias	Eastwell		Salem, Mass.	Pope
LOTHROP, Rev. John	Eastwell		Scituate	Pope

KENT

NAME OF THE EMIGRANT	ENGLISH PARISH NAME	SHIPS NAME	NEW ENGLAND TOWN	VARIOUS REFERENCE
WARD, Miles	Erith		Salem, Massachusetts	Perley Salem 2/101
CLARKE, Jeremy	Farleigh, East		Newport, R. I.	
DAVIS, Dolor	Farleigh, East		Barnstable, Massachusetts	N.E.G.R. 36/320
PAINE, Moses	Frittenden		Braintree, Massachusetts	N.E.G.R. 65/290
BROWN, William	Frittenden		Sudbury, Mass.	Pope
CALL, Thomas	Faversham		Charlestown, Massachusetts	Pope
GOSMER, John	Fordwich		Southhold, Long Island	Hist. West Chester County
HUDSON, William	Greenwich		Boston, Mass.	Banks Mss.
LEWIS, George	Greenwich		Scituate	Farmer
TEWKSBURY, Henry	Greenwich		Boston, Mass.	Banks Mss.
MERRIAM, George	Hadlow		Concord, Massachusetts	N.E.G.R. 24/64
Joseph	Hadlow		Concord, Massachusetts	N.E.G.R. 24/64
Robert	Hadlow		Concord, Massachusetts	N.E.G.R. 24/64
BRANCH, Peter	Halden, High		Scituate	Pope
HOSMER, James	Hawkhurst		Concord, Massachusetts	N.E.G.R. 24/164
Thomas	Hawkhurst		Concord, Mass. Cambridge, Mass.	N.E.G.R. 24/164

KENT

NAME OF THE EMIGRANT	ENGLISH PARISH NAME	SHIPS NAME	NEW ENGLAND TOWN	VARIOUS REFERENCE
CRUTTENDEN, Abraham	Hawkhurst		Guilford, Conn.	Banks Mss.
FESSENDEN, John	Hawkhurst		Cambridge, Mass.	Cant. Wills
CHITTENDEN, Thomas	Hawkhurst		Scituate	Banks Mss.
William	Hawkhurst		New Haven, Connecticut	Banks Mss.
BACHELOR, Joseph	Hawkhurst		Salem, Mass.	Pope
BORDEN, Richard	Headcorn		Portsmouth, R. I.	Banks Mss.
BISBEACH, Thomas	Headcorn		Cambridge, Mass. Scituate	Pope
ALLEN, John	Herne Hill		Plymouth, Mass.	Pope
WILLARD, George	Horsemonden		Scituate	Genealogy
Simon m. Mary Sharpe	Horsemonden		Cambridge, Mass. 1634	Genealogy
SCUDDER, John	Horton Kirby		Salem, Mass. Southold, L. I.	Banks Mss.
Thomas	Horton Kirby		Salem, Mass.	Banks Mss.
CHURCHMAN, John	Kennington	Lion	Cambridge, Mass.	Banks Mss.
JORDAN, John	Lenham		Guildford	History of Guildford
PARTRIDGE, Rev. Ralph	Lenham		Duxbury	Banks Mss.
PAINE, William	Lenham		Salem, Mass.	Pope
BATE, Clement	Lydd		Hingham, Mass.	Pope

KENT

NAME OF THE EMIGRANT	ENGLISH PARISH NAME	SHIPS NAME	NEW ENGLAND TOWN	VARIOUS REFERENCE
JORDAN, Thomas	Lenham		Guildford	History of Guildford
BATE, James	Lydd		Dorchester	Pope
ATWATER, Joshua	Lenham		New Haven, Connecticut	Genealogy
BROOKS, Robert	Maidstone		New London, Connecticut	N.E.G.R. 61/385
WETHERELL, William	Maidstone		Charlestown, Massachusetts	Wyman
PIERPOINT, Robert	Maidstone		Ipswich, Mass. Roxbury	Aspinwall
GAMLYN, Robert	Malling, East		Roxbury	Lechford
MAYO, John	Malling, East		Roxbury	Pope
PIERPOINT, John	Maidstone		Ipswich, Mass. Roxbury	Aspinwall
WEBB, Richard	Milton (Sittingbourne)		Weymouth, Massachusetts	Pope
SAYER, James	Northbourne		Hercules	Hotten
CHILD, Robert	Northfleet		Lancaster, Massachusetts	Hist. Anct. Hon. Art. Co.
ODIORNE, John	Oxney		Portsmouth, New Hampshire	Strong Funeral Sermon 1848
GOOKIN, Daniel	Ripple		Boston, Mass. Cambridge, Mass.	Genealogy
HOADLEY, John	Rolvenden		Guildford	History of Guildford
PAINE, Thomas	Sandwich	Whale		Plough Company
WARD, Andrew	Sandhurst		Watertown Wethersfield, Connecticut	P.C.C. Brent 113

KENT

NAME OF THE EMIGRANT	ENGLISH PARISH NAME	SHIPS NAME	NEW ENGLAND TOWN	VARIOUS REFERENCE
HOLMES, William	Sandwich	Hercules		N.E.G.R. 75/217 79/108
JENNINGS, Robert	Sandwich	Hercules		N.E.G.R. 75/217 79/108
COLEMAN, Joseph	Sandwich		Charlestown, Massachusetts	Pope
PIERCE, Marmaduke	Sandwich		Salem, Mass.	Lechford
BUNNEY, Thomas	Sandwich		Charlestown, Massachusetts	Wyman
BRIGDEN, Thomas	Sandwich		Charlestown, Massachusetts	Wyman
COLE, Isaac	Sandwich		Charlestown, Massachusetts	Wyman
BEST, John	Sandwich		Salem, Mass.	Pope
WHEELER, Thomas	Sandwich		Sandwich, Mass.	Pope
SMITH, Matthew	Sandwich		Charlestown, Massachusetts	Pope
HATCH, William	Sandwich		Scituate	Pope
JOHNS, William	Sandwich		Cambridge, Mass.	Winthrop
EWELL, Henry	Sandwich		Scituate	Pope
FLETCHER, Moses	Sandwich	Mayflower	Plymouth, Massachusetts	Banks Mss.
KETCHERELL, Joseph	Sandwich	Hercules		N.E.G.R. 75/21 79/208
Simon	Sandwich	Hercules		N.E.G.R. 75/21 79/208
EVEREST, Andrew	Southfleet		York, Maine	Banks Mss.

KENT

NAME OF THE EMIGRANT	ENGLISH PARISH NAME	SHIPS NAME	NEW ENGLAND TOWN	VARIOUS REFERENCE
WHITTEN, Thomas	Smarden	Elizabeth and Anne	Plymouth, Massachusetts	History Martha's Vineyard 3/510
STANBOROUGH, Josiah	Stanstead		Southampton, Long Island	Aspinwall
EATON, William	Staple		Watertown Reading, Mass.	Pope
KINGSNORTH, Henry	Staplehurst		Guilford	History of Guilford
AUSTIN, Jonas	Staplehurst		Cambridge, Mass. Hingham, Mass. Taunton	N.E.G.R. 67/166
PHILLIPS, William	Staplehurst		Hartford, Connecticut	Memor. History Hartford, page 255
GREENHILL, Samuel	Staplehurst		Hartford, Connecticut	Memor. History Hartford, page 241
EWER, Thomas	Stroud		Barnstable, Massachusetts	
MUDGE, Thomas	Stroud		Malden, Massachusetts	N.E.G.R. 53/432
EATON, Jonas	Staple	Hercules	Charlestown, Massachusetts Reading, Mass.	N.E.G.R. 75/21 79/21
WALTERS, Richard	Staplehurst		Lynn, Massachusetts Boston, Massachusetts	N.E.G.R. 66/87 P. C. C. Alchin 327
WHETSTONE, John	Tenterden		Scituate	Banks Mss.
CHAFFINCH, John	Tenterden		Guilford, Connecticut	P. C. C. 19 Pell Banks Mss.
FOED, Edward	Tenterden	Hercules	Scituate	N.E.G.R. 75/218 79/108

KENT

NAME OF THE EMIGRANT	ENGLISH PARISH NAME	SHIPS NAME	NEW ENGLAND TOWN	VARIOUS REFERENCE
SUTTON, George	Tenterden	Hercules	Scituate	N.E.G.R. 75/218 79/108
JENKINS, Edward	Tenterden	Hercules	Scituate	N.E.G.R. 75/218 79/108
TERRY, Stephen	Thanet (St. Lawrence)		Dorchester Windsor	Parish Register
BOYKETE, Gervais	Thannington		Charlestown, Massachusetts	Pope
GRANGER, Stephen	Thannington		Charlestown, Massachusetts	N.E.G.R. 75/217 79/108
STANBOROUGH, Josias m. Frances Gransden	Tonbridge		Southampton, Long Island	Aspinwall
BUSS, William	Tonbridge		Concord	N.E.G.R. 24/164
GOODHUE, Nicholas	Tonbridge	James		Banks Mss.
William	Tonbridge		Ipswich, Mass. 1635	Banks Mss.
WYBORNE, Thomas	Tenterden		Duxbury	Pope
AUSTIN, Jonas	Tenterden		Cambridge, Mass.	Pope
LAPHAM, Thomas	Tenterden		Scituate	Pope
HINCKLEY, Samuel	Tenterden		Scituate	N.E.G.R. 65/318
LEWIS, John	Tenterden		Scituate	N.E.G.R. 66/356
IDDENDEN, Edmund	Tenterden		Scituate	N.E.G.R. 67/38
TILDEN, Nathaniel	Tenterden		Scituate	N.E.G.R. 65/330

KENT

NAME OF THE EMIGRANT	ENGLISH PARISH NAME	SHIPS NAME	NEW ENGLAND TOWN	VARIOUS REFERENCE
TICKNOR, William	Tenterden		Scituate	N.E.G.R. 70/189
ELY, Nathaniel	Tenterden		Cambridge, Massachusetts	Boston T. June 13, 1928
BENNETT, James	Tenterden		Scituate Cambridge, Massachusetts	N.E.G.R. 75/218 79/108
PANTRY, William	Willesborough		Cambridge, Mass. Hartford, Conn.	Banks Mss.
GODFREY, Edward	Wilmington		York, Maine	Banks Mss.
JOHNSON, John	Wilmington		Roxbury 1630	Banks Mss.
PECKHAM, John	Woodnesborough		Newport, Rhode Island	Banks Mss.
PREBLE, Abraham	Wooton		Scituate York, Maine	Banks Mss.
HATCH, Thomas	Wye	Hercules 1634 Castle 1638	Scituate	Genealogy N.E.G.R. 70/256
TILDEN, Thomas	Wye	Anne	Plymouth, Mass.	Banks Mss.
SPROAT, Robert	Wye		Scituate	Banks Mss.
HALL, John	?		Hartford, Connecticut	HallFamily Record p. 1
STANLEY, John	?		Cambridge, Mass. Hartford, Conn.	Genealogy
Thomas	?		Cambridge, Mass. Hartford, Conn.	Genealogy
Timothy	?		Cambridge, Mass. Hartford, Conn.	Genealogy
MANN, William	?		Cambridge, Massachusetts	N.E.G.R. 13/325

KENT

NAME OF THE EMIGRANT	ENGLISH PARISH NAME	SHIPS NAME	NEW ENGLAND TOWN	VARIOUS REFERENCE
WARREN, Richard	?		Charlestown, Massachusetts	
ALCOCK, John	?		York, Maine	Banks Mss.
GOULD, Jarvis	?	Elizabeth	Hingham, Massachusetts	Stackpole Kittery

Total number of Emigrants from Kent is 197 from 59 Parishes.

LANCASHIRE

NAME OF THE EMIGRANT	ENGLISH PARISH NAME	SHIPS NAME	NEW ENGLAND TOWN	VARIOUS REFERENCE
BRECK, Edward	Ashton under Lyne		Dorchester	Boston Transcript
ATHERTON, Humphrey	Atherton (Leigh)		Dorchester Milton	N.E.G.R. 35/67
James	Atherton (Leigh)		Dorchester Milton	N.E.G.R. 35/67
WORTHINGTON, Henry	Atherton (Leigh)		Dorchester	
CRABTREE, John	Broughton (Manchester)		Boston, Massachusetts	Banks Mss.
FARRAR, Thomas	Bromley		Lynn, Massachusetts	N.E.G.R. 61/386
DUNSTER, Henry	Bury		Cambridge, Massachusetts	N.E.G.R. 80/94
WORDEN, Peter	Clayton		Yarmouth	Pope
PRESTON, Roger	Colne		Ipswich, Massachusetts	Parish Register
MORTON, Samuel	Denton		Boston, Mass. Plymouth, Mass.	Genealogy
SMITH, Rev. Ralph	Denton		Plymouth, Mass. Manchester	Biography
CLOVER, John	Eccleston		Dorchester	Suff. Deeds 1/333
BLAISDELL, Ralph	Goosnargh	Angel Gabriel	York, Maine Salisbury	Banks Mss.
SIMPSON, Henry	Goosnargh		York, Maine	Banks Mss.
BLAISDELL, Ralph	Holcombe	Angel Gabriel	York, Maine Salisbury	Banks Mss.
LOVER, John	Knowsley		Dorchester	Suff.Deeds 1/333
WORTHINGTON, Nicholas	Liverpool		Saybrook, Conn.	Farmer
ALLEN, William	Manchester		Salem, Massachusetts	Hist. of Salem 1.

LANCASHIRE

NAME OF THE EMIGRANT	ENGLISH PARISH NAME	SHIPS NAME	NEW ENGLAND TOWN	VARIOUS REFERENCE
DANA, Richard	Manchester		Cambridge, Massachusetts	Parish Register
KINGAN, Roger	Manchester		Block Island, Rhode Island	N.E.G.R. 67/296
HOLME, Obadiah	Manchester		Rehoboth, Massachusetts	N.E.G.R. 64/238
SEWELL, Henry	Manchester		Newbury	N.E.G.R. 66/283
WALKER, Robert	Manchester		Boston, Massachusetts	N.E.G.R. 7/46
ASPINWALL, William	Manchester		Boston, Massachusetts	Leyden Arch.
DOANE, John	Manchester		Plymouth, Mass. Eastham, Mass.	Banks Mss.
MAWDESLEY, Henry	Mawdesley		Dorchester	N.E.G.R. 35/67
John	Mawdesley		Dorchester	N.E.G.R. 35/67
WORDEN, Peter	Newton		Yarmouth	Ply. Col. Rec. 1, Pt. 1, p. 33
PARKE, Robert	Preston		Wethersfield, Connecticut	Hist. of W. Wethersfield
GLOVER, John	Rainhill		Dorchester	Suff. Deeds 1/333
MATHER, Rev. Richard	Toxteth	James	Dorchester	Savage
AMBROSE, Joshua	Toxteth		Dorchester	N.E.G.R. 42/313
Nehemiah	Toxteth		Dorchester	N.E.G.R. 42/312
HENSHAW, Joshua	Toxteth		Boston, Massachusetts	N.E.G.R. 42/312
SMITH, John (Quarter Master) ?	Toxteth		Dorchester	N.E.G.R. 1/95

LANCASHIRE

NAME OF THE EMIGRANT	ENGLISH PARISH NAME	SHIPS NAME	NEW ENGLAND TOWN	VARIOUS REFERENCE
ASPINWALL, Peter	Toxteth (Warrington)		Dorchester	N.E.G.R. 47/342
THOMPSON, Rev. William	Winwick		Dorchester York, Maine Braintree, Mass.	Savage
WOODWARD, Henry	Woolton, Gt.	James	Dorchester	Banks Mss.
John	Woolton, Gt.	James	Dorchester	Banks Mss.
WALES, Nathaniel	?		Dorchester	N.E.G.R. 35/72
CUNLIFFE, Henry	?		Dorchester	Banks Mss.
KENDRICK, George	?	James	Scituate Boston, Mass.	Pope
John	?	James	Boston, Mass.	Savage

Total number of Emigrants from Lancashire is 43 from 22 Parishes.

LEICESTERSHIRE

NAME OF THE EMIGRANT	ENGLISH PARISH NAME	SHIPS NAME	NEW ENGLAND TOWN	VARIOUS REFERENCE
DEACON, John (alias FRANCIS)	Barleston		Plymouth, Massachusetts	Pope
DILLINGHAM, Edward	Bitteswell		Lynn, Mass. Sandwich, Massachusetts	Mayflower Desc. 16/161
John	Bitteswell		Boston, Mass.	Banks Mss
*PABODIE, John	Bitteswell		Duxbury	Banks Mss
CHESTER, Leonard	Blaby		Watertown Wethersfield, Massachusetts	N.E.G.R. 22/338
HOOKER, Rev. Thomas	Blaston		Cambridge, Mass. Hartford, Conn.	Family Record
FISH, William	Bowden Magna		Windsor, Connecticut	Waters 14
BLACKMAN, Rev. Adam	Bowden Magna		Scituate Stratford, Conn.	Banks Mss.
John	Bowden Magna		Cambridge, Massachusetts	Banks Mss.
CLEMENT, Robert	Cosby		Haverhill, Mass.	Genealogy
WEBSTER, John	Cossington		Hartford, Conn.	Banks Mss
HIGGINSON, Rev. Francis	Claybrooke		Salem, Mass.	Savage
SHOTTON, Sampson	Croxton		Braintree, Mass. Newport, R. I.	Lechford
WHITING, Nathaniel	Desford		Lynn, Mass.	Banks Mss
ROBY, Henry	Donnington Castle		Hampton, New Hampshire	N.E.G.R. 60/92
Samuel	Donnington Castle			

* The great-great-great-great-great-great-grandfather of Elijah Ellsworth Brownell - - the Publisher.

LEICESTERSHIRE

NAME OF THE EMIGRANT	ENGLISH PARISH NAME	SHIPS NAME	NEW ENGLAND TOWN	VARIOUS REFERENCE
VEAZIE, William	Gumley		Braintree, Massachusetts	Aspinwall N.E.G.R. 55/380 66/353
HULL, Robert	Harborough (Market)		Boston, Massachusetts	Banks Mss.
ABELL, Robert	Hemington		Boston, Massachusetts Rehoboth, Massachusetts	Boston T. 10, Jan. 1927 P.C.C. 10 St. John
KNOLLYS, Rev. Hanserd	Humberstone		Dover, New Hampshire	N.E.G.R. 19/131
BOSWELL, Isaac	Husbands Bosworth		Salisbury	Banks Mss.
CLEMENT, Robert	Huncote		Haverhill, Mass.	Genealogy
SHEPARDSON, Daniel	Kettleby		Charlestown, Massachusetts	Banks Mss.
ALMY, William (born 1601)	Kilworth (South)		Lynn, Mass. Sandwich, Mass.	Banks Mss.
TILTON, William	Lawford Church		Lynn, Massachusetts	Leic. Marr. Lic.
HOOKER, Rev. Thomas	Markfield		Cambridge, Mass Hartford, Conn.	N.E.G.R. 47/92
PALMES, Edward	Melton Mowbray		New Haven, Connecticut	Visit Leic.
HORTON, Barnabas	Mowsley		Hampton, N. H. Ipswich, Mass. Southold, L. I.	N. Y. Gen. & Biog. Rec. 36/38
TILTON, William	Narborough		Lynn, Mass.	Banks Mss.
PABODIE, Francis	Noseley		Hampton, N. H.	Banks Mss.
*John	Noseley		Duxbury	Banks Mss.
William	Noseley		Duxbury	Banks Mss.

* The great-great-great-great-great-great-grandfather of Elijah Ellsworth Brownell - - the Publisher.

LEICESTERSHIRE

NAME OF THE EMIGRANT	ENGLISH PARISH NAME	SHIPS NAME	NEW ENGLAND TOWN	VARIOUS REFERENCE
COULTMAN, John	Newton Harcourt		Wethersfield, Connecticut Hadley, Mass.	Lechford 280
Thomas	Newton Harcourt		Weathersfield, Connecticut Hadley, Mass.	Lechford 280
ROBBINS, Samuel	Thedingworth		Salisbury	Hoyt 300
SCARBOROUGH, John	Thorpe Satchwell		Roxbury	Banks Mss.
TILTON, William	Thurcaston		Lynn, Massachusetts	Parish Register
FELLOWS, Richard	?		Hartford, Conn.	Hoyt
Samuel	?		Ipswich, Mass.	Hoyt
William	?	Planter	Salisbury	Hoyt
HERRICK, Henry	?		Salem, Mass.	Banks Mss.
BEARDSLEY, William	?	Planter	Concord	C. of A. Hotten
PELTON, John	?		Dorchester	Banks Mss.
GARFORD, Gervais	?		Salem, Mass.	Banks Mss.

Total number of Emigrants from Leicestershire is 44 from 29 Parishes.

LINCOLNSHIRE

NAME OF THE EMIGRANT	ENGLISH PARISH NAME	SHIPS NAME	NEW ENGLAND TOWN	VARIOUS REFERENCE
BELLINGHAM, Richard	Aisthorpe		Boston, Massachusetts	N.E.G.R. 28/14 Lincoln Peds Watkins
William	Aisthorpe		Boston, Mass.	
RISHWORTH, Edward	Alford		Exeter, N. H. York, Maine.	Venn Savage
WILLIX, Balthazar	Alford		Exeter, New Hampshire	N.E.G.R. 68/79
WENTWORTH, William	Alford		Exeter, New Hampshire	N.E.G.R. 22/135
HUTCHINSON, Edward	Alford	Griffin	Boston, Mass	Pope
Samuel	Alford	Griffin	Boston, Mass.	Pope
William	Alford	Griffin	Boston, Mass.	Pope
HEATON, Nathaniel	Alford		Boston, Mass.	Banks Mss.
WIGHT, Thomas	Alford		Exeter	N.E.G.R. 68/
RISHWORTH, Edward	Basingthorpe		Exeter, N. H. York, Maine	
WIGHT, Henry	Alford		Dedham, Mass.	
WARDELL, Thomas	Alford		Boston, Mass. Exeter	Banks Mss.
William	Alford		Boston, Mass. Exeter Portsmouth, R. I.	Banks Mss.
MARSHALL, Christopher	Alford		Boston, Mass. Piscataqua	Banks Mss.
Thomas	Alford		Boston, Mass.	Banks Mss.

LINCOLNSHIRE

NAME OF THE EMIGRANT	ENGLISH PARISH NAME	SHIPS NAME	NEW ENGLAND TOWN	VARIOUS REFERENCE
COLBY, Anthony	Aswarby		Boston, Mass. Cambridge, Mass. Salisbury	Banks Mss.
WHITTINGHAM, John	Boston		Ipswich, Massachusetts	N.E.G.R. 70/
COYE, Matthew	Boston		Boston, Massachusetts	N.E.G.R. 30/111
Richard	Boston		Boston, Massachusetts	N.E.G.R. 30/111
LEVERETT, Thomas	Boston		Boston, Mass.	Savage
WHITING, Rev. Samuel	Boston		Lynn, Massachusetts	N.E.G.R. 14/62
HIBBINS, William	Boston		Boston, Massachusetts	N.E.G.R. 48/74
HOUGH, Atherton	Boston		Boston, Mass.	Banks Mss.
CODDINGTON, William	Boston		Boston, Massachusetts	Banks Mss. N.E.G.R. 28/14
TRUESDELL, Richard	Boston		Boston, Massachusetts	Pope Banks Mss.
BOSWORTH, Daniel	Boston		Ipswich, Mass.	Pope
BURRELL, George	Boston		Lynn, Massachusetts	Pope Banks Mss.
MELLOWES, Oliver	Boston		Boston, Mass.	Banks Mss.
JACKSON, Edmund	Boston		Boston, Mass.	Banks Mss.
CHEESEBOROUGH, William	Boston		Boston, Massachusetts	Family Genealogy
DINELEY, William	Boston		Boston, Mass.	Banks Mss.
FARWELL, Henry	Boston		Concord Chelmsford,Mass.	Genealogy

NAME OF THE EMIGRANT	ENGLISH PARISH NAME	SHIPS NAME	NEW ENGLAND TOWN	VARIOUS REFERENCE
KINGSLEY, Stephen	Boston		Braintree, Mass.	Banks Mss.
CRAM, John	Bilsby		Brookline, Mass. Exeter	N.E.G.R. 68/68
WHEELWRIGHT, Rev. John	Bilsby		Boston, Mass. Exeter	Savage
TOWNE, William m. Joanna Blessing	Braceby		Salem, Massachusetts	N.E.G.R. 10/36
SOMERBY, Anthony	Bytham, Little		Newbury	Pope
Henry	Bytham, Little		Newbury	Pope
KNOLLYS, Hanserd	Cawkewell		Dover, N. H.	
WILSON, Edward	Donington		Salem, Mass.	Lechford
Thomas	Donington		Roxbury	Lechford
William	Donnington Super Bain		Boston, Massachusetts	Lechford
LONGLEY, William	Firsby		Lynn, Mass.	Lechford
STICKNEY, William	Frampton		Boston, Mass. Rowley, Mass.	Genealogy
PORMORT, Philemon	Grimsby		Boston, Massachusetts	N.E.G.R. 53/302
WRIGHT, Thomas	Harrowby		Exeter	N.E.G.R. 68/78
BRADSTREET, Simon	Horbling		Cambridge, Massachusetts	N.E.G.R. 48/169 8/312
BOWLES, John	Hough-on-the-Hill		Roxbury	Hinman

LINCOLNSHIRE

NAME OF THE EMIGRANT	ENGLISH PARISH NAME	SHIPS NAME	NEW ENGLAND TOWN	VARIOUS REFERENCE
BLACKSTONE, Rev. William	Horncastle	Katharine	Weymouth, Mass. Boston, Massachusetts	Bolton Real Founders
LAKE, Capt. Thomas	Irby		Boston, Mass.	Pope
LONGLEY, William	Irby-in-the-Marsh		Lynn, Mass. Groton	Lechford
PARKS, Robert	Keal, East		Wethersfield, Connecticut	Waters 146
DOWSE, Lawrence	Legbourne		Charlestown, Massachusetts	Genealogy
BURCHAM, Edward	Lincoln	Little James	Plymouth, Mass. Lynn, Mass.	Pope
BOWER, George	Manby		Scituate	Banks Mss.
THORNDIKE, John	Scamelsby		Salem, Mass.	Pope
SKELTON, Samuel	Sempringham		Salem, Mass.	Pope
BUCKMASTER, Thomas	Sempringham		Boston, Mass.	Banks Mss.
WHITING, Rev. Samuel	Skirbeck		Lynn, Massachusetts	N.E.G.R. 28/233
INGALLS, Edmond	Skirbeck		Lynn, Massachusetts	N.E.G.R. 50/72
Francis	Skirbeck		Lynn, Massachusetts	N.E.G.R. 50/72 Banks Mss.
HARKER, William	Skirbeck		Lynn, Mass.	Banks Mss.
BOWLES, John	Swineshead		Roxbury	Hinman
WHITTINGHAM, William	Sutterton		Boston, Mass.	Waters 113
PARRATT, Francis	Sutterton		Rowley, Massachusetts	P. C. C. Berkeley 67

LINCOLNSHIRE

NAME OF THE EMIGRANT	ENGLISH PARISH NAME	SHIPS NAME	NEW ENGLAND TOWN	VARIOUS REFERENCE
HETT, Thomas	Stockingham		Hull, Mass.	Aspinwall
SKELTON, Samuel	Tattersall		Salem, Massachusetts	N.E.G.R. 58/350
FISH, Gabriel	Trusthorpe		Exeter, N. H.	Lechford
DEARBORN, Godfrey	Willoughby		Exeter, New Hampshire	N.E.G.R. 68/72
HILL, Valentine	Winthorpe		Boston, Massachusetts	P. C. C. Exton, 16 Banks Mss.
PHILBROOK, Thomas	?		Watertown Hampton, N. H.	N.E.G.R. 38/279
BITFIELD, Samuel	?		Newbury	Banks Mss.
LUMPKIN, Richard	?		Ipswich, Massachusetts	P. C. C. Brent 313
William	?		Yarmouth	P. C. C. Brent 313
KNOWLES, Rev. John	?		Watertown	Savage 3/41

Total number of Emigrants from Lincolnshire is 76 from 34 Parishes.

LONDON

NAME OF THE EMIGRANT	ENGLISH PARISH NAME	SHIPS NAME	NEW ENGLAND TOWN	VARIOUS REFERENCE
VENNER, Thomas	All Hallows Barking		Salem, Massachusetts	Banks Mss.
PRINCE, Thomas	All Hallows Barking	Fortune	Plymouth, Mass. Eastham, Mass.	Savage
JENKS, Joseph	All Hallows London Wall		York, Maine Lynn, Mass.	Banks Mss.
DODD, George	All Hallows London Wall		Boston, Massachusetts	Banks Mss.
PAGE, Thomas	All Hallows Stayning	Increase	Saco, Maine	Banks Mss.
WALDO, Cornelius	All Hallows Honey Lane		Ipswich, Mass. 1650	Banks Mss.
PRESTON, Roger	St. Alphege	Elizabeth	Ipswich, Mass.	Pope
FENN, Robert	St. Alphege		Salem, Mass.	Pope
HARBERT, Sylvester	St. Andrew Holborn		Kittery, Maine Newcastle, New Hampshire	Y. D. 1, 116
BRADLEY, Francis	St. Andrew Holborn	Hector	New Haven, Connecticut Branford, Conn. Fairfield	Banks Mss.
SAMPSON, Henry	St. Andrew Undershaft	May-flower	Plymouth, Massachusetts	Banks Mss.
ALLERTON, Isaac	St. Andrew Undershaft	May-flower	Plymouth, Massachusetts	Banks Mss.
GREGSON, Thomas	St. Augustine		New Haven, Connecticut	Farmer
FREEMAN, Samuel	St. Anne Blackfriars		Watertown	Banks Mss.
GRANGER, Launcelot	St. Antholin		Ipswich, Mass. Newbury	Banks Mss.
BROUGHTON, Thomas	St. Bartholomew Exchange		Watertown	Aspinwall
LOVELL, Alexander	St. Bartholomew the Great		Ipswich, Massachusetts	Banks Mss.

LONDON

NAME OF THE EMIGRANT	ENGLISH PARISH NAME	SHIPS NAME	NEW ENGLAND TOWN	VARIOUS REFERENCE
BUMPAS, Edward	St. Bartholomew Great	Fortune	Plymouth, Massachusetts	Banks Mss.
ROGERS, Thomas	St. Bartholomew Great	Mayflower	Plymouth, Massachusetts	Banks Mss.
KIBBY, Henry	St. Bennet Finck		Dorchester	Waters
WOODWARD, George	St. Botolph Billingsgate			Pope
EDWARDS, William	St. Botolph Aldgate		Hartford, Connecticut	Banks Mss.
WATERS, Richard	St. Botolph Aldgate		Salem, Massachusetts	Waters Gleanings
PLACE, William	St. Botolph Aldgate		Salem, Massachusetts	Waters Gleanings
GORTON, Samuel	St. Botolph Aldgate		Boston, Massachusetts	Genealogy
PEDDOCK, Leonard	St. Catherine Coleman St.		Boston Bay	Banks Mss.
NEGOOSE, Benjamin	St. Botolph Aldersgate		Boston, Massachusetts	Banks Mss.
GAUNT, Peter	St. Bridget		Scituate	Banks Mss.
BURT, Hugh	St. Clement Eastcheap	Abigail	Lynn, Massachusetts	Aspinwall
EATON, William	St. Dunstan in-the-East		Watertown	N.E.G.R. 15/29 P.C.C. 107 Carr
TOMLINS, Edward	St. Dunstan in-the-West	Susan and Ellen	Lynn, Massachusetts	Banks Mss.
HICKS, John	St. Faith under Paul's		Weymouth, Mass. Newport, Rhode Island	Austin & History Weymouth
HILTON, Edward	St. George Botolph Lane		Dover, New Hampshire	Hubbard
LYNDE, Simon	St. George Botolph Lane		Boston, Massachusetts	Suff. Deeds 1/42

LONDON

NAME OF THE EMIGRANT	ENGLISH PARISH NAME	SHIPS NAME	NEW ENGLAND TOWN	VARIOUS REFERENCE
KILHAM, Augustine	St. George Botolph Lane		Salem, Mass. Ipswich, Mass.	Banks Mss.
GOVE, John	St. Giles Cripplegate		Charlestown, Massachusetts	Banks Mss.
TREADWELL, Thomas	St. Giles Cripplegate		Dorchester Ipswich, Mass.	Banks Mss.
CROUCH, William	St. Giles Cripplegate		Charlestown, Massachusetts	Waters
GOODYEAR, Stephen	St. Gregory		New Haven, Connecticut	Banks Mss.
PARKER, Basil Als. BROOKS, Thomas	St. Gregory		Kittery, Maine	Banks Mss.
BOREMAN, Thomas	St. Helen Bishopsgate		Ipswich, Massachusetts	N.E.G.R. 62/303
KEMPTON, Ephraim	St. John Walbrook		Scituate	Banks Mss.
TITUS, Robert	St. Katherine by-the-Tower	Hopewell	Boston, Mass. Rehoboth, Mass. Weymouth, Mass.	Hotten
BLACKLEDGE, John	St. Katherine Cree		Boston, Massachusetts	Aspinwall 223
CONANT, Christopher	St. Lawrence Jewry	Anne	Plymouth, Mass. Charlestown, Massachusetts	Pope
Roger	St. Lawrence Jewry		Cape Ann Salem, Mass.	Genealogy
HOLYOKE, Edward	St. Lawrence Jewry		Lynn, Massachusetts	Banks Mss.
BARNARD, Bartholomew	St. Margaret Westminster		York, Maine Boston, Mass.	Banks Mss.
OAKES, Edward	St. Margaret Westminster		Cambridge, Massachusetts	Aspinwall
Urian	St. Margaret Westminster		Cambridge, Massachusetts	Aspinwall

LONDON

NAME OF THE EMIGRANT	ENGLISH PARISH NAME	SHIPS NAME	NEW ENGLAND TOWN	VARIOUS REFERENCE
FORRETT, James	St. Margaret Westminster			Banks Mss.
WHITNEY, John	St. Margaret Westminster		Watertown	Amer.Hist. Soc. 1928
KING, Daniel	St. Martin Le Grand		Lynn, Massachusetts	Aspinwall
SOANCE, John	St. Martin Ludgate		New Haven, Connecticut	Essex Inst. 27/-
BRINLEY, Lawrence	St. Martin Pomeroy		Newport, Rhode Island	Banks Mss.
JONES, William	St. Martin in-the-Fields		New Haven, Connecticut	
BEARD, Thomas	St. Martin?		Salem, Mass.	Pope
LOW, Anthony	St. Mary Aldermanbury		Boston, Massachusetts	Aspinwall
John	St. Mary Aldermanbury		Boston, Massachusetts	Aspinwall
EVANCE, John	St. Mary Aldermanbury		New Haven, Connecticut	Waters EssexNotes
BUTLER, Stephen	St. Mary Whitechapel		Boston, Massachusetts	Banks Mss.
WITCHFIELD, John	St. Mary Whitechapel	Lion	Dorchester Windsor	Banks Mss.
LAMBERTON, George	St. Mary Whitechapel		New Haven, Connecticut	N.E.G.R. 68/283
BOURNE, Nehemiah	St. Mary Whitechapel		Charlestown, Massachusetts	N.E.G.R. 8/139 27/28
HAWKINS, Thomas	St. Mary Whitechapel		Dorchester	N.E.G.R. 8/140 27/28
BRADBURY, Thomas	St. Mary Whitechapel		York, Maine Salisbury	Genealogy
HAWKINS, Abraham	St. Mary Whitechapel		Charlestown, Massachusetts	Banks Mss.

LONDON

NAME OF THE EMIGRANT	ENGLISH PARISH NAME	SHIPS NAME	NEW ENGLAND TOWN	VARIOUS REFERENCE
JACKSON, Edward	St. Mary Whitechapel		Cambridge, Mass. Newton, Mass.	N.E.G.R. 66/84
John	St. Mary Whitechapel		Cambridge, Mass. Newton, Mass.	N.E.G.R. 66/84
HALL, John	St. Mary Whitechapel		Charlestown, Massachusetts	Banks Mss.
SMITH, John	St. Michael Crooked Lane	Whale	Boston, Massachusetts	Plough Company
JUPE, Anthony	St. Michael Crooked Lane	Whale	Boston, Massachusetts	Plough Company
CRISPE, John	St. Michael Crooked Lane	Whale	Boston, Massachusetts	Plough Company
BINCKS, Bryan	St. Michael Crooked Lane	Plough	Sagadahoc Boston, Mass.	Plough Company
JOHNSON, Peter	St. Michael Crooked Lane	Plough	Sagadahoc Boston, Mass.	Plough Company
HICKFORD, John	St. Mary Bow		Scarboro, Maine	Josselyn
HOPKINS, Stephen	St. Mary Whitechapel	May- flower	Plymouth, Massachusetts	Banks Mss.
WARD, Benjamin	St. Mary Whitechapel		Boston, Massachusetts	Banks Mss.
BEECHER, Thomas	St. Mary Whitechapel	Talbot	Boston, Massachusetts	Banks Mss.
BALL, Allen	St. Mary le Bow		New Haven, Connecticut	N.E.G.R. 54/97
HENCHMAN, Daniel	St. Mary Somerset		Boston, Massachusetts	Banks Mss.
DOTEY, Edward	St. Mary le Strand	May- flower	Plymouth, Massachusetts	Banks Mss.
HEATON, Nathaniel	St. Mary le Strand		Boston, Massachusetts	Banks Mss.
FOOTE, Nathaniel	St. Mary Bothaw		Hartford, Connecticut	College of Arms
STODDARD, Anthony	St. Michael le Quern		Boston, Massachusetts	Banks Mss.

LONDON

NAME OF THE EMIGRANT	ENGLISH PARISH NAME	SHIPS NAME	NEW ENGLAND TOWN	VARIOUS REFERENCE
GOVE, John	St. Nicholas Acon		Charlestown, Massachusetts	Banks Mss.
FEAKE, Robert	St. Nicholas Acon		Watertown Greenwich, Conn.	Banks Mss.
Tobias	St. Nicholas Acon		Watertown	Banks Mss.
KIRTLAND, Nathaniel	St. Olave Silver Street		Lynn, Massachusetts	N.E.G.R. 14/241
COLLINS, Edward	St. Peter le Poor		Cambridge, Massachusetts	Essex Inst.27/
PITT, William	St. Peter ad Vincula Tower	Fortune	Plymouth, Massachusetts	Banks Mss.
HOLLAND, Nathaniel	St. Sepulchre		Watertown	P.C.C. 9 Pell
OLDHAM, John	St. Stephens Coleman Street	Anne	Plymouth, Massachusetts	Banks Mss.
WORLEY, Ralph	St. Swithin		Charlestown, Massachusetts	Aspinwall
BURTON, Stephen	St. Thomas the Apostle		Bristol, Rhode Island	N.E.G.R. 60/28
WHITMAN, Robert	Trinity, Holy Minories		Ipswich, Massachusetts	Pope
TILLEY, William	Trinity, Holy Minories		Barnstable, Massachusetts	Pope
FOGG, John	Foster Lane		Boston, Mass.	Aspinwall
CHAULKLEY, Robert	Spitalfields		Charlestown, Massachusetts	Pope
TINCKER, John	Bread Street		Boston, Mass.	Aspinwall
WILLIAMS, Hugh	Burnaby Street		Boston, Mass. Block Island, R.I.	Pope
DYER, William	Strand		Boston, Mass. Dorchester	Winthrop
ADAMS, Ferdinando	St. Katherine		Dedham, Mass.	Wyman

LONDON

NAME OF THE EMIGRANT	ENGLISH PARISH NAME	SHIPS NAME	NEW ENGLAND TOWN	VARIOUS REFERENCE
BURROUGHS, Rev. George	Staple Inn		Salem, Mass.	Banks Mss.
TYNG, Edward			Boston, Mass.	Pope
William			Boston, Mass.	Pope
GRAY, John			Boston, Mass. Yarmouth	Pope
CUTTING, Capt. John			Newbury	Farmer
STEVENSON, Marmaduke			Boston, Mass.	Banks Mss.
ATWOOD, John			Plymouth, Mass.	Banks Mss.
PRIEST, Digory		Mayflower	Plymouth, Mass.	Banks Mss.
BIDGOOD, Richard			Boston, Mass.	Boston T.
GLOVER, Rev. Josse			Cambridge, Massachusetts	Col. Soc. Mass.25/18
PERKINS, Rev. William			Topsfield	N.E.G.R. 10/211
BROWN, John			Hampton, New Hampshire	N.E.G.R. 6/232
WINTER, John			Watertown	Boston T.
SWIFT, William			Watertown	Banks Mss.
JAMES, William			Boston, Mass.	Lechford
HILTON, William			Dover, N. H.	Hubbard
POOLE, Henry			Boston, Massachusetts	N.E.G.R. 46/244

LONDON

NAME OF THE EMIGRANT	ENGLISH PARISH NAME	SHIPS NAME	NEW ENGLAND TOWN	VARIOUS REFERENCE
MORLEY? James			Charlestown, Massachusetts	Visit. London N.E.G.R. 15/123 17/111
SMITH, Robert			Boston, Massachusetts	N.E.G.R. 40/63
MERRIAM, Nathaniel	Saint Mary Somerset	Plough		Genealogy N.E.G.R. 53/21
PATTISHALL, Edmund	St. Mary le Strand		Boston, Massachusetts	Banks Mss.
WRIGHT, Richard			Plymouth, Mass.	Pope
SCOTT, Robert			Boston, Mass.	Aspinwall
BENDALL, Edward			Boston, Mass.	Aspinwall
KIBBE, Louis			Boston, Mass.	Pope
ARNOLD, Richard			Chelsea	Pope
HOWES, Samuel			Scituate	Aspinwall
FORREST, Edward				Aspinwall
BLOOMFIELD, James			Boston, Mass.	Aspinwall
LINNELL, Robert			Scituate	Pope
MATSON, Thomas			Braintree, Mass.	Pope
CRACKBONE, Gilbert			Cambridge, Massachusetts	History Cambridge page 519
CLARKE, John			Newbury	Pope
COLLIER, William			Plymouth, Mass.	Pope

LONDON

NAME OF THE EMIGRANT	ENGLISH PARISH NAME	SHIPS NAME	NEW ENGLAND TOWN	VARIOUS REFERENCE
LECHFORD, Thomas			Boston, Mass.	Lechford
KNOWER, Thomas			Charlestown, Massachusetts	Pope
EPPES, Daniel			Ipswich, Mass.	Pope
SEDGWICK, Robert			Charlestown, Massachusetts	Savage
BURCHARD, Thomas			Edgartown, Massachusetts	History Martha's Vineyard
PADDY, William			Plymouth, Mass.	Pope
PESTER, William			Salem, Massachusetts	Essex Court Files
BURTON, Thomas			Boston, Mass.	Pope
CARTER, Joseph			Newbury	Pope
CHEEVER, Ezekiel son of William, Linen-draper			Boston, Massachusetts	Savage
WESTON, Thomas		Charity	Weymouth, Mass.	Bradford
FOOTE, Joshua			Boston, Mass. Providence, R. I.	Pope
VERNON, Daniel			Kingston, R. I.	Austin 402
WARNER, John			Providence, R. I.	Austin 408
NANNEY, Robert			Boston, Mass.	Savage
FURBER, William			Dover, N. H.	Farmer
LIGHTFOOT, Francis			Lynn, Mass.	Farmer
BILLINGTON, John		May-flower	Plymouth, Massachusetts	Bradford

LONDON

NAME OF THE EMIGRANT	ENGLISH PARISH NAME	SHIPS NAME	NEW ENGLAND TOWN	VARIOUS REFERENCE
IOWLAND, John		May-flower	Plymouth, Massachusetts	Banks Mss. Bradford
OGG, Ralph			Plymouth, Mass. Salem, Mass.	Pope
NEALE, Capt. Walter			Portsmouth, New Hampshire	Banks Mss.
MITH, William			Charlestown, Massachusetts	N.E.G.R. 38/71
REENE, John		James	Charlestown, Massachusetts	Dexter Eng. and Holland page 425 Wyman 1/563
RATT, Abraham			Boston, Mass.	Banks Mss.
OWNING, Emanuel	St. Michael Cornhill		Salem, Massachusetts	Winthrop Papers
James	St. Michael Cornhill		Salem, Massachusetts	History of Salem
EXTER, Gregory			Providence, Rhode Island	Records Stationers Co. London
YRES, John			Salisbury	New York G. & B.Rec.
UTHERFORD, Henry			New Haven, Connecticut	Banks Mss.
UGUR, Nicholas			New Haven, Connecticut	Banks Mss.
OXWELL, Richard	St. Bride?		Boston, Mass. Scituate Barnstable, Mass.	Banks Mss.
ILLIAMS, Rev. Roger			Salem, Mass.	Pope
ROWNE, John		Talbot	Salem, Mass.	Savage
Samuel		Talbot	Salem, Mass.	Savage

LONDON

NAME OF THE EMIGRANT	ENGLISH PARISH NAME	SHIPS NAME	NEW ENGLAND TOWN	VARIOUS REFERENCE
TAYLOR, Samuel			Ipswich, Mass.	Banks Mss.
VANE, Sir Henry		Abigail	Boston, Mass.	Winthrop
OLCOTT, Thomas			Hartford, Conn.	Savage
BOYLSTON, Thomas m. Sarah (————)		Defence	Charlestown, Massachusetts	Savage
HANDFORTH, Nathaniel			Lynn, Mass.	Pope
HOWLAND, Arthur			Duxbury	
Henry			Duxbury	
John		May-flower	Plymouth, Mass.	
NORTON, George		Talbot	Salem, Mass.	Pope
SOUTHWORTH, Constant			Plymouth, Mass. (1628)	
Thomas			Plymouth,Mass.	
STORY, George			Boston, Mass.	Winthrop
ALLEN, Arnold			Casco Bay	Mass.Hist. Coll.7/362
WRIGHT, Robert			Boston, Mass.	Banks Mss.
STILEMAN, Elias	St. Andrew Undershaft		Salem, Mass. Portsmouth, R. I.	Banks Mss.
Richard			Cambridge, Mass. Salem, Mass. Andover	Banks Mss.
MORRIS, Richard			Boston, Mass.	Banks Mss

LONDON

NAME OF THE EMIGRANT	ENGLISH PARISH NAME	SHIPS NAME	NEW ENGLAND TOWN	VARIOUS REFERENCE
IARRIS, Nathaniel		Whale	Boston, Massachusetts	Plough Company
BROWNE, Richard			Watertown	Hubbard 187
CLARKE, William			Watertown	Banks Mss.
'URNER, Robert	?		Boston, Mass.	Banks Mss.
ELMORE, Edward	St. Mary Bow		Cambridge, Mass. Hartford, Conn. Northampton, Massachusetts	Banks Mss.
JURNELL, John	?		Dorchester	Banks Mss.
'OWELL, Michael	St. Margaret Pattens		Dedham, Massachusetts	Banks Mss.
ROWNELL, *Ann (Bourne)			Braintree, Mass. Portsmouth, R. I.	
*Thomas	St. Mary Cole		Braintree, Mass. Portsmouth, R. I.	Banks Mss.
INDALL, James	St. Leonard Foster Lane		Duxbury	Waters 743
ARTHOLOMEW, William		Griffin	Ipswich, Mass. Boston, Mass.	Banks Mss.
ERCE, Abraham	?		Plymouth, Mass. 1627 Duxbury	Banks Mss.
ECK, William		Hector	New Haven, Connecticut	Savage
AMMOND, Benjamin		Griffin	Boston, Mass. Sept. 18, 1634	Hammond Gen. p. 565
Elizabeth (widow) (children; Elizabeth, Martha, Rachel and Benjamin)		Griffin	Boston, Mass. Sept. 18, 1634	Hammond Gen. p. 565 Drakes "Boston"

Total number of Emigrants from London is 203 from 67 Parishes.

he great-great-great-great-great-grandparents of Elijah Ellsworth Brownell - - the publisher.

MIDDLESEX

NAME OF THE EMIGRANT	ENGLISH PARISH NAME	SHIPS NAME	NEW ENGLAND TOWN	VARIOUS REFERENCE
BRIGHT, Henry	Bow		Watertown	Bond
*PIERCE, Richard	Bow		Prudence I'd., Rhode Island	Aspinwall
MORGAN, Benedict	Clerkenwell St. James	Fortune	Plymouth, Massachusetts	Banks Mss.
VINES, Richard	Clerkenwell St. James		Saco, Maine Barbados	Banks Mss.
NEWHALL, Anthony	Fulham		Lynn, Mass.	Waters 84
Thomas	Fulham		Lynn, Mass.	Waters 84
BUGBEY, Richard	St. John Hackney		Roxbury	
SEAGAR, Lawrence	Hampton	James		Hotten
REDKNAP, Joseph	Hampton		Lynn, Massachusetts	Suff. Deeds 1/99 Sewall Diary
TIFFANEY, Humphrey	St. John Hackney		Rehoboth, Massachusetts	Banks Mss.
GARDINER, Peter	Hammersmith		Roxbury	Aspinwall
NEEDHAM, Edmund	Hampstead			Hart. Memorial page 2.
ANTHONY, John	Hampstead		Portsmouth, R. I.	Austin 4
GRAY, Henry	Hackney		Fairfield, Connecticut	N.E.G.R. 61/386
John	Hackney		Fairfield, Connecticut	N.E.G.R. 61/386
BRENTON, William	Hammersmith		Newport, R. I.	Savage

* The great-great-great-great-great-grandfather of Elijah Ellsworth Brownell - - the Publisher.

MIDDLESEX

NAME OF THE EMIGRANT	ENGLISH PARISH NAME	SHIPS NAME	NEW ENGLAND TOWN	VARIOUS REFERENCE
COLE, James	Highgate		Saco, Maine Plymouth, Mass.	Genealogy
SNOW, Nicholas	Hoxton	Anne	Plymouth, Mass.	Banks Mss.
DENNISON, William	Holborn		Charlestown, Massachusetts	Banks Mss.
ATKINSON, Luke	Islington		New Haven, Connecticut	Banks Mss.
SCOTT, Richard	Limehouse		Boston, Mass.	Banks Mss.
BROWN, Henry	Limehouse		Boston, Mass.	Pope
HODGES, John	Limehouse		Charlestown, Massachusetts	Wyman
WARREN, Richard	Shoreditch (S. Leonard)	May-flower	Plymouth, Massachusetts	Morton Banks Mss.
GRAVES, Mark	Shoreditch (S. Leonard)		Rowley, Massachusetts	Banks Mss.
POLLEY, George	Shoreditch (S. Leonard)		Woburn, Massachusetts	Banks Mss.
DOWNING, Dennis	Spitalfields		Kittery, Maine.	Banks Mss.
HAMMOND, Lawrence	Spitalfields			Banks Mss.
CHAFFEE, Matthew	Stepney		Boston, Mass. Newbury	Banks Mss.
JONES, Lewis	Stepney		Roxbury	Banks Mss.
PIERCE, William	Stepney (Ratcliffe)		Boston, Massachusetts	Banks Mss.
CRISP, George	Stepney		Eastham, Mass.	Nauset
DOANE, John	Stepney		Eastham, Mass.	Nauset
STEPHENS, William	Stepney		Salem, Mass. Gloucester, Mass.	Banks Mss.

MIDDLESEX

NAME OF THE EMIGRANT	ENGLISH PARISH NAME	SHIPS NAME	NEW ENGLAND TOWN	VARIOUS REFERENCE
PALSGRAVE, Richard	Stepney		Charlestown, Massachusetts	Boston T. 25 Oct. '22 19 Nov. '22 16 Sep. '25
GRAVES, Thomas	Stepney (Ratcliffe)		Charlestown, Massachusetts	Banks Mss.
BIBBLE, John	Stepney		Boston, Mass.	Lechford
FOSTER, William	Stepney		Charlestown, Massachusetts	Waters 82
STEPHENS, Robert	Stepney	Planter	Braintree, Mass.	Pope
VASSALL, William	Stepney		Salem, Massachusetts	Dudley Banks Mss.
LANNIN, James	Stepney	Planter		Hotten
GRIFFITH, Joshua	Stepney		Lynn, Mass.	Pope
COLLINS, Henry	Stepney		Lynn, Mass.	Pope
WILLOUGHBY, Francis	Stepney		Charlestown, Massachusetts	Withington Mss. Essex Inst.
LOCKE, William	Stepney (Wapping)		Charlestown, Massachusetts	Banks Mss.
DAVIS, Nicholas	Stepney (Wapping)		Charlestown, Massachusetts York, Maine	Banks Mss.
MARCH, John	Stepney (Shadwell)		Charlestown, Massachusetts	Banks Mss.
COYTMORE, Thomas	Stepney (Wapping)		Charlestown, Massachusetts	Pope
PAINE, Edward	Stepney (Wapping)		Charlestown, Massachusetts	Pope
CHITTENDEN, Thomas	Stepney (Wapping)		Scituate	Pope
AVERY, Matthew	Stepney (Wapping)		Charlestown, Massachusetts	Pope

MIDDLESEX

NAME OF THE EMIGRANT	ENGLISH PARISH NAME	SHIPS NAME	NEW ENGLAND TOWN	VARIOUS REFERENCE
ROBERTS, William	Stepney (Wapping)		Charlestown, Massachusetts	Town Records
GARDINER, Lyon	Stepney		Long Island, New York	Banks Mss.
GILLAM, Benjamin	Stepney		Boston, Mass.	Banks Mss.
TRERICE, Nicholas	Stepney (Wapping)		Boston, Massachusetts	Banks Mss.
ADAMS, John	Stepney (Wapping)	Fortune	Plymouth, Massachusetts	Banks Mss.
SHRIMLTON, Henry	Stepney Bethnal Green		Boston, Massachusetts	Farmer
BROWN, Hugh	Stepney (Ratcliffe)		Salem, Massachusetts	Banks Mss.
BASSETT, William	Stepney Bethnal Green	Fortune	Plymouth, Massachusetts	Banks Mss.
DAMERILL, Humphrey	Stepney		Boston, Mass.	Banks Mss.
HOLDEN, Randall	Stepney		Warwick, R. I.	Banks Mss.
KNIGHT, Philip	Stepney		Charlestown, Massachusetts	Banks Mss.
TERRILL, Roger	Stepney (Wapping)		Milford, Connecticut	Banks Mss.
COLLAMORE, Isaac	Stepney (Ratcliffe)		Boston, Massachusetts	Aspinwall
FLAVELL, Thomas	Stepney	Fortune	Plymouth, Mass.	Banks Mss.
PALMER, William	Stepney	Fortune	Plymouth, Mass.	Banks Mss.
PRINCE, Thomas	Stepney	Fortune	Plymouth, Massachusetts	Parish Register
TILDEN, Thomas	Stepney	Anne	Plymouth, Mass.	Banks Mss.
ARNOLD, Jasper (or Shoreditch)	Stepney	Abigail		Banks Mss.

MIDDLESEX

NAME OF THE EMIGRANT	ENGLISH PARISH NAME	SHIPS NAME	NEW ENGLAND TOWN	VARIOUS REFERENCE
WRIGHT, Richard	Stepney (Ratcliffe)		Boston, Massachusetts (1630)	Banks Mss.
HAYWARD, William	Stepney (Limehouse)		Charlestown, Massachusetts Braintree, Mass.	Banks Mss.
RAINSBOROUGH, William	Stepney (Wapping)		Charlestown, Massachusetts	Banks Mss.
RICHARDSON, John	Stepney (Ratcliffe)		Woburn, Massachusetts	Mass. Col. Rec. 2/86
CORNWELL, William	Stepney (Ratcliffe)		Roxbury Hartford, Conn.	Banks Mss.
HABORNE, George	Stepney		Exeter Hampton, N. H.	Pope
NOWELL, Increase	Stepney (Wapping)		Charlestown, Massachusetts	Somerby Mss.
GRIFFIN, Hugh	Stepney		Sudbury, Mass.	Banks Mss
KING, Daniel	Uxbridge		Lynn, Mass.	Aspinwall
NICHOLAS, Randall	Uxbridge		Charlestown, Massachusetts	Pope

Total number of Emigrants from Middlesex is 79 from 22 Parishes.

NORFOLK

NAME OF THE EMIGRANT	ENGLISH PARISH NAME	SHIPS NAME	NEW ENGLAND TOWN	VARIOUS REFERENCE
PAGE, Robert	Acle		Salem, Massachusetts	N.E.G.R. 66/183
SUTTON, John	Attleboro		Hingham, Massachusetts	Cushing Mss.
WARD, Thomas	Bedingham		Dedham, Mass.	Banks Mss.
MINGAY, Jeffrey	Bedingham		Dedham, Mass.	Banks Mss.
THAXTER, Thomas	Briggham		Hingham, Mass.	Pope
IRESON, Edward	Buckenham		Lynn, Mass.	Banks Mss.
SMITH, Henry	Buckingham		Dedham, Mass.	Pope
ROPER, John	Buckingham		Dedham, Mass.	Hotten
BAYES, Thomas	Burgh-Apton		Dedham, Mass. Edgartown, Mass.	History Martha's Vineyard
KNIGHT, George	Burgh-Apton		Hingham, Massachusetts	Cushing Mss.
LAWES, Francis	Carleton Rode		Salem, Massachusetts	Banks Mss.
CROWE, John	Carleton Rode		Charlestown, Massachusetts Yarmouth	Banks Mss.
HEARD, Luke	Claxton		Ipswich, Massachusetts	N.E.G.R. 36/353 Banks Mss.
ALLEN, Rev. John	Colby		Dedham, Mass.	Pope
CHAPMAN, Ralph	Diss		Duxbury	Banks Mss.
FOLGER, John	Diss		Dedham, Mass.	Banks Mss.
BUXTON, Thomas	Diss		Salem, Mass.	Banks Mss.
JONES, Thomas	Elsing	Mary Ann	Newbury	Pope

NORFOLK

NAME OF THE EMIGRANT	ENGLISH PARISH NAME	SHIPS NAME	NEW ENGLAND TOWN	VARIOUS REFERENCE
PAINE, Stephen	Ellingham (Great)		Hingham, Massachusetts	Cushing Mss. Banks Mss.
GOFFE, Edward	Ellingham (Great)		Cambridge, Massachusetts	Banks Mss.
TRUE, Henry	Filby		Salisbury	Banks Mss.
GIBBS, Henry	Frenze		Charlestown, Massachusetts Hingham, Mass.	Banks Mss.
PITTS, Edmond	Hackford		Hingham, Massachusetts	Banks Mss.
KNIGHT, Ezekiel	Harleston		Salem, Mass. Braintree, Mass.	Banks Mss.
HOUCHIN, Jeremiah	Harleston		Dorchester	Pope
SMITH, Henry	Hempenall		Charlestown, Massachusetts	Pope
FOULSHAM, Adam	Hingham		Hingham, Massachusetts	Cushing Mss.
John	Hingham		Exeter, New Hampshire	Cushing Mss.
HOBART, Edmond	Hingham		Charlestown, Massachusetts Hingham, Mass.	Wyman
CHUBBOCK, Thomas	Hingham		Charlestown, Massachusetts Hingham, Mass.	Daniel Cushing Mss.
SMITH, Ralph	Hingham		Charlestown, Massachusetts Hingham, Mass.	Daniel Cushing Mss.
PECK, Joseph	Hingham		Hingham, Massachusetts	Cushing Mss.
Rev. Robert	Hingham		Hingham, Massachusetts	Cushing Mss.
SKOULDING, Robert	Hingham		Hingham, Massachusetts	Cushing Mss.
SUCKLING, Thomas	Hingham		Hingham, Massachusetts	Cushing Mss.

NORFOLK

NAME OF THE EMIGRANT	ENGLISH PARISH NAME	SHIPS NAME	NEW ENGLAND TOWN	VARIOUS REFERENCE
CHAMBERLIN, Henry	Hingham		Hingham, Massachusetts	Cushing Mss.
BAXTER, Richard	Hingham		Hingham, Massachusetts	Cushing Mss.
BUCK, James	Hingham		Hingham, Massachusetts	Cushing Mss.
BEALE, John	Hingham		Hingham, Massachusetts	Cushing Mss.
COOPER, Anthony	Hingham		Hingham, Massachusetts	Cushing Mss.
Thomas	Hingham		Hingham, Massachusetts	Cushing Mss.
LINCOLN, Samuel	Hingham		Hingham, Mass. Salem, Mass.	Cushing Mss.
Thomas	Hingham		Hingham, Massachusetts	Cushing Mss.
CUSHING, Mathew	Hingham		Hingham, Massachusetts	Cushing Mss.
Theophilus	Hingham		Hingham, Massachusetts	Cushing Mss.
FARROW, John	Hingham		Hingham, Massachusetts	Cushing Mss.
GATES, Stephen	Hingham		Hingham, Massachusetts	Cushing Mss.
PITTS, Edmond	Hingham		Hingham, Massachusetts	Cushing Mss.
Leonard	Hingham		Hingham, Mass. Boston, Mass.	Cushing Mss.
William	Hingham		Hingham, Massachusetts	Cushing Mss.
JACOB, Nicholas	Hingham		Hingham, Massachusetts	Cushing Mss.
GILMAN, Edward	Hingham		Hingham, Massachusetts	Cushing Mss.

NORFOLK

NAME OF THE EMIGRANT	ENGLISH PARISH NAME	SHIPS NAME	NEW ENGLAND TOWN	VARIOUS REFERENCE
JAMES, Francis	Hingham		Hingham, Massachusetts	Cushing Mss.
Philip	Hingham		Hingham, Massachusetts	Cushing Mss.
MITCHELL, Edward	Hingham		Hingham, Massachusetts	Cushing Mss.
HAWKES, Adam	Hingham		Hingham, Massachusetts	Parish Register
TOWER, John	Hingham		Hingham, Massachusetts	Cushing Mss.
HUNTING, John	Hingham		Dedham, Massachusetts	N.E.G.R. 63/360
MOREFIELD, John	Hingham		Hingham, Massachusetts	Cushing Mss.
TUFTS, John	Hingham		Hingham, Massachusetts	Cushing Mss.
IBROOKE, Richard	Hingham		Hingham, Mass.	
THOMPSON, Edmund	Holkham		Salem, Mass. 1637	N.E.G.R. 62/303
REX, Thomas	Kenninghall		Salem, Mass.	Lechford
William	Kenninghall		Boston, Massachusetts	N.E.G.R. 61/208
ALLEN, Bozoun	Lynn, Kings		Hingham, Mass. Boston, Mass.	Banks Mss.
GRUBB, Thomas	Lynn, Kings		Boston, Mass.	Lechford
KEMPSTER, Daniel	Needham		Cambridge, Mass.	Pope
JENNEY, John	Norwich	Little James	Plymouth, Massachusetts	Mayf.Desc. 10/129
UNDERWOOD, James	Norwich		Salem, Massachusetts	Mass.Arch. (Dom.) Vol. 9
WALKER, William	Norwich		Salem, Mass.	Pope

NORFOLK

NAME OF THE EMIGRANT	ENGLISH PARISH NAME	SHIPS NAME	NEW ENGLAND TOWN	VARIOUS REFERENCE
TORY, William	Norwich		Boston, Mass.	Pope
IERCE, John	Norwich		Watertown	Pope
YERS, Samuel	Norwich		Charlestown, Massachusetts	Savage
AKER, John	Norwich		Charlestown, Massachusetts	Pope
ETCALF, Michael	Norwich		Dedham, Massachusetts	N.E.G.R. 19/26
ICKERSON, William	Norwich		Boston, Mass. Yarmouth	Banks Mss.
LIVER, Thomas	Norwich		Salem, Mass.	Drake
OGGET, Thomas	Norwich		Weymouth, Mass. Concord Marshfield, Mass.	Pope
AWES, Francis	Norwich		Salem, Mass.	Banks Mss.
UZBY, Nicholas	Norwich		Watertown	N.E.G.R. 66/87
OWARD, Thomas	Norwich		Norwich, Connecticut	N.E.G.R. 78/336
UNTINGTON, Simon (died 1633 in route to America, see page 124)	Norwich		Roxbury Saybrook, Connecticut	N.E.G.R. 5/163 Banks Mss.
UDKIN, William	Norwich		Hingham, Massachusetts	Cushing Mss.
ILLIAMS, Robert	Norwich		Roxbury	N.E.G.R. 34/69
ATES, Stephen	Norwich		Hingham, Massachusetts	N.E.G.R. 3/401,31/ Boston T. 16 Sept.'25
EAD, John	Norwich		Charlestown, Massachusetts	Wyman
AIRFIELD, Daniel	Norwich		Salem, Mass. Boston, Mass.	Banks Mss.

NORFOLK

NAME OF THE EMIGRANT	ENGLISH PARISH NAME	SHIPS NAME	NEW ENGLAND TOWN	VARIOUS REFERENC
GEDNEY, John	Norwich		Salem, Massachusetts	Essex Ins 16/241
SCOTTOW, Joshua	Norwich		Boston, Massachusetts	Banks Mss.
Thomas	Norwich		Boston, Massachusetts	Banks Mss.
GREENFIELD, Samuel	Norwich	Mary Ann	Salem, Mass. Ipswich, Mass. Hampton, N. H.	Banks Mss.
JACOB, Nicholas	Norwich		Hingham, Massachusetts	Banks Mss.
WILLET, Thomas	Norwich		Plymouth, Mass. New York Rehoboth, Mass.	N. Y. G. & B. Jan. '29
GREENWOOD, Nathaniel	Norwich		Braintree, Mass.	Savage
DAVISON, Nicholas	Norwich		Charlestown, Massachusetts	Banks Mss.
WEBSTER, Thomas	Ormsby, Great		Hampton	N.E.G.R. 21/1
PALMER, William	Ormsby, Great		Newbury Waterbury Hampton	N.E.G.R. 68/269
MARSTON, John	Ormsby, Great		Salem, Massachusetts	N.E.G.R. 27/292
Robert	Ormsby, Great		Hampton, N. H.	Banks Mss
Thomas	Ormsby, Great		Hampton, N. H.	Banks Mss
William	Ormsby, Great		Salem, Mass.	Banks Mss
DOW, Henry	Ormsby, Great		Watertown Hampton	History Hampton
NUDD, Thomas	Ormsby, Great		Hampton, New Hampshire	History Hampton

NORFOLK

NAME OF THE EMIGRANT	ENGLISH PARISH NAME	SHIPS NAME	NEW ENGLAND TOWN	VARIOUS REFERENCE
MOULTON, John	Ormsby, Great		Hampton Newbury	History of Hampton
Robert	Ormsby, Great		Hampton Newbury	History of Hampton
Thomas	Ormsby, Great		Newbury Hampton York, Maine	Banks Mss.
ESTOW, William	Ormsby, Great		Hampton, N. H.	Banks Mss.
PHILLIPS, Rev. George	Rainham (St. Martin)		Watertown Waltham	Boston T. 6 Apr. '25
FULLER, Giles	Redenhall		Dedham, Mass. Hampton	N.E.G.R. 55/193
Mathew	Redenhall		Plymouth, Massachusetts	N.E.G.R. 55/411
Samuel	Redenhall	May-flower	Plymouth, Massachusetts	N.E.G.R. 55/193
TUTHILL, John	Saxlingham		Southold, Long Island	Moore Indexes Southold
CARVER, Richard	Scratby		Watertown	Pope
FLAGG, Thomas	Shipdam		Watertown	Genealogy
PETTENGILL, Richard	Shotesham		Newbury	N.E.G.R. 55/194
SMITH, Richard	Shropham		Ipswich, Mass.	Banks Mss.
BAXTER, Gregory	Sporle		Roxbury	Banks Mss.
CUTLER, John	Sprowston		Hingham, Massachusetts	Cushing Mss.
METCALF, Michael	Tatterford		Dedham, Mass.	Banks Mss.
CHAPLIN, Rev. Clement	Thetford		Cambridge, Mass.	Pope

NORFOLK

NAME OF THE EMIGRANT	ENGLISH PARISH NAME	SHIPS NAME	NEW ENGLAND TOWN	VARIOUS REFERENCE
CLARKE, William	Thetford		Roxbury	N.E.G.R. 56/84
WILTON, David	Topcroft		Dorchester Windsor Northampton, Massachusetts	College of Arms
Nicholas	Topcroft		Dorchester Windsor Northampton, Massachusetts	College of Arms
PETTENGELL, Richard	Topcroft		Newbury	
TUFTS, Peter	Wilby		Charlestown, Massachusetts	Waters
FULLER, Thomas	Wortwell		Dedham, Massachusetts	N.E.G.R. 55/196
MOORE, Jeremy	Wymondham		Hingham, Massachusetts	N.E.G.R. 55/378
PACKER, Samuel	Wymondham		Hingham, Massachusetts	Cushing Mss.
LINCOLN, Stephen	Wymondham		Hingham, Massachusetts	Cushing Mss.
Thomas	Wymondham		Hingham, Massachusetts	Cushing Mss.
RIPLEY, William	Wymondham		Hingham, Massachusetts	Cushing Mss.
HOBART, Thomas	Wymondham		Hingham, Massachusetts	Cushing Mss.
SWETT, Benjamin	Wymondham		Newbury	Parish Register
John	Wymondham		Newbury	Parish Register
JAMES, Gardey	Winfarthing		Charlestown, Massachusetts	Pope
YOUNGS, Christopher	Yarmouth		Salem, Massachusetts	N.E.G.R. 52/246

NORFOLK

NAME OF THE EMIGRANT	ENGLISH PARISH NAME	SHIPS NAME	NEW ENGLAND TOWN	VARIOUS REFERENCE
TOWNE, William	Yarmouth		Salem, Massachusetts	N.E.G.R. 10/36 21/15
TOPPAN, Abraham	Yarmouth		Newbury	N.E.G.R. 26/434
MILWARD, Thomas	Yarmouth		Newbury	Boston T. 6 Apr. '25
TRACY, Stephen	Yarmouth	Anne	Duxbury	Mayfl.Desc. 10/143
SYMONDS, John	Yarmouth		Salem, Mass.	Banks Mss.
GOODALE, John	Yarmouth		Newbury	Pope
GALT, William	Yarmouth		Salem, Mass.	Pope
ASKEW, John	Yarmouth		Cambridge, Mass.	Pope
FELTON, Benjamin	Yarmouth		Salem, Massachusetts	N.E.G.R. 52/
Nathaniel	Yarmouth		Salem, Massachusetts	N.E.G.R. 52/
BURROUGHS, John	Yarmouth		Salem, Mass.	Hotten
LEEDS, Richard	Yarmouth		Dorchester	Pope
TOWN, Edmond	Yarmouth		Salem, Mass.	Pope
KERRY, Henry	Yarmouth	John and Dorothy	Salem, Massachusetts	Hotten
WILLIAMS, William	Yarmouth	John and Dorothy	Watertown	Hotten
MEAVE, Richard	Yarmouth	Mary Ann	Salem, Mass.	Pope
SCRUGGS, Thomas	Yarmouth		Salem, Mass.	Banks Mss.
RIME, Mark	Yarmouth		Rowley, Mass.	Banks Mss.

NORFOLK

NAME OF THE EMIGRANT	ENGLISH PARISH NAME	SHIPS NAME	NEW ENGLAND TOWN	VARIOUS REFERENCE
BUFFUM, Robert	Yarmouth		Salem, Mass.	Banks Mss
SKERRY, Francis	Yarmouth		Salem, Massachusetts	History of Salem 1/390
WALLER, Christopher	Yarmouth		Salem, Mass.	Banks Mss
Matthew	Yarmouth		Salem, Mass.	Banks Mss
William	Yarmouth		Salem, Mass.	Banks Mss
WRIGHT, Isaac			Hingham, Massachusetts	Cushing Mss.
TUTTLE, Henry			Hingham, Massachusetts	Cushing & Banks Mss
LARGE, William			Hingham, Massachusetts	Cushing Mss.
SMART, John			Hingham, Massachusetts	Cushing Mss.
WELDON, Capt. Robert			Salem, Massachusetts	Boston T. 6 Apr. '25
LUDKIN, George			Hingham, Massachusetts	Cushing Mss.
BUTTS, Thomas			Portsmouth, Rhode Island	Austin 34
STOWELL, Samuel			Hingham, Mass.	Banks Mss
HUNTINGTON, Margaret(Baret) widow of Simon (see page 119) Children: Ann, William, Christopher, Simon, Thomas				

Total number of Emigrants from Norfolk is 168 from 42 Parishes.

NORTHAMPTONSHIRE

NAME OF THE EMIGRANT	ENGLISH PARISH NAME	SHIPS NAME	NEW ENGLAND TOWN	VARIOUS REFERENCE
QUINCY, Edmund	Achurch		Boston, Massachusetts	N.E.G.R. 36/318
MEAKINS, Thomas	Achurch		Boston, Mass.	Pope
BEEBE, James	Addington Magna		Hadley, Massachusetts	Banks Mss.
STANBURY, Josiah	Ashby, Canon's		Lynn, Mass.	Pope
CHURCH, Richard	Ashton		Boston, Mass.	Banks Mss
BALSTON, Jonathan	Barnwell		Boston, Massachusetts	P.C.C. Pell 174 Pell 72 Nabbes 201
ROOT, Thomas	Badby		Salem, Mass. Hartford, Conn.	Root Gen. 93/107
LYNE, Henry	Badby		New Haven, Connecticut	N.E.G.R. 70/
AMES, Thomas	Barton, Earl's		Salem, Massachusetts	N.E.G.R. 63/164
BURGESS, Thomas	Barton, Earl's		Charlestown, Massachusetts	Aspinwall
GORHAM, John	Benefield		Yarmouth Barnstable, Mass.	N.E.G.R 52/
Ralph	Benefield		Yarmouth Barnstable, Mass	N.E.G.R 52/
AMES, Edmund	Barton, Earl's		Watertown	N.E.G.R 63/164
William	Barton, Earl's		Salem, Mass.	Pope
COOPER, Thomas	Bowden, Parva		Boston, Mass.	Pope
BEEBE, John	Broughton		Hadley, Massachusetts	Hartford Prob. Rec. 1/96

* The great-great-great-great-great-grandfather of Elijah Ellsworth Brownell - - the Publisher.

NORTHAMPTONSHIRE

NAME OF THE EMIGRANT	ENGLISH PARISH NAME	SHIPS NAME	NEW ENGLAND TOWN	VARIOUS REFERENCE
JOHNSON, James	Broughton		Boston, Massachusetts	Town Rec. N. London Douglas Genealogy
SIMPKINS, Nicholas	Burcot		Dorchester Boston, Mass. Cambridge, Mass.	Banks Mss.
WADSWORTH, William	Buckby, Long		Cambridge, Mass. Hartford, Conn.	Day Hist. Disc. 1843
SISSON, George	Burton, Latimer		Portsmouth, Rhode Island	Banks Mss.
COLEMAN, Thomas	Cotterstock		Newbury Hampton, N. H. Nantucket, Mass.	Aspinwall
SANDYS, Henry	Culford		Boston, Mass.	Banks Mss.
OXENBRIDGE, Rev. John	Daventry		Boston, Mass.	Farmer
MAKEPEACE, Thomas	Daventry		Boston, Mass.	Banks Mss.
LOVELL, Alexander	Daventry		Westfield, Mass.	Banks Mss.
FRANKLIN, Josiah	Ecton		Boston, Massachusetts	N.E.G.R. 11/17
WARD, Andrew	Faxton		Watertown Wethersfield, Connecticut	Banks Mss.
BELCHER, Edward	Guildsborough		Boston, Massachusetts	N.E.G.R. 60/127
DUDLEY, Thomas	Hardingstone		Boston, Massachusetts	N.E.G.R. 56/206
BOSWELL, Isaac	Husbands Bosworth		Salisbury	Banks Mss.
GARFIELD, Edward	Kilsby		Watertown	27/253
VARNUM, George	Lilbourne		Ipswich, Mass.	Banks Mss.
TEW, Richard	Maidford		Newport, R. I.	Austin 394

NORTHAMPTONSHIRE

NAME OF THE EMIGRANT	ENGLISH PARISH NAME	SHIPS NAME	NEW ENGLAND TOWN	VARIOUS REFERENCE
DOXEY, Thomas	Moulton		New London, Connecticut	Banks Mss.
SARGENT, William	Northampton		Charlestown, Massachusetts	Lechford
COREY, Giles	Northampton (S. Sepulchre)		Salem, Massachusetts	N.E.G.R. 54/344
SUMNER, Henry	Northampton		Woburn, Mass.	Pope
HERBERT, John	Northampton		Salem, Mass.	Pope
HOLMAN, William	Northampton (All Saints)		Cambridge, Massachusetts	Paige Hist.Camb.
RYDER, Samuel	Northampton (All Saints)		Plymouth, Massachusetts	N.E.G.R. 79/316
ADAMS, Richard	Northampton		Salem, Mass.	Pope
DAWES, William	Northampton (S. Sepulchre)		Braintree, Massachusetts	Banks Mss.
SILSBEE, Henry	Northampton (All Saints)		Salem, Massachusetts	Duren S. Family
WADE, Jonathan	Northampton		Charlestown, Massachusetts	Mass. Col. Rec. 3/154
THOMPSON, John	Preston Parva		Stonington	Banks Mss.
DENISON, George	Preston		Roxbury	Lechford
BLISS, Thomas	Preston Parva		Braintree, Mass. Rehoboth, Mass.	Banks Mss.
WRIGHT, Anthony	Preston Parva		Sandwich, Massachusetts	Banks Mss.
CHECKLEY, John	Preston Parva		Boston, Massachusetts	Drake's Boston
William	Preston Parva		Boston, Massachusetts	Drake's Boston

NORTHAMPTONSHIRE

NAME OF THE EMIGRANT	ENGLISH PARISH NAME	SHIPS NAME	NEW ENGLAND TOWN	VARIOUS REFERENCE
TUTTLE,				
Richard	Ringstead		Boston, Massachusetts	College of Arms
William	Ringstead		Boston, Massachusetts	College of Arms
BOSWORTH, Zacheus	Stowe (IX Churches)		Boston, Massachusetts	Banks Mss.
DENISON, George	Scaldwell		Roxbury	Lechford
CORWIN, Matthias (children; John, Martha and Theophilus)	Sibbertoft		Ipswich, Mass. 1634	P. F. 135
HUNT, Robert	Sudborough		Charlestown, Massachusetts	Wyman
WOODHULL, Richard	Thenford		Brookhaven, Long Island	P. F. 110
JONES, Edward	Tichmarsh		Boston, Mass.	Lechford
GOULD, John	Towcester		Charlestown, Massachusetts	Pope
LORD, Thomas	Towcester	Elizabeth and Ann	Cambridge, Mass. Hartford, Conn.	Boston T. 21 Apr. '25
SHEPARD,				
Rev. Thomas	Towcester		Charlestown, Massachusetts	N.E.G.R. 70/189
William	Towcester		Taunton New Haven, Connecticut	Essex Inst.64/236
REEVES,				
Thomas	Towcester			Banks Mss.
William	Towcester			Banks Mss.
BURTON, Boniface	Warmington		Lynn, Mass. Reading, Mass.	Waters 172
JONES, Edward	Welling-borough		Boston, Massachusetts	Lechford
PAINE, Thomas	Whittlebury		Watertown Edgartown, Massachusetts	History Martha's Vineyard

NORTHAMPTONSHIRE

NAME OF THE EMIGRANT	ENGLISH PARISH NAME	SHIPS NAME	NEW ENGLAND TOWN	VARIOUS REFERENCE
CORWIN, George			Salem, Mass. 1638	Corwin Genealogy
DUDLEY, Thomas	Yardley Hastings		Boston, Massachusetts	N.E.G.R. 66/340
HILL, John	?		Guildford, Connecticut	Smith History Guildford Page 20
WELBY, George	?	Susan and Ellen	Lynn, Mass. Southampton, Long Island	Pope

Total number of Emigrants from Northamptonshire is 71 from 42 Parishes.

NORTHUMBERLAND

NAME OF THE EMIGRANT	ENGLISH PARISH NAME	SHIPS NAME	NEW ENGLAND TOWN	VARIOUS REFERENCF
WALKER, Augustine	Berwick		Charlestown, Massachusetts	Wyman
FENWICK, George	Brinkthorn		Saybrook, Connecticut	Visit. Northumberland
HALL, Edward	Heddon		Cambridge, Mass	Pope
CHISHOLM, Thomas	Newcastle on Tyne		Cambridge, Massachusetts	N.E.G.R. 61/59 58/79 59/242
CUTTER, William	Newcastle on Tyne		Cambridge, Massachusetts	N.E.G.R. 61/69
WINSHIP, Edward	Newcastle on Tyne		Cambridge, Massachusetts	N.E.G.R. 61/69
BAINBRIDGE, Guy	Newcastle on Tyne		Cambridge, Massachusetts	N.E.G.R. 61/69
BITTLESTON, Thomas	Newcastle on Tyne		Cambridge, Massachusetts	N.E.G.R. 61/69
ERRINGTON, Abraham	Newcastle on Tyne		Charlestown, Massachusetts	N.E.G.R. 38/79 59/242 Pope
STEVENSON, Andrew	Newcastle on Tyne		Charlestown, Massachusetts	N.E.G.R. 38/79 59/242 Pope
TRUMBULL, John	Newcastle on Tyne		Charlestown, Massachusetts	N.E.G.R. 38/79 59/242 Pope
ERRINGTON, Thomas	Newcastle on Tyne		Salem, Mass. Lynn, Mass. Charlestown, Massachusetts	Pope
SILL, John	Newcastle on Tyne		Cambridge, Massachusetts	Pope
READ, William	Newcastle on Tyne		Dorchester Scituate Woburn, Mass.	Banks Mss.

NORTHUMBERLAND

NAME OF THE EMIGRANT	ENGLISH PARISH NAME	SHIPS NAME	NEW ENGLAND TOWN	VARIOUS REFERENCE
HOLMES, Robert	Newcastle on Tyne		Cambridge, Massachusetts	Pope
STEVENSON, John	Newcastle on Tyne		Boston, Massachusetts	Banks Mss.
BITTLESTONE, William	Newcastle on Tyne		Cambridge, Massachusetts	Paige
CUTTER, Richard	Newcastle on Tyne		Cambridge, Massachusetts	Paige
COPELAND, Lawrence	?		Braintree, Mass.	

Total number of Emigrants from Northumberland is 19 from 4 Parishes.

NOTTINGHAMSHIRE

NAME OF THE EMIGRANT	ENGLISH PARISH NAME	SHIPS NAME	NEW ENGLAND TOWN	VARIOUS REFERENCE
STARBUCK, Edward	Attenboro		Dover, New Hampshire	Farmer Banks Mss.
HUTCHINSON, Richard	Arnold		Salem, Mass.	Banks Mss.
WHELDON, Gabriel	Arnold		Yarmouth Lynn, Mass. Malden, Mass.	Banks Mss.
NODDLE, William	Bole		Salem, Mass.	Banks Mss.
GREGORY, Henry	Brompton Sulney		Boston, Mass. Springfield	N.E.G.R. 23/306
ODINGSELLS, Thomas	Epperstone		Salem, Mass.	Lechford
HEATHERSAY, Robert	Gotham		Concord, Mass. Charlestown, Massachusetts Exeter, Dover York, Maine	Banks Mss.
MORTON, George	Harworth	Anne	Plymouth, Mass	Dexter
WADSWORTH, Christopher	Mansfield		Duxbury	Banks Mss.
HUTCHINSON, Richard	Muskham, North		Salem, Massachusetts	N.E.G.R. 22/247
SQUIRE, George	Nottingham		Concord	Notts. Marr. Lic.
CONKLING, Ananias	Nottingham		Salem, Mass. Southold, L. I.	N.E.G.R. 61/386
John	Nottingham		Salem, Mass. Southold, L. I.	N.E.G.R. 61/386
AYER, Peter	Nottingham		Haverhill, Massachusetts	History of Hampstead N. H.2/744
GREGORY, John	Nottingham		Duxbury	Pope

NOTTINGHAMSHIRE

NAME OF THE EMIGRANT	ENGLISH PARISH NAME	SHIPS NAME	NEW ENGLAND TOWN	VARIOUS REFERENCE
FROST, William	Nottingham		Fairfield	Lechford Plaine Dealing
BLOOD, James	Nottingham		Lynn, Mass. Concord	Banks Mss.
COWLISHAW	Nottingham		Boston, Mass.	Banks Mss.
CONKLING, John	Nuthall		Salem, Mass. Southold, L. I.	Notts. Marr. Lic.
MALTBY, John	Retford, East			Boston T. 2313, 1924
Robert	Retford, East			Boston T. 2313, 1924
William	Retford, East			Boston T. 2313, 1924
BLOOD, Robert	Ruddington		Lynn, Mass. Concord	Essex Deeds 1/24
BREWSTER, William	Scrooby	May-flower	Plymouth, Massachusetts	Savage
SOUTHWORTH, Edward	Sturton	Anne	Plymouth, Mass.	Banks Mss.
ROBINSON, Isaac	Sturton		Barnstable, Mass Tisbury, Mass.	History Martha's Vineyard
SHAW, Roger	Willoughby		Cambridge, Mass. Hampton, N. H.	Banks Mss.
BOWLES, Joseph	Worksop		Wells, Maine	N.E.G.R. 52/185
FITZRANDLE, Edward	?		Scituate	Pope

Total number of Emigrants from Nottinghamshire is 29 from 17 Parishes.

OXFORDSHIRE

NAME OF THE EMIGRANT	ENGLISH PARISH NAME	SHIPS NAME	NEW ENGLAND TOWN	VARIOUS REFERENCE
BOREMAN, Samuel	Banbury		Ipswich, Mass. Wethersfield, Connecticut	Genealogy
NEWMAN, Rev. Samuel	Banbury		Dorchester	Pope
SUMNER, William	Bicester		Dorchester	N.E.G.R. 8/128D P. F. 76
STEPHENS, John	Caversham		Newbury	N.E.G.R. 60/60
SALTER, Sampson	Caversham		Newport, Rhode Island	N.E.G.R. 60/61
JONES, Thomas	Caversham		Newbury	N.E.G.R. 60/60
BENSON, John	Caversham		Hingham, Massachusetts	N.E.G.R. 60/60
KEENE, Matthew	Checkenden	Confidence	Hingham, Massachusetts	Aspinwall 249
AVERY, William	Chipping Norton		Ipswich, Massachusetts	N. Y. Gen. & Biog. Rec.59/294
BETTS, John	Claydon		Cambridge, Mass.	Brainerd
Thomas	Claydon		Hartford, Conn. Wethersfield, Connecticut	Brainerd
WESTON, Edmond	Cornwell		Duxbury	Banks Mss.
STEPHENS, John	Eynsham	Confidence	Newbury	Pope
William	Eynsham	Confidence	Newbury	Pope
BENSON, John	Eynsham	Confidence	Hingham, Massachusetts	Pope
WHITTON, James	Hook Norton		Hingham, Mass.	Aspinwall

OXFORDSHIRE

NAME OF THE EMIGRANT	ENGLISH PARISH NAME	SHIPS NAME	NEW ENGLAND TOWN	VARIOUS REFERENCE
WOODHULL, Richard	Mollington		Brookhaven, Long Island	N.E.G.R. 45/146
MAYO, John	Newington, North		Nauset, C. C.	Banks Mss.
PRINCE, John	Oxford		Watertown Hull, Mass.	Banks Mss.
FLOYD, John	Oxford		Scituate	Aspinwall
BLAND, Bridget	Oxford		Charlestown, Massachusetts	Aspinwall
JONES, Robert	Reading		Hingham, Mass.	Aspinwall
LARKIN, William	Reading		Reading, Mass.	Pope
WILDER, Edward	Shiplake		Hingham, Mass.	Genealogy
Thomas	Shiplake		Charlestown, Massachusetts Lancaster, Mass.	Genealogy
COBBETT, Thomas	Thame		Lynn, Massachusetts	Mather 1/518
SUTTON, Ambrose	Westwell		Charlestown, Massachusetts Newport, R. I.	Lechford

Total number of Emigrants from Oxfordshire is 27 from 16 Parishes.

RUTLAND

NAME OF THE EMIGRANT	ENGLISH PARISH NAME	SHIPS NAME	NEW ENGLAND TOWN	VARIOUS REFERENCE
HINMAN, Edward	Barrow		Stratford, Conn.	Banks Mss.
VEAZIE, William	Caldecot		Braintree, Mass.	Aspinwall
JOHNSON, Isaac	Clipsham		Boston, Mass.	Savage
Isaac	Luffenham, South		Boston, Massachusetts	Savage
SMITH, Robert	Manton		Boston, Mass.	Banks Mss.
FLETCHER, John	Stretton		Wethersfield, Connecticut Milford	Banks Mss.
BACON, Andrew	Stretton		Hartford Conn.	Savage
Nathaniel	Stretton		Barnstable, Massachusetts Middletown	Banks Mss.
FLOWER, Lamerock	Whitwell		Hartford, Conn.	

Total number of Emigrants from Rutland is 9 from 7 Parishes.

SHROPSHIRE

NAME OF THE EMIGRANT	ENGLISH PARISH NAME	SHIPS NAME	NEW ENGLAND TOWN	VARIOUS REFERENCE
THOMPSON, Thomas	Burford		Farmington, Connecticut	Banks Mss.
GROSVENOR, John	Bridgenorth		Roxbury	N.E.G.R. 72/131
WESTON, Thomas	Hughley	Charity	Weymouth, Mass.	Banks Mss.
MORE, Elinor	Shipton	Mayflower	Plymouth, Massachusetts	Parish Register
Jasper	Shipton	Mayflower	Plymouth, Massachusetts	Parish Register
Richard	Shipton	Mayflower	Plymouth, Massachusetts	Parish Register
MACKWORTH, Arthur	Shrewsbury		Portland, Maine	Banks Mss.
CLEEVES, George	Shrewsbury		Portland, Maine	Banks Mss.
BRUEN, Obadiah	Shrewsbury		Swampscott, Massachusetts Gloucester, Mass. New London, Connecticut	Pope
LEWIS, Thomas	Shrewsbury		Saco, Maine	Banks Mss.
HOPKINS, Edward	Shrewsbury		Hartford, Conn.	Waters
PRICE, Richard	Shrewsbury		Boston, Mass.	Pope
SMITH, Abraham	Sidbury		Charlestown, Massachusetts	Pope
TYLER, Nathaniel	Shrewsbury		Lynn, Mass.	Pope

Total number of Emigrants from Shropshire is 14 from 6 Parishes.

SOMERSETSHIRE

NAME OF THE EMIGRANT	ENGLISH PARISH NAME	SHIPS NAME	NEW ENGLAND TOWN	VARIOUS REFERENCE
HARVEY, William	Ashill		Taunton	Waters Gleanings 645
MORTON, Thomas	Axbridge		Merry Mount	Banks Mss.
FRYE, Adrian	Axbridge		Kittery,Maine	Banks Mss.
ADAMS, Henry	Barton, St. Dav.		Braintree, Massachusetts	Genealogy
BICKNELL, Zachary	Barrington		Weymouth, Mass.	Banks Mss.
WOOREY, Ralph	Bedminster		Charlestown, Massachusetts	Banks Mss.
BARNARD, Methuselah	Batcombe		Weymouth, Massachusetts	N.E.G.R. 67/382
MARTIN, Robert	Batcombe		Weymouth, Massachusetts	N.E.G.R. 67/382
TABOR, Timothy	Batcombe		Weymouth, Massachusetts	N.E.G.R. 67/382
READE, William	Batcombe		Weymouth, Mass. Boston, Mass.	N.E.G.R. 67/382
ADAMS, Richard	Batcombe		Weymouth, Mass.	Pope
HEARD, John	Batcombe		York, Maine	Banks Mss.
ENDRED, John	Brent, South		Boston, Mass.	Banks Mss.
STREET, Nicholas	Bridgewater		Taunton	N.E.G.R. 46/256 Banks Mss.
BALCH, John	Bridgewater		Salem, Massachusetts	Farmer Perley
LINDON, Henry	Bridgewater		New Haven, Connecticut	Banks Mss.
NORTON, Nicholas	Broadway		Weymouth, Mass. Edgartown, Massachusetts	History Martha's Vineyard

SOMERSETSHIRE

NAME OF THE EMIGRANT	ENGLISH PARISH NAME	SHIPS NAME	NEW ENGLAND TOWN	VARIOUS REFERENCE
HOLBROOK, Thomas	Broadway		Weymouth, Massachusetts	N.E.G.R. 58/305
POOLE, Edward	Broadway			
PINNEY, Humphrey	Broadway		Windsor, Connecticut	Stiles History Windsor
AMES, John	Bruton		Bridgewater	Hinman
William	Bruton		Braintree, Massachusetts	N.E.G.R. 49/273
LAMPREY, Henry	Cannington		Boston, Mass. Hampton York, Maine	Banks Mss.
GILLETTE, Jonathan	Chafcombe		Dorchester Windsor	New York G. & B. Record
Nathaniel	Chafcombe		Dorchester Windsor	New York G. & B. Record
HILL, John	Chafcombe		Dorchester	N.E.G.R. 58/157
DEANE, John	Chard		Taunton	Genealogy
Walter	Chard		Taunton	Genealogy
HILL, John	Chard		Dorchester	N.E.G.R. 58/157
PINNEY, Thomas	Chard		Weymouth, Mass.	Banks Mss.
BOULTER, Nathaniel	Chewton Keynsham		Hampton, New Hampshire	Banks Mss.
SHEPARD, John	Charlton Mackrell		Braintree, Massachusetts	Banks Mss.

SOMERSETSHIRE

NAME OF THE EMIGRANT	ENGLISH PARISH NAME	SHIPS NAME	NEW ENGLAND TOWN	VARIOUS REFERENCE
HASKELL, Mark	Charlton Musgrove		Salem, Massachusetts	Banks Mss.
Roger	Charlton Musgrove		Salem, Massachusetts	Banks Mss.
William	Charlton Musgrove		Salem, Massachusetts	Banks Mss.
DIMMOCK, Thomas	Chesterblade		Weymouth, Mass. Barnstable, Mass.	Banks Mss.
COLE, William	Chew Magna			Lechford
MINOR, Thomas	Chew Magna		Stonington, Connecticut	N.E.G.R. 13/163 Diary
BAGNALL, Walter	Chewton		Braintree, Mass. Richmond Island	Banks Mss.
DODGE, William	Chinnock Middle		Salem, Massachusetts	N.E.G.R. 46/383
GAYLORD, William	Chilthorne Domer	Mary and John	Dorchester	Banks Mss.
TILLEY, John	Chilthorne Domer	Mary and John	Dorchester	Banks Mss.
MATTOCK, James	Clapton		Boston, Massachusetts	Boston Town Rec.
SPOORE, John	Clapton		Boston, Massachusetts	Boston Town Rec.
IRISH, John	Clisdon		Duxbury	Austin N.E.G.R. 39/28
SLOCUM, Giles	Cleeve, Old		Portsmouth, Rhode Island	N.E.G.R. 70/284 78/396
TRASK, Osmand	Coker, East		Salem, Mass. Beverly, Mass.	Pope
William	Coker, East		Salem, Massachusetts	N.E.G.R. 54/279

SOMERSETSHIRE

NAME OF THE EMIGRANT	ENGLISH PARISH NAME	SHIPS NAME	NEW ENGLAND TOWN	VARIOUS REFERENCE
DODGE,				
Richard	Coker, East		Beverly, Mass.	Genealogy
William	Coker, East		Salem, Massachusetts	N.E.G.R. 54/279
MEIGS, John	Combe (S. Nicholas)		Weymouth, Mass. New Haven, Connecticut	Banks Mss.
FRYE,			Weymouth, Massachusetts	Banks Mss. Pope
George	Combe (S. Nicholas)			
William	Combe (S. Nicholas)		Weymouth, Massachusetts	Banks Mss.
ROSSITER, Edward	Combe (S. Nicholas)	Mary and John	Dorchester	Banks Mss.
TORREY,				
Philip	Combe (S. Nicholas)		Roxbury	Pope
William	Combe (S. Nicholas)		Weymouth, Massachusetts	Pope
WEEKS, Leonard	Compton Martin		Greenland, New Hampshire	Genealogy
PATTEN, Nathaniel	Crewkerne		Dorchester	Lechford
BARTOLL, John	Crewkerne		Marblehead, Massachusetts	Lechford
CHUBB, Thomas	Crewkerne		Salem, Massachusetts	Perley History of Salem
POMEROY, Eltweed	Crewkerne		Dorchester	Genealogy
HULL, Rev. Joseph	Crewkerne		Weymouth, Mass.	Genealogy
MOSIER, Hugh	Cucklington	James	Portland Newport, R. I. Portsmouth, R. I.	Banks Mss.
JONES, Richard	Dinder		Dorchester	Pope
WEST,				
Bartholomew	Evercreech		Newport, R. I.	Banks Mss.
Stephen	Evercreech		Newport, R. I.	Banks Mss.

SOMERSETSHIRE

NAME OF THE EMIGRANT	ENGLISH PARISH NAME	SHIPS NAME	NEW ENGLAND TOWN	VARIOUS REFERENCE
COLE, William	Farrington Gourney			Lechford
ROCKWELL, William	Fitzhead	Mary and John	Dorchester	Genealogy
DYER, George	Fitzhead	Mary and John	Dorchester	Banks Mss.
KINGMAN, Henry	Frome		Weymouth, Mass.	Banks Mss.
RAYMOND, John	Glastonbury		Salem, Mass. Beverly, Mass	
William	Glastonbury		Salem, Mass.	
OTIS, Richard	Glastonbury		Dover, New Hampshire	N.E.G.R. 5/177 5/223
OFFLEY, Davis	Glastonbury		Boston, Mass.	Pope
WOLCOTT, John	Glastonbury		Watertown	Pope
GUTCH, Robert	Glastonbury		Salem, Mass.	Banks Mss.
PADDOCK, Robert	Ham, High		Plymouth, Mass.	Banks Mss.
WILLIAMS, Roger	Harptree, West	Mary and John	Dorchester Windsor Boston, Mass.	Banks Mss.
PATTEN, William	Hardington		Cambridge, Mass.	Genealogy
HAYDEN, John	Hinton, Blewet		Dorchester	Stiles Hist. of Windsor Page 369
William	Hinton, Blewet		Windsor, Connecticut	Stiles Hist. of Windsor Page 369

SOMERSETSHIRE

NAME OF THE EMIGRANT	ENGLISH PARISH NAME	SHIPS NAME	NEW ENGLAND TOWN	VARIOUS REFERENCE
POOLE, Edward	Heathcombe		Weymouth, Mass.	Banks Mss.
BALCH, John	Horton		Salem, Mass.	Genealogy
PALFREY, Peter	Horton		Salem, Mass.	Banks Mss.
ARNOLD, William	Ilchester		Hingham, Mass. Providence, R. I.	N.E.G.R. 69/649
HOPKINS, Thomas	Ilchester		Providence, R. I.	Banks Mss.
TABOR, Philip	Kilmington		Plymouth, Mass. Watertown	Banks Mss.
BIBBLE, John	Lympsham		Hull, Mass.	Banks Mss.
JEFFRIES, Thomas	Lympsham		New Haven, Connecticut	Banks Mss.
GARDINER, Thomas	Martock (Hurst)		Salem, Mass.	Banks Mss.
BRADFORD, Robert	Martock		Boston, Mass.	Banks Mss.
ROYCE, Robert	Martock		Stratford, Conn.	Banks Mss.
GYLES, Edmund	Meere		Salem, Mass.	Banks Mss.
GETCHELL, John	Monkton, West		Salem, Mass.	Genealogy
Samuel	Monkton, West		Salem, Mass.	Genealogy
PIKE, Robert	Merriott		Providence, R. I.	Banks Mss.
POOLE, William	Milton		Taunton	Aspinwall
LEACH, Lawrence	Martock (Ash)		Salem, Mass.	Banks Mss.
SYLVESTER, Richard	Northover		Dorchester Weymouth, Mass. Marshfield, Mass.	Banks Mss.

SOMERSETSHIRE

NAME OF THE EMIGRANT	ENGLISH PARISH NAME	SHIPS NAME	NEW ENGLAND TOWN	VARIOUS REFERENCE
COMER, John	Oake			N.E.G.R. 57/110 P.C.C. 76 Ent.
NORMAN, Hugh	Orchard Portman		Plymouth, Massachusetts	Mayf.Desc. 6/103 N.E.G.R. 68/62
LING, Benjamin	Petherton, North		New Haven, Connecticut	Banks Mss. Subsidy
PATCH, Edmund	Petherton, South		Salem, Massachusetts	Banks Mss.
Nicholas	Petherton, South		Salem, Massachusetts	Banks Mss. N.E.G.R. 66/166
WOODBURY, William	Petherton, South		Salem, Massachusetts	N.E.G.R. 66/166
PHELPS, William	Porlock	Mary and John	Dorchester	Banks Mss.
GAYLORD, John	Pitminster		Dorchester	New York G. & B. Record
TREAT, Richard	Pitminster		Wethersfield, Connecticut	N.E.G.R. 58/315
BLAKE, William	Pitminster		Dorchester Springfield	Blake Gen. Pope
SEABURY, John	Porlock		Boston, Massachusetts	History of W. Chester Co., N. Y.
LOWELL, Percival	Portbury		Newbury	Harl. Mss. 1559 Banks Mss
WHITE, Gawen	Quantoxhead West		Scituate	Banks Mss
FLOWER, Lamerock	Saltford		Hartford, Conn.	Banks Mss
ALLEN, George	Saltford		Weymouth, Mass.	Banks Mss

SOMERSETSHIRE

NAME OF THE EMIGRANT	ENGLISH PARISH NAME	SHIPS NAME	NEW ENGLAND TOWN	VARIOUS REFERENCE
EMBLEN, ——	Shepton Mallet		Charlestown, Massachusetts	Banks Mss.
CRANE, Henry	Somerton			Banks Mss.
KNIGHT, Walter	Staplegrove		Salem, Mass.	Banks Mss.
CRANE, Jasper	Spaxton		New Haven, Connecticut Newark, N. J.	Banks Mss.
EVERETT, Andrew	Stogursey		York, Maine	Banks Mss.
TUCKER, Richard	Stogumber		Portland, Maine	Willis' History of Portland
WHITCOMB, John	Taunton		Dorchester	N.E.G.R. 68/63
PARDEE, George	Taunton		New Haven, Connecticut	Holworthy
SAVAGE, Thomas	Taunton		Boston, Massachusetts	Banks Mss. N.E.G.R. 1891
STRONG, John	Taunton		Dorchester	N.E.G.R. 23/294
SWINNERTON, Job	Taunton		Salem, Mass.	Banks Mss.
MANNING, John	Taunton		Boston, Mass.	Banks Mss.
MACEY, George	Taunton		Taunton	Banks Mss.
BILLING, Roger	Taunton		Dorchester	Banks Mss.
William	Taunton		Dorchester	N.E.G.R. 81/158
ELLSWORTH, Josiah	Timberscomb		Windsor	Banks Mss.

SOMERSETSHIRE

NAME OF THE EMIGRANT	ENGLISH PARISH NAME	SHIPS NAME	NEW ENGLAND TOWN	VARIOUS REFERENCE
WOLCOTT, Henry	Tolland	Mary and John	Dorchester	Pope
BIBBLE, John	Wedmore		Hull, Mass.	Aspinwall
CLARKE, James	Wells		Boston, Mass.	Pope
DURSTON, Thomas	Wilton		Charlestown, Massachusetts	Parish Register
JONES, Hugh	Wincanton		Salem, Massachusetts	N.E.G.R. 30/460 66/187
ABBOTT, James	Wincanton		Salem, Massachusetts	N.E.G.R. 30/460 66/187
VINING, John	Wincanton		Salem, Massachusetts	N.E.G.R. 30/460 66/187
DYER, George	Wincanton	Mary and John	Dorchester	Banks Mss.
EYRES, Simon	Woodland, West		Watertown Boston, Mass.	Banks Mss.
FUSSELL, John	Wookey		Weymouth, Mass.	Banks Mss.
LOVELL, Robert	Wookey		Weymouth, Mass.	Banks Mss.
MORGAN, Robert	Wrington		Salem, Mass.	Banks Mss.
NODDY, Doctor (First doctor in Salem; was butcher in England)	Wrington		Salem, Massachusetts	Thomas Morton N. E. Canaan
WORTH, Lionel	Yeovil		Newbury	Banks Mss.
RICHARDS, Thomas	?	Mary and John	Dorchester	Mayflower Desc't. 6/103
PHELPS, George	?		Dorchester	P. C. C. Berkeley 366

SOMERSETSHIRE

NAME OF THE EMIGRANT	ENGLISH PARISH NAME	SHIPS NAME	NEW ENGLAND TOWN	VARIOUS REFERENCE
SHATTUCK, Samuel	?		Salem, Massachusetts	Perley History of Salem
William	?		Watertown	Pope
SAFFIN, John	?		Scituate Boston, Mass.	Pope Banks Mss.
SAWTELLE, Richard	?		Watertown Groton	Banks Mss.
WILLET, Nathaniel	?		Hartford,Conn.	Banks Mss.
LOVELL, William	?	Mary and John	Dorchester	Banks Mss.
TILLEY, Hugh	?	Lion's Whelp	Salem, Mass. Yarmouth	Mass. Col. Rec. 1/101

Total number of Emigrants from Somersetshire is 153 from 78 Parishes.

STAFFORDSHIRE

NAME OF THE EMIGRANT	ENGLISH PARISH NAME	SHIPS NAME	NEW ENGLAND TOWN	VARIOUS REFERENCE
LEONARD, Henry	Bilston		Braintree, Mass. Taunton	N.E.G.R. 5/104
James	Bilston		Braintree, Mass. Taunton	N.E.G.R. 5/104
PADDY, William	Eccleshall		Plymouth, Mass. Boston, Mass.	Banks Mss.
BLAKEMAN, Rev.Adam	Gnosall		Scituate Stratford, Conn.	Banks Mss.
CONKLING, Ananias	Kingswinford		Southold, Long Island	Notts. Marr. Lic.
BOYLSTON, Henry	Lichfield		Charlestown, Massachusetts	N.E.G.R. 7/145
BROUGHTON, Thomas	Longdon		Watertown	N.E.G.R. 40/106
HOLYOKE, Edward	Tamworth		Lynn, Mass.	E. L. S.
CHADBURNE, William	Tamworth		Boston, Mass.	Banks Mss.
PILSBURY, William	?		Dorchester Newbury	Farmer
SOUTHWICK, John			Salem, Mass.	Banks Mss
Lawrence	Tetnall		Salem, Mass. Southold, L. I.	Banks Mss.
HANBURY, William	Wolver-hampton		Duxbury	N.E.G.R. 40/106 Visit Staff.
SANDBROOKE, Thomas	Wolver-hampton		Boston, Massachusetts	Suff. Deeds 3/244

Total number of Emigrants from Staffordshire is 14 from 9 Parishes.

SUFFOLK

NAME OF THE EMIGRANT	ENGLISH PARISH NAME	SHIPS NAME	NEW ENGLAND TOWN	VARIOUS REFERENCE
GILDERSLEEVE, Richard	Aldeburgh		Stamford, Conn.	Banks Mss.
LOVERING, Thomas	Aldham		Watertown	N.E.G.R. 18/336 56/184
FRENCH, John	Assington		Ipswich, Mass.	Linzee 419
Thomas	Assington		Ipswich, Mass.	Linzee 419
Thomas, Jr.	Assington		Ipswich, Mass.	Linzee 419
WYATT, John	Assington		Ipswich, Mass.	Banks Mss.
GURNEY, Edward	Bardwell		Cambridge, Mass.	Banks Mss.
WING, Robert	Bergholt, East	Francis	Boston, Mass.	Banks Mss.
COLE, Edward	Bergholt, East			Waters
JOSSELYN, Thomas	Barham		Hingham, Mass.	
BULLARD, Robert	Barham		Watertown 1634	Boston T. 11 Oct. 1926
COLBY, Anthony	Beccles		Salisbury	
HUBBARD, George	Bergholt, East		Guildford, Conn.	Banks Mss.
READE, John	Blyborough		Braintree, Mass.	Aspinwall
KINGSBURY, Henry	Boxford		Boston, Mass.	Banks Mss.
SAWIN, John	Boxford		Watertown	Aspinwall Suff. Deeds 1/141

SUFFOLK

NAME OF THE EMIGRANT	ENGLISH PARISH NAME	SHIPS NAME	NEW ENGLAND TOWN	VARIOUS REFERENCE
PHILLIPS, Rev. George	Boxford		Watertown	Pope
CRABBE, Richard	Boxford		Watertown Wethersfield, Connecticut Stamford, Conn. Greenwich Oyster Bay, L. I.	History of Wethersfield
COE, Robert	Boxford	Frances	Watertown Wethersfield, Connecticut Stamford, Conn. Greenwich	Genealogy
EDDY, Samuel	Boxted	Handmaid	Plymouth, Massachusetts	Winthrop Mss. W. 7a, 49
GRIGGS, Thomas	Boxted		Roxbury	Linzee 475
TOWNSEND, Thomas	Bracon Ash		Lynn, Massachusetts	N.E.G.R. 29/102
BALLARD, William	Bradwell		Lynn, Massachusetts	N.E.G.R. 61/69
COLLINS, Edward	Bramford		Cambridge, Massachusetts	College of Arms
COOPER, Benjamin	Brampton		Salem, Massachusetts	N.E.G.R. 57/198
KILHAM, John	Brampton		Salem, Mass.	Hotten
BLOSS, Edmond	Brandstone		Watertown	Banks
BARNARD, Robert	Brandstone		Salisbury	Banks Mss.
LOKER, Henry	Bures St. Mary		Sudbury, Massachusetts	N.E.G.R. 64/136
John	Bures St. Mary		Sudbury, Massachusetts	N.E.G.R. 63/280
PARMENTER, John	Bures St. Mary		Sudbury, Massachusetts	N.E.G.R. 68/271
KNAPP, Nicholas	Bures St. Mary		Watertown	Pope

SUFFOLK

NAME OF THE EMIGRANT	ENGLISH PARISH NAME	SHIPS NAME	NEW ENGLAND TOWN	VARIOUS REFERENCE
KNAPP, William	Bures St. Mary		Watertown	Pope
CHILD, Benjamin	Bury St. Edmunds		Roxbury	Linzee 545-7
Ephraim	Bury St. Edmunds		Watertown	Linzee 545-7
William	Bury St. Edmunds		Watertown	Linzee 545-7
NEWGATE, John	Bury St. Edmunds		Boston, Massachusetts	N.E.G.R. 33/58
CHAPLIN, Clement	Bury St. Edmunds		Cambridge, Massachusetts	Chandler Mss. N.E.G.R. 38/343
KNAPP, William	Bury St. Edmunds		Watertown	Boston T.
GOODRICH, John	Bury St. Edmunds		Watertown Wethersfield, Connecticut	Genealogy
BRIGHT, Henry	Bury St. Edmunds		Watertown	N.E.G.R. 13/98
TOWNSEND, William	Bury St. Edmunds		Boston, Massachusetts	Pope
ATKINSON, Theodore	Bury St. Edmunds		Boston, Massachusetts	Pope
COOKE, Peyton	Bury St. Edmunds		Scarboro, Maine	Banks Mss.
WRIGHT, Samuel	Bury St. Edmunds		Springfield	Banks Mss.
GURNEY, John	Bury St. Edmunds		Braintree, Massachusetts	Banks Mss.
BRADSTREET, Humphrey	Capel St. Mary		Ipswich, Massachusetts	N.E.G.R. 65/74
MIXER, Isaac	Capel St. Mary		Watertown	N.E.G.R. 65/380 66/179

SUFFOLK

NAME OF THE EMIGRANT	ENGLISH PARISH NAME	SHIPS NAME	NEW ENGLAND TOWN	VARIOUS REFERENCE
GRIGGS, Humphrey	Cavendish		Braintree, Massachusetts	N.E.G.R. 63/284
LOCKWOOD, Edmond	Combs		Cambridge, Mass.	Banks Mss.
PAINE, Thomas	Cooklie		Salem, Massachusetts	N.E.G.R. 5/332
RAY, Simon	Cowling		Braintree, Massachusetts	N.E.G.R. 69/27
LOCKWOOD, Robert	Combs		Cambridge, Mass.	Banks Mss.
BRADSTREET, Humphrey	Creeting All Saints		Ipswich, Massachusetts	F. Fines Suff. Mch. 21 Eliz.
PARTRIDGE, George	Creeting St. Mary		Bridgewater	Banks Mss.
CODMAN, Robert	Culpho		Salem, Mass. Edgartown, Mass. Hartford, Conn.	History Martha's Vineyard
HINSDALE, Robert	Debenham		Dedham, Mass. Hartford, Conn.	Banks Mss.
KILHAM, Augustine	Dennington		Salem, Massachusetts	Waters Gleanings 2/1403-5 N.E.G.R. 57/197
MOYSE, Joseph	Dennington		Salisbury	Hoyt Old Families 3/992
RAYNER, Edward	Elmsett	Elizabeth	Hempstead, Long Island	N.E.G.R. 166/164
BRAND, Benjamin	Edwardstone		Charlestown, Massachusetts	Banks Mss
RAYNER, Thurston	Elmsett		Watertown	N.E.G.R. 66/166
ROSE, Robert	Elmswell Eye		Wethersfield, Connecticut	Banks Mss

SUFFOLK

NAME OF THE EMIGRANT	ENGLISH PARISH NAME	SHIPS NAME	NEW ENGLAND TOWN	VARIOUS REFERENCE
FIELD, Zachariah	Elmswell Eye		Hartford, Connecticut	Banks Mss.
HUBBARD, Edmund	Finborough Magna		Hingham, Massachusetts	Banks Mss.
BRIDGHAM, Henry	Felsham		Boston, Mass.	Aspinwall
BRUNDAGE, John	Felsham		Fairfield	Banks Mss.
BRIDGHAM, Henry	Flooton		Dorchester	Pope
SMITH, Samuel	Elmsett	Elizabeth	Watertown Wethersfield, Connecticut	Banks Mss.
DANFORTH, Nicholas	Framlingham		Cambridge, Massachusetts	N.E.G.R. 7/315
Thomas	Framlingham		Cambridge, Massachusetts	N.E.G.R. 57/193
COOK, Oliver	Framlingham		Salisbury	N.E.G.R. 65/262
TUTTLE, Henry	Fressingfield		Hingham, Mass.	Banks Mss.
ALDERS (Aldis), Nathan	Fressingfield		Dedham, Massachusetts	N.E.G.R. 64/248
COLBY, Henry	Fressingfield			N.E.G.R. 54/104
BARBER, George	Fressingfield		Dedham, Massachusetts	N.E.G.R. 79/339
BROCK, Henry	Fressingfield		Dedham, Massachusetts	N.E.G.R. 79/339
LUSHER, Eleazer	Fressingfield		Dedham, Massachusetts	N.E.G.R. 79/339
WARE, Robert	Fressingfield		Dedham, Massachusetts	N.E.G.R. 79/339
COLBY, Anthony	Glenham, Parva		Boston, Mass. Cambridge, Mass. Salisbury	P. C. C. 94 Kidd.

SUFFOLK

NAME OF THE EMIGRANT	ENGLISH PARISH NAME	SHIPS NAME	NEW ENGLAND TOWN	VARIOUS REFERENCE
RAY, Simon	Glemsford		Braintree, Mass.	Banks Mss.
RUGGLES, John	Glemsford		Boston, Mass.	Banks Mss.
GALT, Richard	Glemsford		Providence, Rhode Island	N.E.G.R. 22/3
SCOTT, Richard	Glemsford		Boston, Massachusetts	N.E.G.R 60/168
TUCK, Robert	Gorleston		Watertown	Pope
GALE, Richard	Groton		Watertown	Winthrop Papers 1/41
POND, John	Groton		Boston, Mass.	Banks Mss.
Robert	Groton		Dorchester	Banks Mss.
William	Groton		Dorchester	Banks Mss.
BRAYBROOK, John	Groton		Watertown	Banks Mss.
GRIDLEY, Richard	Groton		Boston, Mass.	N.E.G.R. 76/240
PEASE, Henry	Groton		Boston, Mass.	Pope
WINTHROP, John	Groton		Boston, Mass.	Savage
DAGGETT, John	Groton		Watertown	Savage
DIXON, William	Groton		Boston, Mass. York, Maine	Banks Mss.
GAGER, Dr. William	Groton		Charlestown, Massachusetts	Life & Letters of J. Winthrop 2/84

SUFFOLK

NAME OF THE EMIGRANT	ENGLISH PARISH NAME	SHIPS NAME	NEW ENGLAND TOWN	VARIOUS REFERENCE
LEAGER, Jacob	Hadleigh		Boston, Massachusetts	N.E.G.R. 61/255
FELMINGHAM, Francis	Halesworth		Salem, Mass.	Banks Mss.
TAYLOR, John	Haverhill		Lynn, Mass.	Farmer
ROGERS, Rev. Nathaniel	Haverhill		Ipswich, Mass.	
BROWNE, Abraham	Hawkedon		Watertown	Bond
John	Hawkedon	Lyon	Watertown	Bond 124
Richard	Hawkedon		Watertown	Bond 123
NEWGATE, John	Hessett		Boston, Massachusetts	N.E.G.R. 52/42
BLODGETT, Thomas	Haughley	Increase	Cambridge, Mass	Banks Mss.
CARTER, Rev. Thomas	Hinderclay		Dedham, Mass. Woburn, Mass.	P.C.C. Aylett 391
RAY, Simon	Hinsden		Braintree, Massachusetts	N.E.G.R. 64/61
BATTLE(Y), Thomas	Holseley		Dedham, Mass.	Banks Mss.
NEWGATE, John	Horningsheath		Boston, Massachusetts	N.E.G.R. 33/58 (L)
GREENE, Solomon	Hadleigh		Boston, Mass.	Pope
GEORGE, Peter	Hundon		Braintree, Mass	Aspinwall
CLARK, Thurston	Ipswich		Plymouth, Massachusetts	N.E.G.R. 6/253
GREENLEAF, Edmund	Ipswich		Newbury	N.E.G.R. 38/299
FOSTER, Thomas	Ipswich		Boston, Mass.	(L)

SUFFOLK

NAME OF THE EMIGRANT	ENGLISH PARISH NAME	SHIPS NAME	NEW ENGLAND TOWN	VARIOUS REFERENCE
PAUL, Daniel	Ipswich		Boston, Mass. Kittery, Maine	Banks Mss.
PARKHURST, George	Ipswich		Watertown	N.E.G.R. 68/
WINDS, Barnabas	Ipswich		Charlestown, Massachusetts	Banks Mss.
STOWERS, Richard	Ipswich		Charlestown, Massachusetts	Aspinwall
STOVER, Sylvester	Ipswich		York, Maine	Banks Mss.
SCARLET, John	Ipswich		Springfield	N.E.G.R. 63/279
ANDREWS, William	Ipswich		Charlestown, Massachusetts	Pope
DOWNING, Emanuel	Ipswich		Salem, Mass.	Pope
CLEVELAND, Moses	Ipswich		Woburn, Mass.	Banks Mss.
PARKER, Judith, widow	Ipswich		Hampton Charlestown, Massachusetts	Banks Mss.
HAWKES, Matthew	Ipswich		Hingham, Mass.	Banks Mss.
GIRLING, Richard	Ipswich		Cambridge, Mass.	Banks Mss.
TURNER, Robert	Ipswich		Boston, Mass.	Banks Mss.
MARSH, George	Ipswich		Hingham, Mass	Banks Mss.
GALE, Edmund	Ixworth		Cambridge, Mass.	
WINSLEY, Samuel	Knodishall		Salisbury	Banks Mss.
ARNOLD, Thomas	Kelshale		Watertown	N.E.G.R. 69/68
SCARLET, Samuel	Kersey		Boston, Mass.	Pope

SUFFOLK

NAME OF THE EMIGRANT	ENGLISH PARISH NAME	SHIPS NAME	NEW ENGLAND TOWN	VARIOUS REFERENCE
SAMPSON, Robert	Kersey	Arbella	Boston, Massachusetts	Winthrop Mss.
NUTTER, Hate-Evil	Kersey		Dover	Banks Mss.
PAINE, William	Lavenham		Salem, Massachusetts	N.E.G.R. 56/164
ONGE —	Lavenham		Watertown	Pope
HAMMOND, William	Lavenham		Watertown	N.E.G.R. 30/28
READE, Thomas	Lavenham		Sudbury, Massachusetts	N.E.G.R. 56/184
FULLER, John	Lavenham		Cambridge, Massachusetts	N.E.G.R. 49/491
HAMMOND, Thomas	Lavenham		Hingham, Massachusetts	N.E.G.R. 56/184
AYERS, Simon	Lavenham		Watertown	Banks Mss. N.E.G.R. 69/250
LEVERICH, Rev. William	Livermere, Gt.	James	Dover, New Hampshire	Venn. Alumni Cantab.
SALES, John	Lavenham		Charlestown, Massachusetts	Banks Mss.
PACY, Nicholas	Lowestoft		Salem, Mass.	Banks Mss.
FERMAYES, Mark	Lowestoft		Salem, Mass.	Banks Mss.
HAMMOND, Thomas	Lavenham		Watertown	Aspinwall 112
ELDRED, Samuel	Laveñham		Cambridge, Mass. Kingston, R. I. Wickford, R. I.	Banks Mss.
HUBBARD, Samuel	Mendelsham		Newport, R. I.	Banks Mss.
UTTING, Anne, widow	Mendelsham		Roxbury	Banks Mss.

SUFFOLK

NAME OF THE EMIGRANT	ENGLISH PARISH NAME	SHIPS NAME	NEW ENGLAND TOWN	VARIOUS REFERENCE
MOODY, John	Moulton		Hartford, Conn.	Banks Mss.
WEBB, Richard	Nayland		Cambridge, Mass. Hartford, Conn.	Banks Mss.
FIRMIN, John	Nayland		Watertown	Greg. Stone Gen.
PARISH, Thomas	Nayland	Increase	Watertown	Pope C. of A.
WATERS, John	Nayland		Boston, Mass.	Pope
FERMIN, Giles	Nayland		Roxbury	Waters & Emmerton
STERNES, Isaac	Nayland		Watertown	N.E.G.R. 56/183 (L)
KENT, John	Nayland		Dedham, Mass.	Stone Gen.
WARREN, John	Nayland		Watertown	Stone Gen. page 43
KENT, Joshua	Nayland		Dedham, Mass.	Pope
WATERMAN, Richard	Nayland		Salem, Mass.	Banks Mss.
REYNOLDS, Robert	Nayland		Wethersfield, Connecticut	Banks Mss.
HOLTON, William	Nayland		Cambridge, Mass. Hartford, Conn.	Banks Mss.
UFFORD, Thomas	Newbourne		Roxbury Springfield	Suff. Ship Money 1636
STOWERS, John	Parham		Watertown	Mdx. De. 1/16
FIRMIN, Josias	Polstead		Boston, Massachusetts	N.E.G.R. 56/182
BUMSTEAD, Edward	Rattlesden		Roxbury	Pope
WEBB, William	Rattlesden		Roxbury	Pope

SUFFOLK

NAME OF THE EMIGRANT	ENGLISH PARISH NAME	SHIPS NAME	NEW ENGLAND TOWN	VARIOUS REFERENCE
SALTER, George	Rattlesden		Watertown	N.E.G.R. 57/331
MUNSON, Thomas	Rattlesden		Hartford, Connecticut	N.E.G.R. 57/331
KIMBALL, Richard Aet. 39 (b. 1595)	Rattlesden	Elizabeth	Watertown Ipswich, Massachusetts	N.E.G.R. 57/331 Waters Gl. page 1413
GUTTRIDGE, John	Rattlesden		Watertown	N.E.G.R. 57/332
SCOTT, Thomas	Rattlesden	Elizabeth	Ipswich, Massachusetts	N.E.G.R. 53/248
MUNNINGS, George	Rattlesden	Elizabeth	Watertown	J.G.B. Hill Gen. 49
KIMBALL, Henry	Rattlesden	Elizabeth	Watertown	
SALTER, William	Rattlesden		Boston, Massachusetts	College of Arms
BURR, Rev. Jonathan	Redegrave		Dorchester	Pope
STEARNS, Charles	Reydon		Watertown	Militia List 1638
HADLEY, George	Reydon		Ipswich, Mass.	Banks Mss.
CHICKERING, Francis	Ringsfield		Dedham, Massachusetts	N.E.G.R. 64/137
Henry	Ringsfield		Dedham, Massachusetts	N.E.G.R. 64/137
AUSTIN, Francis	Ringsfield		Dedham, Mass. Hampton	N.E.G.R. 63/283
MINOT, George	Saffron Walden		Boston, Mass.	Pope
POLLARD, (Mrs.) Anne (......)	Saffron Walden		Boston, Massachusetts	Savage
CLARK, William	Semer		Roxbury	N.E.G.R. 56/183

SUFFOLK

NAME OF THE EMIGRANT	ENGLISH PARISH NAME	SHIPS NAME	NEW ENGLAND TOWN	VARIOUS REFERENCE
STRATTON, John	Shotley		Salem, Mass.	Pope
YOUNGS, Christopher	Southwold		Salem, Massachusetts	Pope Par. Reg.
John	Southwold		Salem, Massachusetts	Pope Par. Reg.
HEMPENSTALL, Robert	Southwold		Boston, Mass.	(L)
COCKRAN, William	Southwold		Hingham, Massachusetts	N.E.G.R. 57/198
JEGGLES, William	Southwold		Salem, Massachusetts	Waters Gl. page 1409
MOORE, Thomas	Southwold		Salem, Massachusetts	Essex Inst. 64/49
FISKE, David	South Elmham		Cambridge, Massachusetts Watertown	Fiske Family Papers
Rev. John	South Elmham St. James (see next page)		Salem, Mass. Wenham, Mass. Chelmsford,Mass.	Pope
William	South Elmham		Salem, Massachusetts	Fiske Family Papers
CALEF, Robert	Stanstead		Roxbury	Essex Inst. 27/
STOWERS, Richard	Stoke		Charlestown, Massachusetts	N.E.G.R. 63/278
POLLARD, George	Stoke Clere		Duxbury	Pope
BARKER, James	Stradishall		Rowley, Mass.	Banks Mss.
KILBOURNE, George	Stradishall		Rowley, Mass.	Pope
WARD, Dr. John	Stratford St. Mary		Ipswich, Massachusetts	Pope Waters

SUFFOLK

NAME OF THE EMIGRANT	ENGLISH PARISH NAME	SHIPS NAME	NEW ENGLAND TOWN	VARIOUS REFERENCE
JPSON, Stephen	Stonham-Aspal	Increase		Pope
QUILTER, Mark	Stoke-by Nayland		Ipswich, Massachusetts	N.E.G.R. 66/189
HOWLETT, Thomas	South Elmham		Ipswich, Mass.	
ALLOWES, Michael	Shadingfield		Salem, Mass.	Banks Mss.
DEVEREUX, John	Stoke-by Nayland		Salem, Massachusetts	Banks Mss.
PAINE, Robert	Sudbury		Ipswich, Massachusetts	N.E.G.R. 56/181
HAYFIELD, Richard	Sudbury		Ipswich, Massachusetts	N.E.G.R. 30/110
WATERBURY, William	Sudbury		Boston, Massachusetts	N.E.G.R. 64/135
RAY, Simon	Sudbury		Braintree, Massachusetts	N.E.G.R. 63/356 64/57
PARMENTER, Robert	Sudbury		Braintree, Massachusetts	N.E.G.R. 66/176
SANDERS, Martin	Sudbury		Braintree, Massachusetts	N.E.G.R. 66/176
WELD, Daniel	Sudbury		Roxbury	N.E.G.R. 66/176
Capt. Joseph	Sudbury		Roxbury	N.E.G.R. 66/176
Rev. Thomas	Sudbury		Roxbury	N.E.G.R. 66/176
FIRMIN, Giles	Sudbury		Boston, Massachusetts	N.E.G.R. 66/176
RUGGLES, Jeffrey	Sudbury		Boston, Massachusetts	N.E.G.R. 66/176
GRIGGS, Humphrey	Sudbury		Braintree, Massachusetts	N.E.G.R. 56/183

SUFFOLK

NAME OF THE EMIGRANT	ENGLISH PARISH NAME	SHIPS NAME	NEW ENGLAND TOWN	VARIOUS REFERENCE
SMITH, John	Sudbury		Sudbury, Massachusetts	N.E.G.R. 56/182
SHEFFIELD, Edmond	Sudbury		Roxbury Braintree, Mass.	Pope
HAWKINS, Job	Sudbury		Boston, Mass.	Pope
COOPER, Elizabeth	Sudbury		Charlestown, Massachusetts	Pope
NEWCOME, Francis	Sudbury		Braintree, Massachusetts	Banks Mss.
AMBROSE, Henry	Sudbury		Charlestown, Massachusetts Hampton	Banks Mss.
LORD, Robert	Sudbury		Ipswich, Massachusetts	Waters Gen. Glean.
WATERBURY, John	Sudbury		Watertown Stamford, Conn.	N.E.G.R. 64/135
SHEFFIELD, Ichabod	Sudbury		Portsmouth, New Hampshire Braintree, Mass.	N.E.G.R. 77/190
William	Sudbury		Dover Braintree, Mass.	N.E.G.R. 77/190
FISHER, Anthony	Syleham		Dedham, Massachusetts	N.E.G.R. 53/462
Joshua	Syleham		Dedham, Massachusetts	N.E.G.R. 53/462
LUSON, John	Syleham		Dedham, Massachusetts	N.E.G.R. 53/462
COE, Robert	Thorpe Morieux	Francis		Genealogy
LIVERMORE, John	Thurloe, Great	Francis	Watertown	Bond
BOATMAN, Jeremiah	Thorpe		Salem, Massachusetts	Essex Court Rec.
NEWMAN, Robert	Thorpe		Salem, Massachusetts	Essex Court Rec.

SUFFOLK

NAME OF THE EMIGRANT	ENGLISH PARISH NAME	SHIPS NAME	NEW ENGLAND TOWN	VARIOUS REFERENCE
WINCOLL, John	Waldingfield		Kittery, Maine	Waters 77
Thomas	Waldingfield		Watertown	Waters
ROBINSON, — — —	Waldingfield (Little)		Ipswich ?	4 MHS 4/560
APPLETON, Samuel	Waldingfield (Little)		Ipswich, Massachusetts	N.E.G.R. 56/184
BIXBY, Joseph	Waldingfield (Little)		Ipswich, Massachusetts	Banks Mss.
BREWSTER, Nathaniel	Walberswick		New Haven, Connecticut	Aspinwall
PELL, Thomas	Walberswick		New Haven, Connecticut	Aspinwall
CARTWRIGHT, Bethia	Walberswick		Salem, Mass.	Pope
BARRELL, George	Wangford (St. Michaels)		Boston, Massachusetts	N.E.G.R. 61/69 Banks Mss.
COCK, Oliver	Waybread		Salisbury	Pope
FOSDICK, Stephen	Wenham Magna		Charlestown, Massachusetts	Banks Mss.
CLARK, Carew	Westhorpe		Newport, Rhode Island	Col. Soc. Mass.25/20
CLARKE, Dr. John	Westhorpe		Newport, Rhode Island	Col. Soc. Mass.25/20
Joseph	Westhorpe		Newport, Rhode Island	N.E.G.R. 75/277
Thomas	Westhorpe		Newport, Rhode Island	Col. Soc. Mass.25/20
FISKE, Nathan	Weybread		Watertown	Fiske Fam. Papers
GOLDSTONE, Henry	Wickham Skeith		Watertown	N.E.G.R. 13/98

SUFFOLK

NAME OF THE EMIGRANT	ENGLISH PARISH NAME	SHIPS NAME	NEW ENGLAND TOWN	VARIOUS REFERENCE
GARRETT, Herman	Wickham Market		Charlestown, Concord Massachusetts Lancaster, Mass.	Banks Mss.
FISKE, Phineas	Wingfield		Salem, Mass.	Banks Mss.
BACON, Michael	Winston		Dedham, Massachusetts	N.E.G.R. 57/330 58/302
HUNTING, John	Wetheringsett		Dedham, Mass.	Banks Mss.
IVES, Miles	Wiston		Watertown	Pope
HOLGRAVE, John	Woodbridge		Salem, Mass.	Banks Mss.
MARRETT, Thomas	Woodbridge		Cambridge, Massachusetts	Suff. Deeds 1/51
CRAMSWELL, John	Woodbridge		Boston, Massachusetts	Suff. Deeds 1/51
CHANDLER, Edmond	Woodbridge		Plymouth, Mass.	Banks Mss.
ESTEY, Jeffrey	Woolverstone		Salem, Mass.	Banks Mss.
DALTON, Rev. Timothy	Woolverstone		Watertown	Pope
PARKER, Robert	Wolpitt		Boston, Mass. Wethersfield, Connecticut	N.E.G.R. 4/179 56/183
CROSS, John	Wolpitt	Elizabeth	Watertown	Ship List
MERRILL, John	Wherstead		Ipswich, Mass. Newbury	Merrill Genealogy
Nathaniel	Wherstead		Ispwich, Mass. Newbury	Merrill Genealogy
PAINE, Thomas	Wrentham	Mary Ann	Salem, Mass.	Pope
THURSTON, John	Wrentham	Mary Anne	Salem, Mass. Dedham, Mass.	Hotten

SUFFOLK

NAME OF THE EMIGRANT	ENGLISH PARISH NAME	SHIPS NAME	NEW ENGLAND TOWN	VARIOUS REFERENCE
ALLEN,				
Edward	Wrentham		Boston, Massachusetts	Suff. Deeds 1/232
Edward	Wrentham		Dedham, Mass.	
Rev. John	Wrentham		Dedham, Massachusetts	N.E.G.R. 41/68
CHICKERING,				
Henry	Wrentham		Dedham, Massachusetts	N.E.G.R. 69/226
Simon	Wrentham			N.E.G.R. 69/226
PHILLIPS, Rev. John	Wrentham		Rowley, Mass.	Pope
WEST, Thomas	Wrentham		Salem, Massachusetts	Perley Salem 2/149
KILHAM, Augustine	Wrentham	Mary Anne	Salem, Massachusetts	Perley Salem 2/149
BIGELOW, John	Wrentham		Watertown	N.E.G.R. 63/363 Banks Mss.
RAWLINGS, Thomas			Boston, Massachusetts	N.E.G.R. 8/255
HOLDEN,				
Justinian	Lindsey		Cambridge, Mass.	Genealogy
Richard	Lindsey		Cambridge, Mass.	Genealogy
ALBRO, John	?		Portsmouth, Rhode Island	Austin 234
STOCKING, George	?		Cambridge, Mass. Hartford, Conn.	Genealogy
FILER, Walter	?		Dorchester Windsor	Banks Mss.
UNDERWOOD, Martin		Elizabeth	Watertown	

SUFFOLK

NAME OF THE EMIGRANT	ENGLISH PARISH NAME	SHIPS NAME	NEW ENGLAND TOWN	VARIOUS REFERENCE
CUTTING, Richard		Elizabeth	Watertown	
William		Elizabeth	Watertown	
LEWIS, Edmund		Elizabeth	Watertown	
WOODWARD, Richard	?	Elizabeth	Watertown	
BLOOMFIELD, William	?	Elizabeth	Cambridge, Mass.	
SPRING, John	?	Elizabeth	Watertown	
BROWNE, William	?		Salem, Massachusetts	Perley Salem 2/149
STACEY, Hugh	?		Salem, Massachusetts	Perley Salem 2/149
MIX, Thomas	?		New Haven, Connecuticut	Banks Mss.
CHENERY, Richard	?		Watertown Dedham, Mass.	Banks Mss.
BRACKETT, Peter	?		Braintree, Mass.	Banks Mss.
Richard	?		Boston, Mass. Braintree, Mass.	Banks Mss.
STONE, Gregory		Increase	Cambridge, Massachusetts	History of Cuyahoga Co.O.p.385
Simon		Increase	Cambridge, Massachusetts	History of Cuyahoga Co.O.p.385

Total number of Emigrants from Suffolk is 298 from 106 Parishes.

SURREY

NAME OF THE EMIGRANT	ENGLISH PARISH NAME	SHIPS NAME	NEW ENGLAND TOWN	VARIOUS REFERENCE
EATON, Theophilus	Barnes		New Haven, Connecticut	Banks Mss.
LENTHALL, Rev. Robert	Barnes		Weymouth, Massachusetts	Banks Mss.
SWIFT, William	Bermondsey		Watertown	Banks Mss.
CODDINGTON, Stockdale	Bermondsey		Roxbury	Banks Mss.
LEARNED, William	Bermondsey		Charlestown, Massachusetts	
DERBY, Edward	Bisley		Braintree, Massachusetts	N.E.G.R. 39/66 Waters 95
SMITH, John (tailor)	Clandon, West		Boston, Massachusetts	P.C.C. 179 Gray
TAYLOR, Anthony	Cobham		Hampton, New Hampshire	Banks Mss.
DUDLEY, William	Dorking		Guilford, Connecticut	N.E.G.R. 54/95
MULLINS, William, Jr.	Dorking		Marshfield, Massachusetts	Banks Mss.
CODDINGTON, John	Dorking		Boston, Mass. Newport, R. I.	Aspinwall 182
HUSSEY, Christopher	Dorking		Lynn, Massachusetts	Farmer Dow, Hampton, 758
STILLWELL, Nicholas	Dorking		Virginia Long Island	Stillwell Gen. 1/35
FOSTER, Christopher	Ewell		Lynn, Mass.	Aspinwall
HIGLEY, John	Frimley		Windsor	Stiles
SHOVE, Rev. George	Gatton		Taunton	Banks Mss.
HOLMAN, Edward	Godstone	Anne	Plymouth, Massachusetts	Banks Mss.

SURREY

NAME OF THE EMIGRANT	ENGLISH PARISH NAME	SHIPS NAME	NEW ENGLAND TOWN	VARIOUS REFERENCE
SCRANTON, John	Guildford		Boston, Mass. New Haven, Connecticut Guildford	Biog. Hist Penna. Vol. A, 36
SPENCER, John	Kingston		Newbury	N.E.G.R. 44/390 55/110
ELSEY, Nicholas	Merstham		New Haven, Connecticut	Banks Mss.
HALL, Francis (This probably error) (see page 174)	Milford		Guilford, Connecticut	N.E.G.R. 55/180
HALL, William	Milford		Guildford, Connecticut	N.E.G.R. 55/180
WHITFIELD, Rev. Henry	Ockley		Guildford, Connecticut	N.E.G.R. 52/130
CLARKE, Thomas	Rotherhithe			
WHEAT, Joshua	Southwark (S. Saviour)	Elizabeth	Concord	Hotten
ELMES, Rodolphus	Southwark (S. Saviour)	Planter	Scituate	N.E.G.R. 40/306
CURTIS, Henry	Southwark (S. Saviour)		Watertown	N.E.G.R. 61/258
BULL, Henry	Southwark (S. Saviour)	Elizabeth	Newport, Rhode Island	Pope
HARVARD, Rev. John	Southwark (S. Saviour)		Charlestown, Massachusetts	Waters
BIRD, Simon	Southwark (S. Saviour)	Susan and Ellen	Chelsea	Pope Banks Mss.
HEPBURN, George	Southwark (S. Saviour)	Abigail	Charlestown, Massachusetts	Banks Mss.
DICKERMAN, Thomas	Southwark (S. George)		Dorchester	Banks Mss.
MILLETT, Thomas	Southwark (S. Saviour)	Elizabeth	Dorchester Gloucester, Massachusetts	Pope

SURREY

NAME OF THE EMIGRANT	ENGLISH PARISH NAME	SHIPS NAME	NEW ENGLAND TOWN	VARIOUS REFERENCE
HETHERLEY, Timothy	Southwark (S. Olave)		Scituate	N.E.G.R. 39/28
STOUGHTON, Israel	Southwark (S. Olave)		Dorchester	N.E.G.R. 5/350 Add. Mss. 6174
HELME, Christopher	Southwark (S. Olave)		Exeter, N. H. Warwick, R. I.	Banks Mss
MOULTON, Robert	Southwark (S. Olave)		Charlestown, Massachusetts	Banks Mss.
FORD, William	Southwark (S. Olave)	Fortune	Plymouth, Massachusetts	Banks Mss.
NORTON, Francis	Southwark		Charlestown, Massachusetts	Banks Mss.
BULL, Thomas	Southwark	Hopewell		Hinman 402
DEANE, Stephen	Southwark	Fortune	Plymouth, Mass.	Banks Mss.
HICKS, Robert	Southwark	Fortune	Plymouth, Mass.	Pope
NEWDIGATE, John	Southwark		Boston, Massachusetts	N.E.G.R. 44/115
CHAPMAN, Ralph	Southwark		Barnstable, Massachusetts	Boston T. 13 Aug. 1906
CRISP, George	Southwark		Plymouth, Mass.	Aspinwall
WINDSOR, Robert, Jr.	Southwark		Boston, Massachusetts	N.E.G.R. 39/28
BURCHER, Edward	Southwark	Little James	Plymouth, Mass Lynn, Mass.	Banks Mss.
ABDY, Matthew	Southwark (S. Olave)	Abigail	Boston, Massachusetts	Banks Mss.
BRIGGS, Clement	Southwark	Fortune	Plymouth, Mass.	Pope
COBB, Henry	Southwark		Plymouth, Mass.	

* The great-great-great-great-great-grandfather of Elijah Ellsworth Brownell - - the Publisher.

SURREY

NAME OF THE EMIGRANT	ENGLISH PARISH NAME	SHIPS NAME	NEW ENGLAND TOWN	VARIOUS REFERENCE
READE, Esdras	Southwark (S.Mary Overy		Boston, Mass. Salem, Mass.	Banks Mss.
ATWOOD, Harman	Sanderstead		Boston, Massachusetts	Par.Reg. Pope
*MULLINS, William	Stoke near Guildford	May- flower	Plymouth, Massachusetts	Banks Mss.
OFFLEY, Daniel	?		Boston, Massachusetts	Col. Soc. Mass.25/19
STILLWELL, Jasper	?		Guildford, Connecticut	Stillwell Genealogy

Total number of Emigrants from Surrey is 55 from 23 Parishes.

*Ancestor of Elijah Ellsworth Brownell - - the publisher.

S U S S E X

NAME OF THE EMIGRANT	ENGLISH PARISH NAME	SHIPS NAME	NEW ENGLAND TOWN	VARIOUS REFERENCE
EVERDEN, Walter	Battle		Dorchester	Hutch. Coll. #468 Col. Paper 37/70
TUPPER, Thomas	Bury		Lynn, Mass. Sandwich, Mass.	Banks Mss.
SKINNER, Thomas	Chichester		Malden, Mass.	Pope
JEFFREY, William	Chiddingly		Weymouth, Mass. Manchester	Visit. Sussex Austin 121
BANNISTER, Edward	Chiddingly		New Haven, Connecticut	Banks Mss.
TILLINGHAST, Pardon	Clayton		Providence, R. I.	Banks Mss.
HARRADEN, Edward	Edburton		Gloucester, Mass.	Banks Mss.
GEERE, Dennis	Falmer		Lynn, Massachusetts	P.C.C.51 Pembroke
NEWMAN, Robert	Fletching		New Haven, Connecticut	Banks Mss.
DRURY, George	Grinstead, East	Abigail		Banks Mss.
KIDDER, James	Grinstead, East		Cambridge, Massachusetts	J.G.B.Hill Gen.p.81
STOCKBRIDGE, John	Hellingley		Scituate	Banks Mss.
DENNETT, Alexander	Hurst Pierpoint		Kittery, Maine	Marshall
John	Hurst Pierpoint		Kittery, Maine	Marshall
BENJAMIN, John	Heathfield	Lion	Cambridge, Mass. Watertown	Banks Mss.
Richard	Heathfield	Lion	Watertown	Banks Mss.
SCHOLES, George	Houghton		Lynn, Mass.	Aspinwall

SUSSEX

NAME OF THE EMIGRANT	ENGLISH PARISH NAME	SHIPS NAME	NEW ENGLAND TOWN	VARIOUS REFERENCE
PHILATER, Abraham	Hastings		Scarboro, Maine	Josselyn Two Voy. Page 73
MAY, John	Mayfield		Plymouth, Massachusetts	N.E.G.R. 27/113
CHATFIELD, Francis	Pagham		Guildford	N.E.G.R. 70/55
George	Pagham		Guildford	N.E.G.R. 70/55
Thomas	Pagham		Guildford	N.E.G.R. 70/55
HARRADEN, Edward	Petworth		Gloucester, Mass.	Banks Mss.
FREEMAN, Edmund	Pulborough		Lynn, Mass. Sandwich, Mass.	E.L.S.
FENNER, Arthur	Rusper		Providence, Rhode Island	N.E.G.R. 62/200
John	Rusper		Saybrook, Connecticut	N.E.G.R. 62/200
LEADER, Richard	Salehurst		Lynn, Mass. Kittery, Maine	Banks Mss.
TILLINGHURST, Pardon	Seven Cliffs		Providence, R. I.	Austin 202
HARRADEN, Edward	Storrington		Gloucester, Mass.	Banks Mss.
GLOVER, Josse	Sutton		Dorchester	Suff.Deeds 1/65
HYLAND, Thomas	Waldron		Scituate	N.E.G.R. 66/67
NYE, Benjamin	?		Lynn ? Sandwich, Mass.	Banks Mss.

Total number of Emigrants from Sussex is 32 from 24 Parishes.

WARWICKSHIRE

NAME OF THE EMIGRANT	ENGLISH PARISH NAME	SHIPS NAME	NEW ENGLAND TOWN	VARIOUS REFERENCE
WALDRON, Alexander	Alcester		Dover, N. H. Portsmouth, R. I.	Banks Mss.
Edward	Alcester		Ipswich, Mass.	Banks Mss.
George	Alcester		Dover, N. H. Boston, Mass.	Banks Mss.
Isaac	Alcester		Portsmouth, R. I. York, Maine Boston, Mass.	Banks Mss.
Richard	Alcester		Dover, New Hampshire	N.E.G.R. 8/78 Banks Mss.
Samuel	Alcester			N.H.Prob. 1/174
William	Alcester		Dover, N. H. Boston, Mass.	Banks Mss.
HOLYOKE, Edward	Alcester		Lynn, Mass.	Waters 57
WILCOX, Robert	Alcester			N.E.G.R. 29/25
CLEMENT, Robert	Ansley		Haverhill, Massachusetts	Gen. Essex Inst. 53
FARMER, Edward	Ansley		Cambridge, Massachusetts	N.E.G.R. 1/1
BELCHER, Gregory	Aston		Braintree, Massachusetts	N.E.G.R. 60/126
PEAK, Christopher	Birmingham		Roxbury	N.E.G.R. 21/413
William	Birmingham		Scituate	
PENDLETON, Bryan	Birmingham		Watertown Saco, Maine	Banks Mss.
PENN, William	Birmingham		Charlestown, Massachusetts	Pope

WARWICKSHIRE

NAME OF THE EMIGRANT	ENGLISH PARISH NAME	SHIPS NAME	NEW ENGLAND TOWN	VARIOUS REFERENCE
WHITEHEAD, John	Bulkington		New Haven, Connecticut	Pope
FIELD, Derby	Bulkington		Dover, N. H.	Aspinwall
HALL, Francis (See page 168)	Bulkington		New Haven, Connecticut	Aspinwall
WELLES, Thomas	Burmington		Cambridge, Mass. Hartford, Conn.	N.E.G.R. 80/279
MAKEPEACE, Thomas	Burton Dassett		Dorchester	Banks Mss.
WRIGHT, Edward	Castle Bromwich		Sudbury, Massachusetts	Pope
PICKERING, John	Cheylesmore		Salem, Mass.	Aspinwall
WYLLYS, George	Compton Fenny		Hartford, Connecticut	N.E.G.R. 37/33
BOSWORTH, Benjamin	Coventry		Hingham, Mass. Boston, Mass.	Lechford
DAVENPORT, Rev. John	Coventry		New Haven, Connecticut	N.E.G.R. 38/30
POTTER, Humphrey	Coventry		Salem, Massachusetts	N.E.G.R. 39/38
PICKERING, John	Coventry		Salem, Mass.	Aspinwall
CROW, William	Coventry		Plymouth, Mass.	Pope
BACON, William	Coventry		Salem, Massachusetts	N.E.G.R. 39/28
SEWALL, Henry	Coventry		Ipswich, Mass.	Pope
EDSON, Samuel	Fillongley		Salem, Mass.	Edson Gen.
PERKINS, John	Hilmorton		Boston, Mass. Ipswich, Mass.	Banks Mss.
COPP, William	Honiley		Boston, Massachusetts	Banks Mss. P.C.C. 462 Alchin

WARWICKSHIRE

NAME OF THE EMIGRANT	ENGLISH PARISH NAME	SHIPS NAME	NEW ENGLAND TOWN	VARIOUS REFERENCE
GRISWOLD, Edward	Kenilworth		Windsor	Stiles
Matthew	Kenilworth		Windsor	Stiles
UNDERHILL, John	Kenilworth		Boston, Mass. Dover, N. H. New York	Genealogy Field Family
WHITEHEAD, Richard	Knole		Windsor	Banks Mss.
HOWE, John	Ladbrooke		Watertown	Farmer
ALCOTT, Thomas OLCOTT,	Leamington Priors		Boston, Massachusetts	Aspinwall
WHITEHEAD, John	Leamington Priors		New Haven, Connecticut	Aspinwall
KERBY, John	Rowington	Hopewell	Plymouth, Mass. Hartford, Connecticut	History Wethersfield
WESTON, Edmond	Shustoke		Plymouth, Mass.	Banks Mss.
LOKER, Henry	Solihull		Sudbury, Mass.	Banks Mss.
HAWES, Edmund	Solihull		Yarmouth	N.E.G.R. 65/160
BRAGDEN, Arthur	Stratford on Avon		York, Maine	Banks Mss.
CURTIS, John	Stratford on Avon		Stratford, Connecticut	Hinman
William	Stratford on Avon		Stratford, Connecticut	Hinman
NASON, Richard	Stratford on Avon		Kittery, Maine	Hist. of Kittery
ROGERS, William	Stratford on Avon		Wethersfield, Connecticut Southampton, Long Island	N. Y. G. & B. Record 60/102

WARWICKSHIRE

NAME OF THE EMIGRANT	ENGLISH PARISH NAME	SHIPS NAME	NEW ENGLAND TOWN	VARIOUS REFERENCE
GIBBARD, William	Tamworth		New Haven, Connecticut	Banks Mss. Town Rec. N. Haven Vol. 1
HOLYOKE, Edward	Tamworth		Lynn, Mass.	Waters 57
FISH, John	Warwick		Boston, Mass.	Aspinwall
COOPER, Timothy	Weston		Lynn, Mass.	Waters 143
EATON, Theophilus	Wheatley (Over)		New Haven, Connecticut	N.E.G.R. 38/30
HEWETT, Rev. Ephraim	Wraxall		Windsor	Par. Reg.
FISH, John	Wraxall		Boston, Mass.	Aspinwall
SNALL, Thomas	Whitacre		Salem, Mass. Bridgewater	Banks Mss.
STAFFORD, Thomas			Warwick, R. I.	Austin 384
HOLCOMB, Thomas			Dorchester	
NEWMAN, Francis			New Haven, Connecticut	Banks Mss.

Total number of Emigrants from Warwickshire is 61 from 28 Parishes.

WILTSHIRE

NAME OF THE EMIGRANT	ENGLISH PARISH NAME	SHIPS NAME	NEW ENGLAND TOWN	VARIOUS REFERENCE
CARPENTER, Thomas	Amesbury			Pope
LOOKE, Thomas	Alderbury		Lynn, Massachusetts	Banks Mss. Davis Towne Ancestry
GILBERT, John	Bratton		Dorchester Taunton	Banks Mss.
HUNGERFORD, Thomas	Bremhill		New London, Connecticut	Genealogy
WEARE, Nathaniel	Broken-borough		Newbury	Banks Mss.
MACY, Thomas	Chilmark		Salisbury Nantucket, Mass.	Banks Mss.
NOYES, James	Cholderton		Newbury	N.E.G.R. 53/36
Nicholas	Cholderton		Newbury	N.E.G.R. 53/36
PARKER, Rev. Thomas	Cholderton	Susan & Ellen	Newbury Ipswich, Mass.	N.E.G.R. 53/36 ParkerGen.
BAILEY, John	Chippenham	James	Salisbury	Hoyt 1/44
GLOVER, Charles	Chippenham		Salem, Mass. Southold, N. Y.	Banks Mss.
HURLBURT, Thomas	Chippenham		Wethersfield, Connecticut	Banks Mss.
WOODMAN, Edward	Corsham		Newbury	
MOXHAM, Rev. George	Corsham		Dorchester Springfield	
BATT, Nicholas	Devizes		Newbury	Pope
SANGER, Richard	Donhead	Confidence	Sudbury, Mass. Watertown	Banks Mss.
GOODNOW, Edmond	Donhead	Confidence	Sudbury, Massachusetts	Pope

WILTSHIRE

NAME OF THE EMIGRANT	ENGLISH PARISH NAME	SHIPS NAME	NEW ENGLAND TOWN	VARIOUS REFERENCE
STOCKMAN, John	Downton		Salisbury	
CURTIS, Zaccheus	Downton		Salem, Mass.	Hotten
SANDERS, John	Downton		Salisbury	Banks Mss.
WORMSTALL, Arthur	Easton		Saco, Maine	Banks Mss.
MOODY, Lady Deborah	Garsdon		Lynn, Mass. Salem, Mass. Long Island	N.E.G.R. 55/377
GINGELL, John	Hardenhuish		Taunton Lynn, Mass. Salem, Mass.	P.C.C. Alchin 61
SAVERY, Anthony	Highworth		Plymouth, Massachusetts	N.E.G.R. 66/367
Thomas	Highworth		Plymouth, Massachusetts	N.E.G.R. 66/367
SWADDON, Philip	Hilmarton		Watertown Kittery, Maine	Banks Mss.
BELCHER, Andrew	Kingswood		Cambridge, Massachusetts	N.E.G.R. 27/239
EASTMAN, Roger	Langford	Confidence	Salisbury	Genealogy
MUSSELWHITE, John	Langford	James	Newbury	Pope
ROWDON, Richard	Langford	Susan and Ellen	Lynn, Massachusetts	Banks Mss.
LUDLOW, Roger	Maiden Bradley	Mary and John	Dorchester Windsor	Genealogy
WOODMAN, Archelaus	Malford Christian	James	Newbury	N.E.G.R. 54/345
BROWNE, Thomas	Malford Christian	James	Newbury	Pope
OSGOOD, Christopher	Marlborough	Mary and John	Ipswich, Massachusetts	N.E.G.R. 20/27

WILTSHIRE

NAME OF THE EMIGRANT	ENGLISH PARISH NAME	SHIPS NAME	NEW ENGLAND TOWN	VARIOUS REFERENCE
COLEMAN, Thomas	Marlborough	James	Newbury Nantucket, Mass.	N.E.G.R. 11/347
WALKER, Richard	Marlborough	James		Pope
BUTLER, Giles	Marlborough	James		Pope
MORSE, Anthony	Marlborough	James	Newbury	Hotten
William	Marlborough	James	Newbury	Pope
DAVIS, Thomas	Marlborough	James	Newbury	Pope
COUSINS, George	Marlborough	James		Hotten
PARKER, John	Marlborough	James	Boston, Mass.	Pope
EVERED alias WEBB, John	Marlborough	James	Boston, Mass.	Pope
ENGLISH, Maudit	Marlborough	James	Boston, Mass.	Pope
PITHOUSE, John	Marlborough	James		Hotten
RING, Robert	Marlborough	Confidence	Salisbury	Hoyt Families Salis. 297
FOWLER, Philip	Marlborough	Mary and John	Ipswich, Mass. Salisbury, Mass.	Banks Mss.
GERRISH, William	Melksham		Newbury	Banks Mss.
WOODBRIDGE, Rev. Benjamin	Mildenhall		Newbury	Pope
Rev. John	Mildenhall		Ipswich, Mass. Newbury Boston, Mass. Andover	P.C.C. 54 Pemb.

WILTSHIRE

NAME OF THE EMIGRANT	ENGLISH PARISH NAME	SHIPS NAME	NEW ENGLAND TOWN	VARIOUS REFERENCE
PARKER, Rev. Thomas	Mildenhall		Newbury	P.C.C. 54 Pemb.
GODDARD, Thomas	Ogbourne St. George	James		Banks Mss.
AYERS, John	Ogbourne St. George	James	Salisbury Haverhill, Mass.	Banks Mss.
ROWE, Henry	Plaitford			Hotten
PLAISTED, Roger	Preshute		Kittery, Maine	Banks Mss.
MONDAY, Henry	Pewsey		Salisbury	Banks Mss.
JAQUES, Henry	Rodborne		Newbury	Banks Mss.
EVERED, Stephen	Ramsbury	James	Boston, Mass.	Banks Mss.
THATCHER, Anthony	Salisbury	James	Marblehead, Massachusetts Yarmouth	Pope Cuyahoga Co., O. Hist.
Rev. Thomas	Salisbury	James	Boston, Mass. 1635	Pope
WHEELER, John	Salisbury	Mary and John	Newbury Salisbury Hampton	Essex Inst. Vol. 44
BATTER, Edmond	Salisbury	James	Salem, Mass.	Pope
REEVES, Thomas	Salisbury	Bevis	Roxbury	Hotten
WEBB, Henry	Salisbury		Boston, Mass.	Savage
DOW, Francis	Salisbury		Salisbury	Pope
VERIN, Philip	Salisbury		Salem, Mass.	Austin 212
HOLDEN, Randal	Salisbury		Warwick, R. I.	Austin 100

WILTSHIRE

NAME OF THE EMIGRANT	ENGLISH PARISH NAME	SHIPS NAME	NEW ENGLAND TOWN	VARIOUS REFERENCE
AVERY, Christopher	Salisbury		Gloucester, Massachusetts	N.E.G.R. 26/197
BILEY, Henry	Salisbury		Newbury	N.E.G.R. 52/49
BRACKETT, Anthony	Salisbury		Portsmouth, New Hampshire	Banks Mss.
OVIATT, Thomas	Salisbury		Milford	Banks Mss.
VERIN, Joshua	Salisbury		Salem, Mass.	Austin
BATTELEY, Thomas	Salisbury		Dedham, Massachusetts	Pope page 39-296
WEST, Francis	Salisbury		Duxbury	N.E.G.R. 60/142
BATT, Christopher	Salisbury		Newbury	N.E.G.R. 52/49
WHITTIER, Thomas	Salisbury		Newbury	N.E.G.R. 66/250
ANTRAM, Thomas	Salisbury		Salem, Massachusetts	P.C.C. Ruthen 263
WISE, Humphrey	Salisbury		Ipswich, Mass.	Banks Mss.
GOODNOW, John	Semley		Sudbury, Massachusetts	N.E.G.R. 60/60
Thomas	Semley		Sudbury, Massachusetts	N.E.G.R. 60/60
HAYNES, Walter	Semley		Sudbury, Massachusetts	N.E.G.R. 65/295
TREADWAY, Nathaniel	Semley		Sudbury, Massachusetts	N.E.G.R. 65/296
WOODBRIDGE, Rev. Benjamin	Stanton		Newbury	N.E.G.R. 32/292
Rev. John	Stanton		Newbury	N.E.G.R. 32/292

WILTSHIRE

NAME OF THE EMIGRANT	ENGLISH PARISH NAME	SHIPS NAME	NEW ENGLAND TOWN	VARIOUS REFERENCE
JACQUES, Henry	Stanton		Newbury	Boston T. 2778, 3 15 Apr. 1925
TERRY, Stephen	Stockton		Dorchester Windsor	N.E.G.R. 55/223
HAYNES, Walter	Sutton Mandeville		Sudbury, Massachusetts	N.E.G.R. 39/263 47/72
BLANDFORD, John	Sutton Mandeville		Sudbury, Massachusetts	N.E.G.R. 39/195
REDIAT, John	Sutton Mandeville		Sudbury, Massachusetts	N.E.G.R. 39/195 47/72
BIDCOMBE, Richard	Sutton Mandeville		Sudbury, Massachusetts	N.E.G.R. 39/195 47/72
MAYHEW, Thomas	Tisbury		Watertown Edgartown, Massachusetts	History Martha's Vineyard
RUDDOCK, John	Trowbridge		Sudbury, Mass.	Savage.
COGGSWELL, John	Westbury Leigh		Ipswich, Massachusetts	N.E.G.R. 52/213
PIKE, John	Whiteparish	James Apr.1635	Newbury Ipswich, Mass.	N.E.G.R. 66/260
ROLFE, Henry	Whiteparish		Newbury	N.E.G.R. 66/260
John	Whiteparish	Confidence	Newbury	N.E.G.R. 66/260
PARKER, Abraham	?		Chelmsford & Woburn, Mass.	N.E.G.R. 16/41
BARTLETT, Robert	?		Newbury	N.E.G.R. 40/195
BROWNE, Nicholas	Bengeworth		Reading, Mass.	Aspinwall

WILTSHIRE

NAME OF THE EMIGRANT	ENGLISH PARISH NAME	SHIPS NAME	NEW ENGLAND TOWN	VARIOUS REFERENCE
BRUNSON, John	?		Farmington	Banks Mss.
Richard	?		Farmington	Banks Mss.
TURBOT, Nicholas	Bredon		Plymouth, Mass. Wells, Maine	Banks Mss.
Peter	Bredon		Plymouth, Mass. Wells, Maine	Banks Mss.
WYNN, Edward	Broughton		Woburn, Mass.	Pope
LACEY, Lawrence	Broughton		Andover	Banks Mss.
THOMAS, William	Comberton Great	Mary Anne	Newbury	Savage
MOSS, John	Cotheridge		New Haven, Connecticut	Banks Mss.

Total number of Emigrants from Wiltshire is 107 from 44 Parishes.

WORCESTERSHIRE

NAME OF THE EMIGRANT	ENGLISH PARISH NAME	SHIPS NAME	NEW ENGLAND TOWN	VARIOUS REFERENCE
WINSLOW, Edward	Droitwich	May-flower	Plymouth, Massachusetts	Savage
Gilbert	Droitwich	May-flower	Plymouth, Massachusetts	Pope
John	Droitwich	Fortune	Plymouth, Mass.	Pope
Kenelm	Droitwich		Plymouth, Mass.	Savage
WASHBURNE, John	Evesham		Plymouth, Mass. Duxbury	E.A.B.B.
COLEMAN, Thomas	Evesham		Wethersfield, Connecticut	Savage
SOULE, George	Eckington	May-flower	Plymouth, Mass. Duxbury	Soule Genealogy
BROWN, Nicholas	Inkberrow		Lynn, Massachusetts	N.E.G.R. 44/281 66/99
Nicholas	Morton, Abbots		Reading, Massachusetts	Aspinwall
CHECKETT, Joseph	Peopleton		Scituate	Banks Mss.
NASH, Thomas	Ribbesford (Bewdley)		Guildford New Haven, Connecticut	Banks Mss.
WAKEMAN, John	Ribbesford	Fellow-ship	New Haven, Connecticut	College of Arms
HUBBALD, Richard	Ribbesford		Pequonnock, Connecticut	College of Arms
DOOLITTLE, Abraham	Ribbesford (Bewdley)		New Haven, Connecticut Wallingford	Banks Mss.
BLANTON, William	Upton on Severn		Boston, Massachusetts	Pope
JORDAN, Rev. Robert	Worcester		Scarboro, Maine	Pioneers of Maine
ROBERTS, Thomas	Wollaston		Dover	Banks Mss.

Total number of Emigrants from Worcestershire is 17 from 11 Parishes.

YORKSHIRE

NAME OF THE EMIGRANT	ENGLISH PARISH NAME	SHIPS NAME	NEW ENGLAND TOWN	VARIOUS REFERENCE
MUMFORD, William	?		Boston, Massachusetts	N.E.G.R. 28/202
SADLER, Richard	?		Lynn, Mass.	Farmer
SHEPARD, Edward	?		Cambridge, Massachusetts	Thomas Shepard's Ch. Rec.
ROWTON, Richard	Cottingham	Susan and Ellen	Lynn, Massachusetts	Banks Mss.
ACIE, William	Cottington (ham)		Rowley, Massachusetts	P.C.C. Nabbes 162
BRADFORD, William	Austerfield	May-flower	Plymouth, Massachusetts	Hunter
WRIGHT, William	Austerfield	Fortune	Plymouth, Mass.	Par. Reg.
REYNER, Humphrey	Batley		Rowley, Massachusetts	N.E.G.R. 11/237
Rev. John	Batley		Plymouth, Mass. Dover	N.E.G.R. 11/237
BRADLEY, William	Bingley		New Haven, Connecticut	N.E.G.R. 57/134
FUGILL, Thomas	Bossall		New Haven, Connecticut	Farmer
MICHELSON, Edward	Buttercrambe		Cambridge, Mass.	Banks Mss.
JUDSON, Samuel	Bradford		Dedham, Mass.	Pope
BOWER, George	Braithwell		Scituate	Banks Mss.
JEWETT, Joseph	Bradford		Rowley, Mass.	Linzee 435
Maximilian	Bradford		Rowley, Mass.	Linzee 435
TOPPAN, Abraham	Coverham		Newbury	N.E.G.R. 33/66 34/48

YORKSHIRE

NAME OF THE EMIGRANT	ENGLISH PARISH NAME	SHIPS NAME	NEW ENGLAND TOWN	VARIOUS REFERENCE
VINCENT, Philip	Coningsborough		New London, Connecticut	Savage
ROWTON, (ROOTEN), Richard	Cottingham (See below)	Susan and Ellen	Lynn, Massachusetts	Banks Mss.
GILPIN, Anthony	Darrington		Barnstable, Massachusetts	Mayfl. Desc. 1421
DICKERSON, Philemon	Dewsbury		Salem, Mass.	Banks Mss.
TURNER, John	Doncaster	Mayflower	Plymouth, Massachusetts	Banks Mss.
CARVER, John	Doncaster	Mayflower	Plymouth, Massachusetts	Banks Mss.
PINDAR, Henry	Cottingham		Ipswich, Mass.	Banks Mss.
PRUDDEN, Rev. Peter	Egton		Boston, Mass. New Haven, Connecticut	N.E.G.R. 11/237
SHERCLIFFE, William	Ecclesfield		Plymouth, Mass.	Banks Mss.
PRESTON, William	Giggleswick		New Haven, Connecticut	Banks Mss.
MAUDE, Rev. Daniel	Halifax	James	Boston, Mass. Dover	Banks Mss.
WILSON, Nathaniel	Halifax		Roxbury	Aspinwall
WOOD, Jonas	Halifax		Hempstead, Long Island	Aspinwall
*SHAW, Abraham	Halifax		Dedham, Mass.	Lechford
MITCHELL, Mathew	Owram, South	James	Wethersfield, Connecticut Charlestown, Massachusetts Concord Springfield Stamford, Conn.	N.E.G.R. 11/241
ATKINSON, Thomas	Halifax		Concord	Pope

* The great-great-great-great-great-great-grandfather of Elijah Ellsworth Brownell - - the Publisher.

YORKSHIRE

NAME OF THE EMIGRANT	ENGLISH PARISH NAME	SHIPS NAME	NEW ENGLAND TOWN	VARIOUS REFERENCE
REENWOOD, Nathaniel	Heptonstall			
RAPER, James	Heptonstall		Lancaster, Mass.	P. F. 137
ROSBY, Simon	Holme-on-Spalding Moor	Susan and Ellen	Cambridge, Massachusetts	Bartlett
RIGHAM, Thomas	Holme-on-Spalding Moor	Susan and Ellen	Cambridge, Massachusetts	Banks Mss.
UDSON, Ralph	Hull	Susan and Ellen	Cambridge, Massachusetts	College of Arms
HWING, Benjamin	Hull	Susan and Ellen	Cambridge, Mass. Boston, Mass.	College of Arms
HAPMAN, Robert	Hull		Saybrook, Conn.	Hinman
NDREWS, William	Hampsthwaite		Salem, Mass.	Pope
ROTHINGHAM, William	Holderness		Charlestown, Massachusetts	Wyman
ONGFELLOW, William	Ilkley		Newbury	Somerby Mss. V.12
OYES, Matthew	Leeds		Rowley, Massachusetts	N.E.G.R. 61/385
OYNTON, John	Knapton		Rowley, Mass.	Linzee 435
William	Knapton		Rowley, Mass.	
ILSON, Nathaniel	Ovenden		Roxbury	Aspinwall
ODD, Christopher	Pontefract		New Haven, Connecticut	Babcock and Allied Families
ROWN, Francis	Rawcliffe		New Haven, Connecticut	N.H.Gen. Mag. 2/346
ARKER, Thomas	Rowley		Boston, Mass. Rowley, Mass	Lechford
OGERS, Rev. Ezekiel	Rowley		Rowley, Mass.	Savage

YORKSHIRE

NAME OF THE EMIGRANT	ENGLISH PARISH NAME	SHIPS NAME	NEW ENGLAND TOWN	VARIOUS REFERENC
JOHNSON, John	Rowley		Boston, Mass. New Haven, Connecticut	Lechford
LAMBERT, Francis	Rowley		Boston, Mass. Rowley, Mass.	Lechford
PUNDERSON, John	Rowley		Boston, Mass. New Haven, Connecticut	Lechford
SCALES, William	Rowley		Rowley, Massachusetts	N.E.G.R. 66/42
CLARK, Richard	Rowley		Rowley, Massachusetts	N.E.G.R. 58/267
NORTHEND, Jeremiah	Rowley		Salem, Massachusetts	Waters & Emmertor 86
NELSON, Thomas	Rowley		Rowley, Mass.	Pope
BROCKLEBANK, John	Rowley		Rowley, Mass.	Boston T.
Samuel	Rowley		Rowley, Mass.	Boston T.
NORTHEND, Ezekiel	Rowley		Salem, Massachusetts	Waters & Emmertor 86
PALMER, John	Rowley		Rowley, Massachusetts	Waters & Emmertor 88
SWIFT, Thomas	Rotherham		Dorchester	Savage 4/241
EGGLESTON, Bigod	Settrington		Dorchester Windsor, Conn.	N. Y. Biog Rec. 23/99
BINGHAM, Thomas	Sheffield		Norwich, Connecticut	N.E.G.R. 49/333
FIELD, Robert	Sowerby		Boston, Massachusetts	N.E.G.R. 48/335
FAIRBANKS, Jonathan	Sowerby		Dedham, Massachusetts	N.E.G.R. 7/303

YORKSHIRE

NAME OF THE EMIGRANT	ENGLISH PARISH NAME	SHIPS NAME	NEW ENGLAND TOWN	VARIOUS REFERENCE
RESCOTT, John	Sowerby		Lancaster, Mass.	Savage
OOD, Edmund	South Owram		Wethersfield, Connecticut Stamford, Conn. Hempstead, Long Island	Miner Genealogy 50
CADLOCK, William	Sutton in the Forest		Saco, Maine	Banks Mss.
TLEY, Samuel	Thorne		Scituate	G.B.U.
EARSON, Rev. Abraham			Southampton, Long Island	Cotton Mather
IGGLESWORTH, Edward			Charlestown, Massachusetts	N.E.G.R. 11/241
Rev. Michael			Charlestown, Massachusetts	N.E.G.R. 11/241
ENTON, Rev. Richard	Owram, north	James	Wethersfield, Connecticut Stamford, Conn.	N.E.G.R. 11/241
ORTHRUP, Joseph				N.E.G.R. 43/242
RADLEY, William			New Haven, Connecticut	Boston T. 7 Dec. '25
ARNE, Miles			Boston, Mass.	Banks Mss.
IBSON, Rev. Richard			Saco, Maine	Alum. Cantab.
ANISTER, John		William & Francis		Sanborn Plough Company
OXON, George (Rev.)			Dorchester Springfield	Savage

Total number of Emigrants from Yorkshire is 81 from 38 Parishes.

INDEXES

INDEX

of the

Names of Emigrants

who came from

Old England to New England

between 1620 - 1650 inclusive

*he great-great-great-great-great-great-grandparent of Elijah Ellsworth Brownell - - the Publisher.

194

INDEX OF NAMES OF EMIGRANTS
(Continued)

INDEX OF NAMES OF EMIGRANTS
(Continued)

196

INDEX OF NAMES OF EMIGRANTS
(Continued)

INDEX OF NAMES OF EMIGRANTS
(Continued)

INDEX OF NAMES OF EMIGRANTS
(Continued)

* The great-great-great-great-great-grandparent of Elijah Ellsworth Brownell - - the Publisher.

INDEX OF NAMES OF EMIGRANTS
(Continued)

INDEX OF NAMES OF EMIGRANTS
(Continued)

INDEX OF NAMES OF EMIGRANTS
(Continued)

INDEX OF NAMES OF EMIGRANTS
(Continued)

INDEX OF NAMES OF EMIGRANTS
(Continued)

INDEX OF NAMES OF EMIGRANTS
(Continued)

206

INDEX OF NAMES OF EMIGRANTS
(Continued)

INDEX OF NAMES OF EMIGRANTS
(Continued)

208

INDEX OF NAMES OF EMIGRANTS
(Continued)

INDEX OF NAMES OF EMIGRANTS
(Continued)

INDEX OF NAMES OF EMIGRANTS
(Continued)

2 1 2

INDEX OF NAMES OF EMIGRANTS
(Continued)

INDEX OF NAMES OF EMIGRANTS
(Continued)

INDEX OF NAMES OF EMIGRANTS
(Continued)

INDEX OF NAMES OF EMIGRANTS
(Continued)

INDEX OF NAMES OF EMIGRANTS
(Continued)

INDEX OF NAMES OF EMIGRANTS
(Continued)

INDEX OF NAMES OF EMIGRANTS
(Continued)

INDEX OF NAMES OF EMIGRANTS
(Continued)

INDEX OF NAMES OF EMIGRANTS
(Continued)

INDEX OF NAMES OF EMIGRANTS
(Continued)

222

INDEX OF NAMES OF EMIGRANTS
(Continued)

INDEX OF NAMES OF EMIGRANTS
(Continued)

INDEX OF NAMES OF EMIGRANTS
(Continued)

INDEX OF NAMES OF EMIGRANTS
(Continued)

226

INDEX OF NAMES OF EMIGRANTS
(Continued)

* The great-great-great-great-great-great-great-grandparent of Elijah Ellsworth Brownell - - the Publisher.

INDEX OF NAMES OF EMIGRANTS
(Continued)

INDEX OF NAMES OF EMIGRANTS
(Continued)

INDEX OF NAMES OF EMIGRANTS
(Continued)

INDEX OF NAMES OF EMIGRANTS
(Continued)

INDEX OF NAMES OF EMIGRANTS
(Continued)

INDEX OF NAMES OF EMIGRANTS
(Continued)

INDEX OF NAMES OF EMIGRANTS
(Continued)

INDEX OF NAMES OF EMIGRANTS
(Continued)

INDEX OF NAMES OF EMIGRANTS
(Continued)

INDEX OF NAMES OF EMIGRANTS
(Continued)

INDEX OF NAMES OF EMIGRANTS
(Continued)

INDEX OF NAMES OF EMIGRANTS
(Continued)

INDEX OF NAMES OF EMIGRANTS
(Continued)

INDEX OF NAMES OF EMIGRANTS
(Continued)

INDEX OF NAMES OF EMIGRANTS
(Continued)

INDEX OF NAMES OF EMIGRANTS
(Continued)

INDEX OF NAMES OF EMIGRANTS
(Continued)

INDEX OF NAMES OF EMIGRANTS
(Continued)

INDEX OF NAMES OF EMIGRANTS
(Continued)

INDEX OF NAMES OF EMIGRANTS
(Continued)

INDEX OF NAMES OF EMIGRANTS
(Continued)

248

INDEX OF NAMES OF EMIGRANTS
(Continued)

INDEX OF NAMES OF EMIGRANTS
(Continued)

INDEX OF NAMES OF EMIGRANTS
(Continued)

INDEX OF NAMES OF EMIGRANTS
(Continued)

INDEX

of the

Wives and the Children

of

EMIGRANTS WHO CAME FROM OLD ENGLAND TO NEW ENGLAND

between 1620-1650 inclusive

INDEX

of

Parishes in England

from which

Emigrants Came to New England

between 1620-1650 inclusive

(*Arranged alphabetically according to the Shires*)

BEDFORDSHIRE

BERKSHIRE

BUCKINGHAMSHIRE

INDEX OF PARISHES
(Continued)

CAMBRIDGESHIRE

*CHESTER

CORNWALL

CUMBERLAND

DERBYSHIRE

DEVONSHIRE

* The word "Chester" was used by Mr. Banks instead of the word "Cheshire" - - the Publisher

INDEX OF PARISHES
(Continued)

DORSETSHIRE

INDEX OF PARISHES
(Continued)

INDEX OF PARISHES
(Continued)

260

INDEX OF PARISHES
(Continued)

INDEX OF PARISHES
(Continued)

KENT

LANCASHIRE

INDEX OF PARISHES
(Continued)

LEICESTERSHIRE

LINCOLNSHIRE

LONDON

263

INDEX OF PARISHES
(Continued)

INDEX OF PARISHES
(Continued)

NORFOLK

NORTHAMPTONSHIRE

INDEX OF PARISHES
(Continued)

INDEX OF PARISHES
(Continued)

SHROPSHIRE

SOMERSETSHIRE

INDEX OF PARISHES
(Continued)

STAFFORDSHIRE

SUFFOLK

INDEX OF PARISHES
(Continued)

SURREY

SUSSEX

INDEX OF PARISHES
(Continued)

INDEX OF PARISHES
(Continued)

YORKSHIRE

INDEX

of

Parishes in England

from which

Emigrants Came to New England

between 1620-1650 inclusive

(*Arranged Alphabetically*)

INDEX OF PARISHES
(Continued)

273

INDEX OF PARISHES
(Continued)

Page

Bridget, St. 99
Bridgewater 138
Bridport 30
Briggham 115
Brinkthorn 130
Brinspittle 31
Bristol 55-56
Brixham 20
Brixton 20
Broadmayne 31
Broadway 138-139
Broadwindsor 31
Brokenborough 177
Bromfield 42
Bromley 76-87
Bromley Magna ..41-42
Brompton Sulney ...132
Broughton .125-126-183
Broughton (Manchester) 87
Bruton 139
Buckby, Long 126
Buckenham 115
Buckingham 115
Budleigh, East 20
Bulkington 174
Bumpstead Steeple .. 42
Burcot 126
Bures 42
Bures St. Mary.150-151
Burford 137
Burgh-Apton 115
Burghfield 5
Burmington 174
Burnham 7-42
Burnaby Street 103

Page

Burrough Green ... 12
Burton Bradstock .. 31
Burton Dassett 174
Burton, Latimer ...126
Bury 87-171
Bury St. Edmunds..151
Buttercrambe 185
Bytham, Little 95
Bythorne 73

C

Caldecot 136
Cambridge 12
Canfield Magna 42
Cannington 139
Canterbury 76-77
Capel St. Mary 151
Carleton Rode 115
Castle Bromwich ...174
Castle Hedingham .. 42
Catherine, St., Coleman St. 99
Catworth 73
Cavendish 152
Caversham 134
Cawkewell 95
Chafcombe 139
Chaldon 31
Chalfont St. Giles .. 7
Chalgrove 1
Chard 139
Chardstock 31
Charfield 56
Charlton Mackrell ...139

Page

Charlton Musgrove ..140
Chart, Great 77
Chatham 77
Cheadle 14
Checkenden 134
Chelmsford 42-43
Cheselborne 31
Chesham 7-8
Cheshunt 67
Chester 14
Chesterblade 140
Chettle 31
Chew Magna 140
Chewton 140
Chewton Keynsham.139
Cheylesmore 174
Chichester 171
Chiddingly 171
Chiddingstone 77
Chideock 31
Chilmark 177
Chilthorne Domer ..140
Chinnock, Middle ...140
Chippenham 177
Chipping Norton ...134
Cholderton 177
Cholesbury 8
Churston Ferrers .. 21
Clandon, West 167
Clapham 1
Clapton 140
Claxton 115
Claybrooke 90
Claydon 134
Clayton 87-171
Cleeve, Old 140

INDEX OF PARISHES
(Continued)

INDEX OF PARISHES
(Continued)

276

INDEX OF PARISHES
(Continued)

INDEX OF PARISHES
(Continued)

INDEX OF PARISHES
(Continued)

INDEX OF PARISHES
(Continued)

INDEX OF PARISHES
(Continued)

INDEX OF PARISHES
(Continued)

INDEX OF PARISHES
(Continued)

INDEX OF PARISHES
(Continued)

INDEX
of
The Counties and Shires in England
from which
EMIGRANTS CAME TO NEW ENGLAND
between 1620-1650 inclusive

INDEX

of

Names of Forty-four Ships

carrying

Emigrants from England to New England

between 1620-1650 inclusive

ABIGAIL.....1-6-12-19-32-36-37-
45-52-99-108-113-168-169-171.

ANGEL GABRIEL.....5-87.

ANNE.....12-13-14-17-20-43-50-85-
100-103-111-113-123-132-133-
167.

ARBELLA.....48-52-157.

BACHELOR.....31.

BEVIS.....60-62-64-180.

BLESSING.....43-50-58-78.

CASTLE.....74-85.

CHARITY.....106-137.

CONFIDENCE.....5-6-30-34-53-61-
62-63-64-134-177-178-179-182.

DEFENCE.....1-6-12-15-44-52-54-
61-108.

ELIZABETH.....5-8-9-41-45-54-
68-76-86-98-152-153-159-164-
165-166-168.

ELIZABETH and ANNE.....17-62-
83-128.

FELLOWSHIP.....56-184.

FORTUNE.....14-76-98-99-103-
110-113-169-184-185.

FRANCES.....150.

FRANCIS.....39-40-42-47-48-54-
149-162.

GRIFFIN.....17-44-54-67-77-93-
109.

HANDMAID.....150.

HECTOR.....71-98-109.

HERCULES.....61-74-75-76-77-78-
82-83-84-85.

HOPEWELL.....6-9-10-13-49-66-
70-71-100-169-175.

INCREASE.....13-34-39-40-41-46-
47-51-98-155-158-161-166.

JAMES.....5-6-55-60-61-62-67-84-
88-89-107-110-141-157-177-178-
179-180-182-186-189.

Names of Forty-four Ships Carrying Imigrants from England to New England. 1620-1650.

(Continued)

JOHN and DOROTHY.....123.

JONATHAN.....25-60-61.

KATHARINE.....96.

LION.....46-50-80-101-171.

LIONS WHELP.....35-36-37-147.

LITTLE JAMES.....96-118-169.

LYON (See LION).....47-53-54-66-155.

MARTIN.....8-11.

MARY ANN.....115-120-123-164-165-183.

MARY and JOHN.....19-21-22-26-29-30-32-34-35-37-61-63-140-141-143-144-146-147-178-179-180.

MAYFLOWER.....30-39-47-50-55-59-62-77-82-98-99-102-104-106-107-108-111-121-133-137-170-184-185-186.

PLAIN JOAN.....31.

PLANTER.....1-2-6-65-69-70-92-112-168.

PLOUGH.....60-102-105.

SUSAN and ELLEN.....2-6-39-40-41-48-99-129-168-177-178-185-186-187.

TALBOT.....102-107-108.

TRUELOVE.....8-9-10.

WHALE.....60-63-81-102-109.

WILLIAM and FRANCIS.....54-56-60-64-189.

WINTHROP FLEET.....51.

INDEX OF TOWNS

In the Colonies in

Maine, New Hampshire, Massachusetts, Rhode Island, Connecticut, New York and New Jersey

(Numbers Indicate Pages)

290

INDEX OF TOWNS

In the Colonies of Maine, New Hampshire, Massachusetts,
Rhode Island, New York and New Jersey

(*Continued*)

(Numbers Indicate Pages)

INDEX OF TOWNS

In the Colonies of Maine, New Hampshire, Massachusetts, Rhode Island, New York and New Jersey

(*Continued*)

(Numbers Indicate Pages)

INDEX OF TOWNS

In the Colonies of Maine, New Hampshire, Massachusetts,
Rhode Island, New York and New Jersey

(Continued)

(Numbers Indicate Pages)

INDEX OF TOWNS

In the Colonies of Maine, New Hampshire, Massachusetts,
Rhode Island, New York and New Jersey

(*Continued*)

(Numbers Indicate Pages)

INDEX OF TOWNS

In the Colonies of Maine, New Hampshire, Massachusetts, Rhode Island, New York and New Jersey

(*Continued*)

(Numbers Indicate Pages)

INDEX OF TOWNS

In the Colonies of Maine, New Hampshire, Massachusetts, Rhode Island, New York and New Jersey

(Continued)

(Numbers Indicate Pages)